AN ALIEN IN JAPAN

*Mune, who writes
unforgettable poetry.
Angela.*

An
Alien in Japan

ANGELA COOK

THIS BOOK IS PUBLISHED FOR THE AUTHOR
BY LINDEN PUBLISHING SERVICES LIMITED

Copyright © Angela Cook, 2010

ISBN: 978-1-905487-32-5

..

TYPESET BY: Linden Publishing Services in 11.5 on 14 point Adobe Garamond
DESIGNED BY: Susan Waine
PRINTED IN IRELAND BY: Betaprint Limited, Dublin

Contents

CHAPTER ONE

How it all Started

"What the Hell am I doing here?"

The thought jolted into my mind without any warning, like a stab of toothache. A daft thought really, because this 'here' was my home. The house we had once christened The Smallest Republic in the World when we bought it, eighteen years ago. This lovely old house set in three acres of walled garden where our four children had grown up, climbed the ancient Spanish chestnut tree, and made secret camps under rhododendron bushes; where my husband and I had decorated rooms, argued, laughed, and entertained friends. Here I was in the kitchen where I had cooked innumerable meals on the old direct-fuel Aga, tripped over dogs, and turfed the cats off my rocking-chair. On the long scrubbed table I had opened many a bottle of wine to share with other exhausted mothers coming in from their turn on the interminable school runs: "Oh, come on – we might as well – sun's over the yardarm somewhere …" before we embarked on our next bout of busyness – making strawberry jam, harvesting apples from the orchard, working the cider press, checking on the bees, digging new potatoes, or feeding the hens; all the normal, everyday jobs that many mothers living in the country do, and are expected to do. And, I could, and I did. For six years, whilst my son was tiny; sometimes gardening all day long with him toddling beside me, until he started school, and I started my flower shop.

Now I was nearer sixty than fifty, and everything seemed over. Now the long scrubbed table was covered with sales ledgers, bank statements, invoices and order books that I must attempt to rationalise for my accountant. Our children had grown up and left the home, all the dogs had died, except for my own puppy, Serena. The two cats were elderly and incontinent. My husband of twenty-seven years was again involved with yet another woman. Even the Aga now lay in some tip rusting away with a hole in its drum: '... cost too much to repair ... and, anyway, what's the point, with the children gone?'

Outside, a stiff Irish south-westerly blew in off the sea, rattling the windows. Ghostly seagulls blew past, mewling, backed by the cello voice of a foghorn in the bay. Typical Cork weather, I muttered. I trailed next door into the dining room to close over the shutters, and decided to pour myself a Scotch. In the sitting room, with its three great bow windows overlooking the sea, puddles gathered on the window ledges, drowning ants; water blipped and plinked in pans placed on window seats, and a noisy family of mice racketted behind the wainscoting. This once-gracious room now smelled of wet soot and damp wallpaper.

I took a slug of whisky. Once upon a time, Sundays had not been like this. My kitchen had smelled of gravy and roast meat; noisy with voices arguing about whose turn it was not to lay the table, or do the washing-up; husband insisting on 'just ten minutes' shut-eye' before he went to mow the lawn, and remaining predictably comatose for a couple of hours; blackberrying with friends and their children, drinks at the tennis club, scrambled eggs and the telly ... that sort of a Sunday, once upon a time.

Back in the kitchen I sat back in the rocking-chair, watching the Super-Sur splutter, feeling tears of sickening self-pity trickle down my face. The tiny blue flame flickered, and the heater began its rapid flup-flup-flup, signalling an empty gas canister. I stared at it, drearily. Maybe there was another full canister still in the stable? But that entailed traipsing across the soaking yard and fumbling around in the dark to discover if there was one. I was being utterly pathetic. 'Oh, Get ON With It, Woman! I clicked off the Super-Sur and grabbed the empty canister. Anorak on, galoshes on, latch up – a furtive cat bolts through my legs, out into a torrent of rain like small cold pebbles, and then I am out to the stable, hearing its loose half-door banging in the gale. And – thank you, God! – gas there was. That small bit of activity had done me good.

"Now look here," I told myself, firmly, "stop being so wet. All over Ireland, all over the world, for that matter, wives are sitting alone in kitchens; some knit, some take to the bottle, some take Valium, some do courses, or do community work; as I have done over the years – bar the Valium or the knitting. Mentally, I itemised past achievements: committee member of a promotional tourism group, on the local tennis club committee (cooking my speciality), working with Bord Luchtas na hEireann, church rota flower arranging, judge of local Carnival Queen, and I'd even attended an incomprehensible series of lectures on Existentialism at Cork University. Before we came here, my role had been that of prime mover, removing our growing family to follow wherever my husband's jobs took him, four times in England, and thereafter, all over Ireland – Dublin, Waterford, the North, and finally, here to County Cork, where my role had diversified into that of a full-time florist as well as mother, wife, cleaner, cook and gardener.

But now, although I still ran my flower shop, and it had expanded into all sorts of other areas – importing flowers, selling artificial wreaths to the trade, making arrangements for hotels and bars, and so on, I still sat alone each night. Each weekend. So, what the Hell *was* I doing here? The thought refused to go away, determinedly closing in on my brain as if trying to make me understand that this was no whim. This mattered. This was real, and important. At my feet lay the Sunday supplements, some full of stories about young people, teenagers, taking a year out to travel – finding themselves.

The young, the self-confident, out there, free. Wasn't I the foolish one to waste my life, just hanging onto regrets? Sitting here passively, waiting for the phone to ring? Why be such a wimp, staying in a place that no longer felt mine? Because, I need not. The wind continued to buffet the windows, and the foghorn still moaned at intervals, but, gradually, the fog of despair was lifting.

I would do it! I really, actually, would. I would leave here, and go away. Go anywhere! And maybe discover a new, stronger me, and meet people who had never known me as I had been – boring, hard-working old Angela, rejected wife. No, I was going to come alive again.

Six weeks later I stood on the windy deck of a cross-channel ferry, Serena quietly snuggled up in her basket on the passenger seat of my car parked below. I went out on deck, glass of Guinness in hand, watching the coastline of Ireland sink into the mist, until, at last, there was no land to be seen, only the tossing sea, and the gulls swirling in our wake.

"GONE!" I shouted.

A man leaning over the rail beside me turned in surprise. His face was wet with tears.

—~~—

Two years passed, I was still in London, the city of my birth. So much had happened to me since I first came back here, raw, anxious, and utterly ignorant of the most basic modern innovations – spaghetti junctions, Pay & Display, tube ticketing machines, none had been there when I left. But, by now I had found my feet, and was earning a living working in peoples' gardens, enjoying the early morning banter in Covent Garden Flower Market, and selling plants at weekend street markets, as well as designing dried flower arrangements for restaurants and nightclubs. It was hard work, but exhilarating, and often great fun. Maybe sometimes I felt a bit of an anachronism, but I had toughened up.

But. A big but. The maisonette I had bought with a daughter and her friend was now in negative equity, and they wanted to move on. We let it for less than the mortgage and Serena and I went to stay with a much loved god-daughter. Standing in line in a dole queue was a degrading experience. I desperately needed a job; a nice, steady job, with a regular income, and, of course, somewhere to live.

One morning, my friend Sue rang me:

"Hi! How would you fancy becoming a guide at Shakespeare's Birthplace?"

"Me? You have to be joking! Sorry, Sue, but, honestly, I couldn't. I don't remember the half of his plays, let alone those damn sonnets – I loathed them at school."

She was determined. "Look, you can talk, can't you? You'll pick it up in no time. And, listen, if you get it, I know of a little cottage not far from me – bit isolated, but it's been standing empty for a while, I'm sure I could persuade the owner to rent it to you cheap."

"But …"

"So. I'll expect you on Wednesday. I know the administrator at the Birthplace. You just come on down and charm him, okay?"

"What's he like?" I wavered.

Sue giggled. "Very brigadier-ish, but a sweetie, really. Just simper at him, or look like a depressed gentlewoman. Whichever."

"I don't do …" She rang off.

Stratford-upon-Avon, Warwickshire. A small market town devoted to memorabilia of the bard. I sat in a book-lined office, facing an impressive mahogany desk on which rested a leather blotter and an array of silver-framed photos. The Brigadier crossed one impeccably shod foot over the other, and steepled his fingers under his chin.

"One of the first requirements for a really good guide is enthusiasm, right? One must radiate enthusiasm in order to communicate our message to the general public."

He smiled boyishly at me, possibly including me into the charmed inner circle of mesmerisingly good guides.

"In other words, Angela, what I am really telling you is that a good guide must like people, right?"

"Absolutely," I said, sitting forward keenly on my upright chair.

"I do so agree. Absolutely."

But, on this particular afternoon, just over one year later, I confess that I do not like people. Here in this little room there are far too many of the species crowding me, crowding each other, and inevitably all saying exactly the same silly things that they say every single day. This low-ceilinged room is stiflingly hot and airless, and I feel like a caged animal, except that I am sharing my cage with thousands of humans from all quarters of the globe.

As a guide, one sees racial stereotypes come to life day after day; the schoolchildren from one nation invariably push, shove, fight and squeal their way through the building, passing through it on average within three minutes, and once, a record, in fractionally under one minute; young matrons from another land drip furs and heavy gold jewellery, shifting uneasily on high-heeled shoes over the uneven seventeenth-century floorboards whilst chattering in shrill hoarse voices during the introductory speech and leaving behind a cloying scent of musky perfume. Then come the droves of solid, serious citizens demanding to know the provenance of each artefact on show, consulting their Baeddeckers and brochures, fingers following them line by line. These are all too ready to argue and debate every issue, ignoring the cross jangle of the curator's keys at closing time. Without fail we are besieged by coachloads of bulbous hordes who ask about potential ravages to the oak beams by termites, and, invariably there is always one who lowers her voice a fraction to enquire how they went to the bathroom in those days, which induces much snickering and burst of "Trust you! You are awful!"

"Remember, Angela, it is your duty to ensure that every visitor feels special," the administrator had urged me, using that special voice with which he presumably had once urged men to go over the top.

After eighteen months' work here I had personally spoken to more than a million of the earth's inhabitants, both singly and in groups, been photographed for folks back home – 'O my God, I didn't know you were real! – recorded, lost my voice more times than I could count, and alternately sweated or froze according to the seasons. Today, I had not been relieved in the main room at the Birthplace for well over an hour, and was feeling hoarse and aggrieved when the deputy-deputy chief guide bustled in with news of another large group coming in. He caught my expression, and faltered.

"I know, I know ... it's just that some of the other ladies are taking a rather long tea-break, actually. I'm sorry. But, if you'd just do this one last lot of visitors?"

As I opened my mouth, the Japanese tour guide came in, followed by some fifty or so tourists. She smiled at me, and I weakened, for we all liked the Japanese tourists, finding them invariably courteous, receptive, quiet, and interested.

"No problem, Tom," I told him.

When I had finished the introductory address, the whole group was still looking expectant, as was their translator, so I started telling them about how life would have been in a medieval town in the fourteenth and fifteenth centuries – the daily way of life, their dress, taxes, sports, and feudal customs. Unusually, this was greeted with a round of applause, and one woman presented me with a little origami bookmark.

"For you. We enjoy," she said, and, bowing, the group passed through to the next room. Their translator stayed for a moment and I said what a pleasure it always was to talk to such charming people.

"I only wish I could speak your language, so that I could communicate better," I told her.

"You should come to Japan, and learn our language. Also, we too have many beautiful old buildings, and much history that would interest you."

Driving back to my little cottage that evening, her words came back to me, and later, walking Serena across the Cotswold meadows, I wasn't seeing the cottages or the cows and sheep grazing, I was envisaging temples, women in kimonos, geisha girls ... the absurd concept simply wouldn't go away.

Nor did it leave me in the following weeks. As more and more Japanese tourists visited the Birthplace, it always seemed to be me on duty, explaining bits of our history, relating it to some of the quirks of British nature and manners, and expounding about our culture, our monarchy, love of gardening and family pets, and the present-day struggles to break loose from the insularity often apparent in an island race, which seemed to strike a chord with them.

Sometimes I told myself to stop daydreaming about such an impractical scheme. But perhaps it was not so impractical after all? So very few British guides spoke Japanese, and those who could were well paid, and always in work. On the other hand, I had my job, the little cottage was now cosy with bits and bobs of my own furniture in it, my dog and I had made good friends in the neighbourhood, and my children, although all living in Ireland, came over to see me whenever they could. So wouldn't it be crazy to leave all this for a hare-brained idea? But the fascination with all things Japanese persisted. I wondered what they were really like ? Kindly? Or cruel? Did they have a sense of humour? Did they love, hate, gossip, grumble, laugh or weep, like us? And, just how did they live, these delightful people, in their own land?

───※───

'What if?' is such a sorry statement. My poor much-travelled furniture returned to storage. My beloved Serena went to live with my daughters back in Ireland. I handed in my notice to an incredulous chief guide, organised a month's worth of tuition at EuroCentre in a town called Kanazawa, and booked my plane ticket to Japan.

Driving to Heathrow, my daughter repacked my overnight case, her way of not fussing.

"You'll be fine, Ma. It'll be a fantastic experience. And, you're good at languages, so you'll pick it up. And, if, well, if you don't like it, you can always come back early, and I'll meet you, and … it'll be fine, I'm sure it will. You'll love it." I nodded. I couldn't say much because I was feeling so sick. Clutching my overnight case I passed through the barrier, turning for one last wave.

The plane gathered momentum, and its wheels left English soil; under its shadow, bright sunlight glinted on traffic jams and caught gleaming new office blocks, red-roofed suburban estates, stretches of wheatfields and small towns. Across the sea to France, where I changed planes and my overnight bag was removed to be placed in the hold on grounds of its weight. As we left Europe, a polite young French steward approached with a tray of food. I was feeling more positive. I had done it – was actually on my way to Japan, at last.

"No thank you," I told him, "no food. Could you bring me a glass of champagne?" He beamed. "Certainly, Madame."

The screen announces that we have passed a time zone, and we are all brought a soft white scarf. "To repose yourself, Madame." The lights are lowered, but I have a window seat and sit staring out at an incredible landscape; beneath this tiny capsule, the world has been transformed into an ice rink on which someone has been skating, dancing in giddy, exultant loops and swirls, swerving through the snow duvet, skimming ice pinnacles flushed a rosy pink as we cross continents of snow and ice, leaving an isobar, or maybe an anti-cyclone; neatly piped ridges of fluff that became purple thunder clouds. And still the skater danced on, zig-zagging across cobalt lakes, dancing towards the roof of the world. I seemed to be the only person still awake; all the other passengers had spread their scarves across their faces, their deep breathing making little billows in the cloth.

At Osaka airport the queue marked ALIENS' EMBARKATION was long. After seventeen hours of travelling I wondered what time it was, or even, having crossed two date lines, what day? We all shuffled slowly forward. Most of the line seemed to be German businessmen. At last I stood in front of the immigration officer who was subjecting my immigration documents to intensive scrutiny.

"You have TOURIST visa!" he barked at length.

"Well, I am a student," I said. "I have come to Japan to study for six months. I wrote it on the form, OK?"

"No OK. You are only tourist. Not student. An ALIEN. You stay three months, and then you leave. NOT six months. You change form now, and you sign."

"But, look here, I have registered with a college in Japan …"

Behind me, the queue shifted feet and sighed. I didn't want to be difficult. And, I was tired. The official shoved a biro across the desk.

"You change date of departure, and you sign here," he ordered.

I signed. Presumably the college would have a quiet word with the Authorities and settle it later, once I got there.

In the Arrivals hall I reclaimed my wheels and big black suitcase. All I needed was my overnight case. And a loo. Chatting, the remaining passengers collected their luggage and left. The conveyor belt stopped. I stood, alone, in the hall. Two officials approached.

"You go Customs now," they said, pointing helpfully. I explained that I was waiting for another case. The smaller of the two clapped his hands. "All finish now," he said.

"But, where is my case?"

"I think it lost," his colleague remarked.

There was a short silence. I reflected that I was now on Japanese soil and it behoved me to show dignity and self-control.

"That," I said, summoning up unusual restraint, "is most unfortunate."

The true awfulness of the situation was gradually dawning on me.

"You see, in that case are all contact numbers, addresses, and my travel route, all written out in English, and Japanese!"

They spoke rapidly to each other, and nodded.

"It is indeed most unfortunate."

Our voices echoed through the empty hall, giving a sense of stately unreality. We three stood looking at each other.

"I am going to Kanazawa," I told them, desperately. "I must get to Kanazawa."

The smaller of the two men brightened.

"Kanazawa, eh? Kanazawa my home. Very nice town, but very far. Where you stay?"

I couldn't tell him. The name of the hotel where I was supposed to spend my first night was in the Japanese brochure, in the missing case. I could visualise the buff folder that contained the right bus number to take me to a railway station in Osaka, together with phrases written phonetically to enable me to buy a train ticket, and yet another slip of paper that I must hand to a cab driver to drive me to the hotel in Kanazawa. Plus emergency phone numbers to ring if anything went wrong, and, of course, my toothbrush and make-up, all efficiently packed by my dear daughter. Why hadn't I had the common sense to keep them out and carry them with me?

"What can I do?" I faltered, trying not to show the tears I could feel welling up. "I mean, I can't speak Japanese, and, and I don't know anyone here, and ..."

The larger official came to a decision.

"I help you. Come, please."

We went through Customs up concrete stairs and along passages to his office, hazy with cigarette smoke. He beckoned me to a chair and lit up the first of many cigarettes.

"I am Mr Oki. You stay with people in Kanazawa? Host family?"

I nodded.

"I find them for you. You know their name?" He reached for the telephone.

That at least I could remember.

"Kitamura-san," I told him, triumphantly.

"Their address?"

I shook my head, and he sighed.

"Japan has many, many Kitamura," he told me, resignedly.

Thank the Lord, Customs & Excise has a lavatory.

Half an hour passed. An hour, and Mr Oki was still on the phone, resolutely working his way through columns of Kitamuras, all living in Kanazawa, population 432,000. His secretary was also busy, locating my missing case. She discovered it, still in Paris. Mr Oki dialled on and on, chain smoking. By 7 pm, he was almost invisible behind a cloud of smoke and had loosened his collar, but was still determinedly on my case, becoming progressively more and more hoarse – as an ex-guide I remembered the feeling. His smile, when he looked over at me, remained in place:

"No problem, I find them ..."

And, at 7.15 pm, he did. His face broke into a broad grin, and he gave me the victory sign, launching into a flurry of staccato Japanese, waving his half-smoked cigarette triumphantly:

"Hai! Hai, Cook-san, Igirisu-jin? Hai, Osaka imasu! Hai, hai," and much more before he closed the conversation, bowing to the receiver with a final, "domo arigato gozaimasu," and, "Sayonara!"

That lovely man had saved me, staying on long after his shift should have ended. Now, he knew which hotel I was registered to stay in, and set to work to get me there, telling me which bus I must take to get to Osaka train station, and carefully writing out directions for me to give the cab driver when I got to Kanazawa. He took me to the ticket vending machine to buy my bus ticket and left me at the stop. Finally, he gave me his home phone number:

"More problem, you phone me."

It was now 8 pm, approximately four hours since I had landed. I waited at the bus stop:

"Mr Oki, I can't even begin to thank you enough …"

"No problem. Enjoy your stay in my country! Be happy in Japan." Bowing, he left, vanishing in the crowded street. The right bus arrived, on time to the minute, and after the requisite number of stops, some forty minutes later, I started walking down the aisle.

"Hankyo eki, desuka?" I asked the driver, reading from Mr Oki's notes. He shook his head.

"Iie, Hankyo hoteru desu."

"I don't want the hotel. I want the railway station."

"Hoteru desu," he insisted.

It was raining heavily. I stayed on the bus, determined not to lose touch with the last safe place to which Mr Oki had directed me. The driver took a look at my face, rolled his eyes, and got down from his cab. I watched him walk up and down on the pavement, speaking to passers-by, gesticulating. Only a few hours in Japan, and I was proving a major nuisance to everybody unlucky enough to encounter me. Now I was wrecking the famous regularity of Osaka's bus service. The engine kept on turning, traffic roared round us, other passengers sat immobile, and the driver was getting very wet. He returned, bringing with him a tiny man, almost invisible under a large black umbrella. All could see of him were navy pin-striped trousers and highly polished brown shoes. The umbrella spoke:

"I was in America. I speak very fine English. Madam, where you want?"

"I want Osaka Hankyo eki," I told him, from the step of the bus.

"OK. I take you," he said, pulling my suitcase onto the pavement.

"Arigato," said the driver, gratefully, re-boarding his bus. The big black umbrella and my case took off at a canter along the wet street, and I ran after it. If the last piece of my luggage disappeared, what the Hell would I do?

"You know Chicago?" the man called over his shoulder.

"No," I panted. "I'm English."

"Ah! Sherlock Holmes live in Baker Street, Rondon, no?"

"Um. Yes."

I was soaking wet, rain dripping off my hair and nose. We arrived at a crossing and, having caught up with the umbrella man I started to cross, seeing a gap in the traffic, but was grabbed and rebuked.

"Tcha! Dangerous, Madam. You wait with me." So we waited until the crossing emitted the sound of a cuckoo.

Without that kindly stranger I would probably never have found the station, and I certainly couldn't have discovered the right platform where each section was marked according to where my ticket had reserved my seat. He got me onto the train, and even located a couple who were travelling to Kanazawa, to make sure I got off at the right stop; finally, he bought me a small wooden box from a platform attendant. Umbrella now neatly furled, he handed it through the door to me.

"Cookies for your journey," he announced. "Have a swell time in Kanazawa!"

The train pulled away, leaving him waving on the platform.

Later, the wife of the couple approached and untied the ribbons on the wooden box. It contained sections of miniscule brightly coloured edibles, and transparent shrimps, approximately the size of a fingernail. She reached into the box and split a splinter of wood into two pieces, pointing to my mouth. Chopsticks! Each morsel tasted either faintly salty, or faintly sugary, more like a perfume than a real taste. I dozed under the benign gaze of the couple.

Kanazawa at last. It was still pouring with rain at midnight as I showed Mr Oki's note to the cab driver. Taxi drivers in Japan, I had been told, do not expect tips, and this surly man certainly did not merit one, pulling out, meter already ticking, as I lugged case and wheels over to the boot, heaved them in, and clambered into the cab. He only got out to stand by me as I repeated the manoeuvre in reverse, waiting for his fare. However, mission accomplished. I was in Kanazawa, at the right hotel, entirely due to Mr Oki and my unknown helper. I was without a nightie, hairbrush, or make-up. But I did have my duty-free bag. I poured a generous slug of Scotch into the toothmug provided and slid under the quilt. Tomorrow, or today, or whatever day it was, was another day.

I woke up to bright sunlight, and the sound of a phone purring rthymically.

"Cook-san?" enquired a female voice.

"Yes, er, hai?"

"My name is Miss Homma, from EuroCentre course. We have been very worried for you. Are you well?"

"Oh! Yes thank you. It was just that my bag was left in Paris, and …"

"So, it was not fault of the Japanese airline." The voice sounded reproving. "Kitamura-san tell me you had problems, and we feel very worried. Please be here at two o'clock to meet with me."

"Certainly. Yes, of course I …"

She rang off before I could ask her what time, or day, it was.

Nobody at reception spoke any English, and, of course, breakfast was long over, but I discovered a very sophisticated kettle-cum-thermos complete with two green tea bags on my locker. However, my tummy not being accustomed to hot spinach on waking, I left the brew in the cup.

Miss Homma sounded formidable. There was no way I was going to meet her, or my hosts, with bird's-nest hair, grotty teeth and naked face. I set out to discover a chemist shop in Kanazawa, determined not to lose my way back. It would have been very helpful if I could have deciphered the name of the hotel written in flowing Japanese script over the door, but my only clue was a frieze of magnolias in the lobby. Perhaps it was called 'The Magnolias'?

The streets were lined with shrines and temples, with little side roads full of tightly shuttered houses, some with linen banners fluttering over the doors. There was a smell of fried rice, fish, and incense. I did not see any other foreigner, but inside a fruit and vegetable market I spotted the magic word 'Pharmacist.' Yes! I bought a toothbrush, but couldn't find a hairbrush. A young male assistant approached me, bowing. His female colleagues remained shyly behind the counter. He spoke no English, but miming achieved first some face cream, and then blusher, eye-shadow, and mascara. The toothpaste I found myself. Next he ushered me to a chair, set up a mirror, and invited me to experiment with different brands of foundation cream, whilst helpfully painting each of his nails in different shades to see which I preferred. One of the other girls came forward, diffidently, and presented me with a paper bag of tissues and cotton wool. "Service, lady," she murmured. I only needed one other item. Nerves, scrappy food and champagne had not agreed with me. I needed a laxative. The young man hovered over me, painting yet another fingernail for my inspection,

"Do you have Milk of Magnesia?" I asked him.

His brow wrinkled. "Mirruku? In café, madam."

"No. Not milk. It's a laxative." I got up and prowled once more along the shelves, followed anxiously by the young chemist. I tried another tack.

"Your delicious Japanese food I am not used to. I need medicine for the toilet."

"Aaa!"

He darted to the back of the shop and returned, beaming, with a small, prettily labelled bottle of lavender toilet water.

There is a limit to the powers of mime. I bought the toilet water.

A few doors away, a glass-fronted shop had a design of scissors etched on its windows. I saw a line of women sitting under dryers, and the thought of clean, well-set hair was irresistible. I went in, running fingers through my dishevelled hair.

" Please, could you give me a shampoo and set?"

"Shampu settu desu ka?"

"Hai?"

"Hai, so desu."

Wonderful! I sat down at the end of a row of women, all with magazines on their laps. They all looked at me. And at my blonde hair.

12 pm … 12.30 pm, and so far, only one woman had left the queue.

I had to be back at the hotel to meet Miss Homma at two o'clock, having relocated the hotel. At 12.45 pm I got up and approached a girl who was blow-drying a client's hair.

"Sorry. I must go now. But I come back, OK?"

Of course, she did not understand. All at once, my patience, never my strongest point, ran out. I was going to get my hair done, come what may. The events of the past day seemed surreal, Alice-through-the-looking-glass-like. In this one small thing I was going to be in charge of my own destiny. Jet lag was making me slightly mad. I began to mime.

"Look here," I told the girl, rubbing my fingers yet again vigorously through my hair.

"But, later. Right?" I pointed to the clock and raised three fingers in the air.

I walked to the door, opened it, and marched out. On re-entering, I unwrapped my new lipstick, grabbed a magazine, and drew a clock face on it, short hand on three, long hand on twelve. The ladies under dryers withdrew their heads and gazed at me in wonderment. The hairdresser's hand dryer was now fluttering pages of magazines, but having got this far, I was unstoppable. I repeated the performance. One finger raised I walked out the door. Three fingers raised I came back in.

"Got it? Do you understand? Later, OK?"

There was a complete silence. I had done my all.

Now, I stood in the middle of the room, making daft washing motions and looking imploringly at the assistant.

Suddenly, a lady in the queue stood up and clapped. The rest of the line followed her example, all laughing merrily, and all clapping. Idiotically, I bowed to the assembled ladies, and, still laughing, they all bowed back.

Immediately I was seated at a row of basins, a young girl solicitously tucking a rug over my knees. I felt that my entertainment had been rewarded, and relaxed as the seat floated into the perpendicular, as if I were at the dentist's. All at once, I was startled by a sharp blow on the centre of my skull. I sat up, indignantly:

"Oi! Stop that at once! Don't you dare …"

The girl jumped, and the customers were once again convulsed. They were not assaulting this mad foreigner, merely beginning a vigorous massage before washing my hair.

I later learned that each salon has its own special massage. This one had a technique: first pounding the skull, and then working the way down to the nape of the neck, finishing up with a firm manipulation of the shoulders. It was wonderfully effective; the strain had left my neck, and my slight headache had gone away.

Curiously, they dried the hair before putting in curlers; given my baby-fine Western hair I knew the set wouldn't last, but I didn't care. At least it was clean, slightly set, and brushed. I left the salon with a quarter of an hour to spare, and rewarded the kind ladies with a final bow, and a 'domo arigato' before retracing my steps. I was right about the duration of the set. It had fallen out by the time I found the hotel again. But I had been wrong in my assessment of Miss Homma. She was charming, and spoke good English. I explained fully the disaster of the missing case, and she emphasised again that no blame could be put upon the Japanese Authorities.

This was apparently of cultural importance.

Later, armed with a note from her, I tried to find the helpful chemist, but, perhaps over-confident, I lost my way. A nice woman took me by the arm, rather as if I was a lost five-year-old, and insisted on walking us to a police station, some two miles away. In the wrong direction. She then walked all the way back with me, only leaving my side when the hotel came into view, some hundred yards from where she had met me. No other foreign student had arrived, but with the help of reception I bought myself a sandwich from a vending machine, and went to bed.

Next morning I was spot-on on time for breakfast, eating the fullest Western breakfast on the menu.

"Cook-san?"

I followed the waiter to Reception and, under his guidance, picked up the receiver.

My younger daughter.

"Ma? How are things? Are you OK?"

Already, I was so far from being able to explain how different things felt.

I gabbled on about the amazing views from the plane, and reassured her that I was grand, perfectly alright, and had even got my hair done!

"Fantastic, Ma! It sounds great!"

"This is an amazing land, darling! The kindness! Well, it puts us to shame, honestly it does."

Miss Homma materialised at my elbow.

"You should come now, Cook-san. Kitamura-san has arrived to collect you."

I looked round and saw a very small, middle-aged couple standing in the foyer, smiling warily. He was skinny and balding, she, standing a pace or two behind her husband, had a worried, but pretty face.

"Got to go, love! I'm being collected. Love you lots … I'll write."

I replaced the receiver, and went to meet my hosts for the next four weeks.

CHAPTER TWO

With the Kitamuras

"THE KITAMURAS do not speak any English, Cook-san," Miss Homma informed me, propelling me towards the couple. I stopped moving and looked at her in horror:

"But … but EuroCentres assured me there would always be at least one family member who could speak a bit of English," I stuttered.

She was undeterred.

"You will learn better like this."

Kitamura-san (male) insisted on carrying my heavy case, heaving it into the boot of their car, together with a bag of fruit I had bought that morning in the market. They then ushered me into the back seat of their immaculate car, which had a white cotton cover, lacy anti-macassars, and white frilly cushions edged with broderie anglaise. I recalled my own mobile dustbin back at home and felt faintly mortified.

Conversation was, perforce, limited. I think the Kitamuras have, between them, some fifteen words of English, and my Japanese vocabulary is probably no greater. I managed a "Kirei desu" (how pretty) when we got to their home, a modern, plastered, two-storey house with red curly pantiles, reached through bushes all tightly clipped into different shapes. Their husky dog, Taro, was tied up to his kennel near the porch, and leapt out, snarling, as I got out of the car.

"Abunai!" warned Mr Kitamura, proudly. He pointed to his teeth and made biting motions. No problem. Patting was out of the question. I had not come to Japan to acquire tetanus in my first week. Inside the porch, Kitamura-san sat down on the wooden step, and shuffled off her shoes. In her stockinged feet, she pointed at my outdoor shoes, and I too slipped them off, standing on the concrete floor. She looked worried. Obviously I had done something wrong. Finally, I understood that it is incorrect to place feet on the concrete; one has to sit on the step before placing shoes neatly side by side – facing the front door on the concrete surface – before swivelling round on haunches to receive house slippers.

"Kore wa anata no surippa desu." Relieved, Mrs Kitamura handed me my own house slippers.

The interior was disappointingly Western in appearance; reminiscent of the early 1950s: beige square rug on teak parquet, grey moquette three-piece suite, glass-topped coffee table, a large TV on castors, wooden shelves containing trophies and a brass clock. There was even an aspidistra! Through an opening I could make out a G-plan dining table with four matching chairs and a long narrow kitchen, all formica and glass-fronted cabinets. The loo was downstairs, beside a windowless room where the washing machine and vegetables were kept.

My room was upstairs; again, it could have been the spare room of any suburban London villa, except for an array of gorgeously dressed Japanese dolls on the bookcase; a heavy wooden bed, mirrored wardrobe and chest of drawers, and a school desk under the window. These boasted pristine net curtains and yellow drapes. I stood in my room, feeling rather disappointed at the lack of Oriental mystery. Even the smell of this house rang a bell; attar of roses air freshener, maybe allied to a faint whiff of joss stick.

There was no trace of the West in our evening meal, however. At six o'clock I was called to the table and discovered that the Kitamuras had laid on a spread to put an Irish wake to shame. Everywhere were little bowls containing different segments of food. Mr Kitamura, whose name I now know to be Hoshiri, sat at the head of the table, noisily slurping thin soup. For such a serious, skimpy little man, he had an astonishingly loud slurp.

Both plied me with food, but Naoko Kitamura seemed unable to sit down and eat with us; floral pinafore covering her blouse and long skirt, she fluttered to and fro, now bringing sauce, now grapes, then beer, alighting on the edge of her seat for mere seconds before darting off in search of something else. Occasionally, she would pick up her chopsticks in a meditative sort of way, imprison a sliver of raw whitebait, and then replace them in her bowl as she thought of something else her husband or I might like, and after a few minutes of covertly watching my lack of prowess with chopsticks, she slipped away again and produced a spoon and fork. The feast was truly magnificent: boiled eggs, raw onion rings, sliced ham, sliced apples, raw fish, some long white vegetable tasting of damp rabbit, tofu, boiled green vegetable stalks tied into tiny bundles, and minute shrimps which the Kitamuras dipped into bowls of tea. Hoshiri-san ate doggedly on, at last sitting back in his chair with a contented smile. His wife promptly bustled away and returned with three bowls of sticky white rice. Her husband held the bowl close to his chin and shovelled the contents rapidly into his mouth before holding it out again for replenishment. Naoko-san, hovering between him and her rice steamer, was ready, refilling his bowl to the brim. I cut into my rice with the spoon. It came out moulded into a soggy, glutinous lump.

"Thank you, but, no. Not another bowlful ..."

It would have been dead useful stuff to have had when my car radiator sprang a leak last year.

Seated together on the sofa, whilst her husband gazed at the telly, Naoko-san thumbed through her photograph albums, showing me views of Japan and snapshots of relations.

I say: "Aa, so desuka," and "kirei," or just "mmm-hmm," at intervals, but she, taking her responsibilities as teacher, looks up words in a dictionary and makes me repeat them after her. No way will she allow me to help her clear the table or wash up. Hoshiri-san smiles over at me from time to time, and offered me a delicious little cake made of, I think, marzipan and chestnut, with a cristallised cherry on top. By now, my eyes were glazing over with fatigue, and I said goodnight.

"Oyasumi nasai, Kitamura-san."

"Oyasumi nasai, Cook-san," they choroused.

When I passed by the door to locate the bathroom, they had vacated the sofa and armchair, and were kneeling side by side, watching the TV screen.

I discovered that the toilet roll played 'Für Elise' when pulled twice.

Breakfast was on the table at seven. The television set had been turned towards the kitchen, and was showing an early morning game show. A male commentator, wearing a smart grey suit, with a red feather in his buttonhole, was being fearfully jolly to his panelists, two young women wearing kimonos, and two youths clad in sweatshirts and jeans. Hoshiri was drinking soup, noisily. Naoko, dictionary to hand, plied me with salad and fish stew. Outside, their dog yipped.

"Could I just have coffee, please?"

"Kohii dake?" her face broke into an anxious frown.

"Hai. Er, kohii dake, arigato."

Hoshiri-san tutted and pushed the bowl of fish stew towards me. Perhaps it would be considered rude to refuse? I helped myself, sparingly. Reassured, he turned back to the screen, where participants and audience alike were pealing with laughter. Naoko-san was once more busy with her dictionary:

"Today wa, National holiday, Nihon ni. We go, er … visit one thousand houses with you."

I was chewing on a chunk of seaweed that had concealed itself in the stew.

"Omoshiroi desuka?" she asked, dextrously filling my rice bowl whilst my attention was distracted.

Dear God, I thought, I know the Japanese are renowned workaholics, but surely, setting out to see one thousand houses on one national holiday was excessive for playaholics? Nonetheless, it behoved me to be grateful.

"Omoshiroi desu," I agreed, meekly. Very interesting.

Before we left, Hoshiri-san, now wearing a tracksuit and brown Gucci slip-ons, exercised Taro. He and the dog disappeared full tilt round the corner, Hoshiri dragged at the end of the rope, as Taro, husky ears flattened and curly plumed tail outstretched, galloped ahead.

I absolutely insisted on helping my hostess clear the table, then carefully rinsing the bowls under a running tap as I had seen her do, before placing them in the dishwasher. Naoko-san seemed distressed by this, and implored me to prepare for our trip. It was going to be a scorcher. I changed into a summer frock and sandals, collected my camera, and was ready and waiting by the time Hoshiri-san drove the car out.

We drove through forests of cypress and winding roads edged with overhanging clumps of gigantic bamboo, then through small villages where many houses were made of some sort of wattle and daub. The sky was an unbroken blue, and a kite wheeled overhead. It was unbelievably hot and I was sticking to the broderie anglaise cushions, but all car windows remained tightly shut. Neither of the Kitamuras seemed to notice, chatting together happily. I was starting to feel faint. How on earth was I going to be able to traipse round a thousand houses? I reckoned that ten would finish me. And who were the occupants? Relatives? Or friends? Even as an ex-guide, I could not envisage bowing to one thousand of them.

At long last we drove into a car park halfway up a mountain. Hoshiri-san parked, and mercifully opened the doors.

"Edo-Mori desu, Angela-san. Here you will see one thousand houses of Japan!"

Within this pine forest were replicas of a thousand-years' worth of Japanese architecture.

We visited house after house … sandals off, slippers on. Cypress pillars, ornate carvings, stone lions and dragons. Slippers off, sandals on … on and on we went, climbing up log steps set between trees, to see yet more and more houses. Mosquitoes zoomed down, crickets chinked. Huge butterflies, willow-green and peach-coloured, fought and died in flapping disarray beside our path; they were almost sparrow-sized, buffeting each other in mid-air and collapsing in pitiful flutters among the pine needles. Japanese groups stepped on them, oblivious. Still we climbed on, up through the sweltering heat, passing only one Westerner, towering above his companions.

"Gee, isn't this just something!" he called out to me. I agreed.

"But how much further do we have to go? I'm whacked."

"Just you wait till you get to the next one. Like, there's some old guy who talks to Buddha twice a year …"

"What?"

But my only contact with the Western world had walked on, now out of sight, lost below among the pine trees. We continued climbing up the mountain, clambering over tree roots, until at last we came to a small wooden house near the summit. Its roof appeared to be of bark, and it had no discernible chimney, but, from a hole in the centre, a column of smoke wreathed out. More smoke spewed out through an opening, marked by two upright wooden poles. The interior was very dark, lit only by a fire burning in a pit in the centre of the room. Over this pit hung a kettle, and, on a wooden platform, an old man squatted, his eyes glazed as if in a trance. He took no notice of our entry but continued to drone on in a cracked, high-pitched voice, some uninflected homily or chant, still seemingly unaware of our presence. I was motioned to kneel beside the fire, while the Kitamuras took their places on the platform. Over their heads was a photograph showing a triangle with sparks descending in a shower. The kettle steamed, and the burning wood gave off a curious aromatic scent. Still the old man continued his chant. Naoko-san poured water from the kettle into three bowls of thin green tea, whilst her husband addressed the ancient. Now, he too sipped his tea, muttering a response, and gesturing at the photograph.

"Aaa, so desuka!" they breathed.

There was something mesmeric about him; all alone, hidden at the top of a dense forest, there in the semi-darkness, with the acrid scent of the wood fire. I took a cautious sip of my tea.

"Buddha!" declaimed the old man, suddenly, pointing upwards.

"Hai, Buddha!" intoned Hoshiri, reverentially, gazing at the photograph.

"Aaa, Buddha!" Naoko said softly.

A mosquito stung me sharply on the calf, and I slapped it.

"I'm sorry, but I can't see Buddha in that photo," I whispered. "I don't understand."

The spell was broken. We bowed and left the hut. Naoko tried to explain the significance of the photograph. On some date every October, apparently, Buddha rains down sparks of gold dust onto that old man in the hut during the night. The triangle in the photo was the mountain we had climbed, and the sparks were the gold dust. I think I do believe it. I feel certain that something curious does occur, in the silence of the night, in that eerie place.

We returned to the car after taking snaps of each other beside the stone lions that guarded the gates.

Mr Oki had not taken the day off. He telephoned to tell me my missing case had now arrived in Osaka, and he would be sending it on to the Kitamuras by special courier. It should arrive tomorrow. Oh, Mr Oki! You are a marvellous man! I must decide on a suitable present to send him.

We had another tussle, Naoko and I, over the washing-up. Again, I scrupulously rinsed all bowls under a running tap before stacking the dishwasher, and again, she protested, this time, wringing her hands in dismay.

"Now, look, Naoko-san," I struggled to explain. "Watashitachi ga dishu washu surunai, er … machine ga dishu washu suru ne huh?" (I wasn't doing it, she wasn't doing it, the dishwasher was). Puzzled, she reached into her pinafore and produced her dictionary, Hoshiri peering over her shoulder.

"Dishu washu … dishu washu?" She muttered.

They both burst out laughing.

"Iie, Shokusen ja arimasen."

It wasn't a dishwasher?

It had stacking racks, it looked like a dishwasher, it sat where a dishwasher usually sits. However, I should have known. This is Japan, where so much is not what it seems, at least to Western eyes.

"So, what is it?"

Naoko smiled proudly. "Dish dryer, this," she explained, extracting all the greasy crocks and running hot water and washing liquid over them in the sink.

Humbly, I took each one from her and stacked them in the dish dryer, recognising that my regular drying of unwashed bowls must have reinforced the standard Japanese belief that Westerners' habits of cleanliness fall far short of their own.

Naoko is a Mistress in the art of the Tea Ceremony, and teaches students twice a week in a special Tea Ceremony room, an eight-mat tatami room, reached through sliding ricepaper doors. This is a sacred room, and must not be entered wearing even slippers. Inside it are zabuton (cushions) placed around a low carved table, and a small circular charcoal grate for boiling the kettle. At one end of the room is a tokonoma (alcove) in which the family's scroll hangs. Usually Naoko would place one or two flowers in a vase on the polished cypress step in front of it.

I am constantly amazed by how bare a Japanese room is. To them, our rooms must seem brimful of clutter. The Kitamuras' bedroom contains absolutely no furniture at all. They sleep on quilts spread on the floor, which are rolled up and put away in a cupboard. This room also is covered in tatami. One can always tell where any member of the household is from the presence of their slippers outside the relevant door, and their position. I am still uncertain at what angle slippers should face in order to indicate occupation of the loo; if one leaves them side by side, facing the door, it facilitates the slipping on of plastic slippers, obligatory footwear for every loo, but then these have to left facing the toilet seat. Extricating one foot from the plastic slipper on the way out means the waggling of a stockinged foot over the door lintel, hopefully making connection, and then executing a little hop backwards to locate the other house slipper, being careful on no account to sully the house slipper by entering the smallest room by a millimetre. The final manoeuvre – that of replacing the plastic slippers neatly, side by side, I can only accomplish by bending down in hopscotch position, and then flipping them just beyond the angle of the door opening. Chez Kitamura, this all has to be done to background accompaniment of the musical toilet roll, designed never to allow the bashful to escape unnoticed.

I retired to my airless room as the last strip of peach fades behind the purple mountain, reflecting that even the Japanese crickets are better organised than their Mediterranean counterparts; none of that chaotic chirruping from a rabble of independent souls! Here, outside my window, they chime rhythmically, in unison. Taro rattles his claws on the netting of his run, and starts to bark. The first stars twinkle in a navy blue sky. I wonder if they are the same stars I knew over Shakespeare's country?

I am just beginning to get accustomed to early rising, and can even face a smidgen of chicken soup at 7 am, but getting up at 6.15 minus my usual cuppa was really difficult. I asked Naoko where to go to buy a thermos flask. She stared at me in surprise. "You want morning picnic?"

Drawing has never been my forte, but desperate measures call for desperate means: I drew two pictures, one of me in bed, the sun peeping over the horizon, and the best depiction of a Teasmade I could manage. The second piece de resistance showed me, still abed, drinking tea with a beatific grin from ear to ear. "Aa, so desu!" Naoko lifted up a trap-door in her kitchen floor and produced an electric thermos, still encased in its original box. It is now plugged in beside my bed, and I can make tea, or coffee, whenever I want. It buzzes when the water boils, and water comes out of a funnel at the side when the lid is pressed. A teabag and a spoonful of powdered milk: I can now face the world of a morning.

The Kitamuras are very anxious to make me feel at home, and are always asking if I am happy, and, do I like their food? This morning, refreshed by my tea, I prepared a sentence to vary the inevitable "oishii desu" as a response to their query, remarking that, back at home, I often ate fruit for breakfast. There was a stunned silence. Hoshiri gazed at me in horror, a piece of raw fish suspended from his chopsticks. Naoko let out a little honk of horror.

"Well," I amended, wondering how I had caused such a reaction, "not always, you know, just sometimes."

Naoko, brow furrowed, produced the dictionary. I put on my glasses. The word for fruit is 'kudamono'. The word for children, 'kodomo'. Tension relaxed, we got on with breakfast in relieved silence. Breakfast over, things move with clockwork precision. 7.30, Hoshiri takes Taro for his morning constitutional. 7.45, he changes into his suit. 7.50, he is in the car outside the front door, with Naoko standing at the gate, bowing and calling goodbye as we drive away, me in the back seat, he listening to classical Noh chant on his cassette. He drops me at the foot of the Shakyo Centre steps, and I climb up beside a winding waterfall, in driving rain, hearing the birds squeaking and frogs gurgling in the bushes on either side, praying that one won't hop out in my path. I am laden with my satchel, handbag, welly boots in a plastic carrier bag, and an umbrella. Five minutes later, I enter the college, panting, and hope there will be time for a coffee before the first class begins.

This first day of the course is an assessment of skills in Japanese. There are three teachers deputed to do this – concensus, Japanese style. Most of the assembled foreign students had apparently studied Japanese, either already here or in their own countries. We are all given a form to fill out. One glance at this, and I had no problem. The contents were totally incomprehensible. I assessed myself as a complete beginner. Summoned to the classroom to meet the teachers, all seated behind desks ranged in a semi-circle, I told them that I knew absolutely no Japanese, and should start from scratch. I also explained that I wanted to learn their language in order to guide Japanese visitors back in England. We chatted for a few minutes about me, my journey to Japan, and my misadventures over the missing suitcase. All of them seemed very friendly and welcoming.

They assigned me to Class Hana II, taught by the Senior Tutor, Kamada-san. Our lessons are scheduled to start at 9 am, and finish at 1 pm, Monday to Friday: four lessons, with two breaks of ten minutes, and one lasting twenty minutes, separating the classes. 'Hana' apparently means flower; our classroom door has two silk carnations sellotaped to the door. Later that day we all went to hear an interesting lecture given by a leading journalist on the history of the town of Kanazawa, and its county, Ishikawa Prefecture.

Tuesday morning. The students are drinking coffee in the students' salon, and mentally sizing each other up. Class of Hana II consists of an elderly German couple, the Schulzes – he a retired sea captain, she a neatly dressed ex-school teacher. There was another ex-sea captain, a bearded American called Mel, and a seventy-year-old Englishman who preferred to be known as Australian, plus four attractive young women, a Venezuelan, Natasha, Anjela, a German, an Italian girl, and Tara who was nineteen and came from Canada. Senior tutor burst through the door, like a bullet from a gun, breathing enthusiasm. The Brigadier would have loved her. Without wasting a moment, she launched into her first mime, and we were all soon greeting her and each other in Japanese, giving our nationality, and practising bowing. Within the next quarter of an hour, she had galloped through the first two lessons in our textbook, gesturing and miming until the bell released us for the first ten-minute break. Queuing up for boiling water with our mugs of Nescafé, tongues loosened.

"My God," Tara said, "do you think it's all going to be like this?"

"It is simply a question of readjustment to the Eastern mentality," Frau Schulz observed.

"I fear I am going to be a slow adjuster," I remarked, pressing the urn button. The bell summoned us back before I could take more than a sip. The same tutor awaited us, raring to continue. Now she walked briskly to the door, opened it, disappeared, came back, closed it, and returned to her desk.

"Hai?" she queried.

"Door?" "Iie." "Open?" "Iie." "Walk?" "Iie."

The teacher, still smiling encouragingly, continued to shake her head. Suggestions came thick and fast.

"Shut?" "Handle?" "Leave?"

"Bloody charades!" Mel exploded.

"We do NOT say that," the teacher said, reprovingly.

It was the first indication we had that she could actually speak English, and Mel looked slightly chastened. Kamada-san, looking disappointed, wrote the answer on the blackboard: 'Kimasu': I come.

She then gave a repeat performance, beaming. "Kimasu!" we chorused. But once again, she shook her head, and returned to the door. Three trips later, her smile was still fixed in position, but Frau Schulz, concentrating intently, had broken her pencil, and Mel was rumbling.

"I give up," I said.

The teacher clicked her tongue. "Ikimasu!" she announced, chalking it on the board. "I go!"

By the time her class was over we all sat, stupefied. Kamada-san bowed to us and 'ikimas'd' smartly from the classroom. I no longer felt like coffee. I stood glumly by the rain-drenched window, hearing unseen birds still squeaking in the bushes. The only other smoker in the room was Bertram Pocock, the Australian. He produced a Zippo and lit my cigarette.

"Don't worry, it'll get better, you'll see," he reassured.

The next two lessons were given by a very pretty young teacher, Taniguchi-san. She was tiny, with long wavy hair, sparkling dangly earrings, and a beautiful smile. She never seemed to walk anywhere, running breathlessly into the classroom, and darting to and fro from desk to student to blackboard like some exotic little hummingbird. Having introduced herself she seemed to grasp that we were all punch drunk with undigested Japanese and began to explain the content of the first two lessons, using a mixture of Japanese and English, writing up all new words on the board. Old Captain Schulz, breathing heavily, took copious notes. I scribbled down as much as I could before Taniguchi, now writing at top speed, rubbed it out and wrote some more. The German girl, Anjela, sitting on one side of me, took lovely, sensible notes with headings neatly underlined. Finally, just at the end of class, we were shown a video covering all the material we had supposedly learned that morning. Had we but been shown this at the start, I reflected, much more of what we had laboured to understand would have been clearer. However, such was not the method, and this procedure was rigorously followed throughout the course, no matter how much we protested. Nor were we ever told which particular lesson would be covered the next day, as sometimes teachers would skip the chapter order in the textbook, thereby leaving students diligent enough to have boned up in advance completely baffled. Taniguchi assigned us our exercise homework, and, as the bell rang, treated us to another of her glorious smiles and flew out. Barely exchanging a word, we all packed up our books as if in a trance, and left. The close of day one.

I squelched through the still teeming rain all the way to the second bus stop, feeling that I could not cope with the gathering of chattering schoolgirls waiting outside the Centre. They all wore the national uniform of schoolgirls throughout Japan; different coloured sailor jackets in navy, green, or wine, with pleated skirts. En masse, they sounded like a flock of falsetto starlings. I could not make out one word of what they were saying.

If anything, the pace of instruction seemed to intensify over the next days. Not only are the teachers expecting us to grasp an inordinate amount of knowledge, the lessons are also designed to show us the culture, or gender difference in the use of language. It would seem that here, men are still overtly in ascendance, even expressed in language. We were taught that, language-wise, men may demand, but ladies should request. For instance, on entering a café, men say to the waitress "Cha, kudasai". Women, on the other hand, should use the honorific for the Japanese word for tea: "O'cha, kudasai" accompanied by deprecating little bow, reminiscent of a pigeon on a ledge. Our teacher advised that here, to gain an end, women should flutter, whilst men may stride. Fifteen aliens sat, wordless, absorbing this concept.

At lunchtime, I walked to the main department store, Daiwa

Depato, and hesitantly practiced my new-found skills. No one understood me, but I was amazed at the display in the huge food hall – eat your heart out, Messrs Fortnum and Mason ... or Harrods!

I bought a delicious sort of crepe and sat on a step surrounding the central fountain in Daiwa Depato watching people shopping before leaving to catch the bus back to the Kitamuras. As usual, the bus arrived on time to the minute. Once, it arrived two minutes late, and the waiting passengers all consulted their watches! Buses in Kanazawa are all single storey, very clean, and desperately overcrowded. It seems that there is no law stating how many people can be on a bus at any one time; the quota is reached only when the sliding doors refuse to shut. The sole unwritten law relates to fresh air. Whenever I open a window, even a crack, and take my first gasp of fresh air, many other hands reach out to shut it. So the aged bus, belching out exhaust fumes, buckets along with all windows fugged up, and passengers wedged together in a sweaty mass.

If getting on is difficult, it is nothing to the trials of leaving at the right stop. Locating the wall button is hard enough, making contact with it on the crowded bus can be impossible. Over the weeks I became more ruthless, and, having missed out on my stop in Hikarigaoka a few times, I learnt how to make a snaking jab for the button in time to duck and wriggle my way through almost impenetrable wedge of souls standing in the aisle.

"Sumimasen, er, sumimasen, gomen nasai ... oh, sorry, oops! Sumimasen ..."

The elderly are the most proficient exiters; tiny little old ladies, clad in kimono and wooden geta, advance along the gangway like midget storm troopers, bony heads and elbows battering a passageway at waist level, their umbrellas pinioning any feet that might block their escape.

After one week of homeward journeys I reflected that, were my kidneys to pack up in later years, it would have comparatively little to do with the sun setting too often over the yardarm.

Since the Kitamuras lived approximately forty-five minutes' bus drive from the centre of Kanazawa, many passengers usually had disembarked, and I could see out sufficiently to recognise certain landmarks. For the first few days, everything went like clockwork. I boarded the No. 18 bus outside Daiwa Depato, shed several pounds on the journey, and got off with the few remaining passengers outside a small parade of shops. On the fourth day, the rain was torrential, visibility nil, and all passengers were stuck together in a heaving, clammy mass. The driver, an elderly man of dyspeptic mien, chewed strong peppermints and drove through the puddles with one foot on the accelerator, the other on the footbrake. More and more passengers fought their way out over my sodden shoes; half an hour went by, but, when I rubbed the window I didn't recognise any of the streets. I was now practically the only person still on the bus. Two more stops, and I was the sole passenger.

Now we left the main road, and began a series of swooping curves. Halfway up a mountain, the bus came to a halt outside a large building, and the driver turned an enquiring face to me. I cleared my throat.

"Hikarigaoka?"

He shook his head, pressing the button to open the exit door. Cataracts of rain washed down the mountain path.

"But … doko wa Hikarigaoka?" I asked, desperately. The driver, exasperated, burst into a flood of incomprehensible Japanese.

"I AM AFRAID I DO NOT UNDERSTAND YOU" I said, loudly.

He slid the door shut to keep out the rain, and we gazed at each other in silence, each wondering how best to communicate. With a courtesy unknown in similar Western circumstances, he waved me to a bench, and I sat down. The driver took out another peppermint and chewed it. The silence continued. Slowly, a thought formed in his mind. He lent forward, smiling.

"Bus stoppu!" he indicated the sign, waving his hands in the opposite direction, "busu stoppu Hikarigaoka!" I got out.

"Soon, more busu, Hikarigaoka?" I queried, weakly, from the rough track.

"Hai, hai!" he called out, making sweeping motions with white-gloved hands. Whereupon he turned the bus around and sped off down the mountain. I stood there for half an hour, before starting to walk down the mountain road. Some time later, I regained a main road, and followed it downhill. One hour later still, I got to the Kitamuras. They had already started supper. Hoshiri looked up from his rice bowl, smiling benignly. Beside him was a piece of paper, and the dictionary. "Bussy laddi?" he enquired. Crossly, I stomped over to read what he had written: 'Busy lady'.

"Much study," Naoko observed, serving up my persimmon, hamburger, soup, and rice. Later, I took a hot shower and retired to study. Perhaps I had made a silly mistake. Perhaps it had not been a No. 18 bus after all. The Kitamuras were really sweet people. It was just a pity I couldn't explain things to them. I opened my notebook, looked at the chapter covering the next day's lessons, and changed my mind. I would get into bed and re-read my old copy of The Hobbit.

Next day, trudging up the steps to the Centre, I was feeling apprehensive. I should have covered so much last night: mastering the days of the week, months of the year, ordinal dates of the month (1st, 2nd, 3rd, etc.) and revised the innumerable methods of counting, ie. people, or things, and books, and long thin things, plus learning how to tell the time. The art of counting in Japan has many pitfalls. I can only explain this by saying that they count visually, not just numerically. Therefore, you employ one set of named numbers for people: one person is 'hitori' (pronounced 'shtori') two are 'futari, three people become 'san nin'. Then, they differentiate between long thin things, which are counted: 'ippon', 'nihon' 'sanbon', and the counting of people (perhaps excluding Scandinavians) who aren't long thin things. Then, to count light, flat things, like stamps, postcards, or shirts: 'ichi-mai' 'ni-mai'. Inanimate objects are counted as 'hitotsu' 'futatsu', 'mittsu'. Animals have their own numerical system, 'ippiki', and so on. I remember feeling surprised on learning that a rose and a bottle of beer came in the same category of long, thin things. I arrived a few minutes early in the students' salon and tried to force the lesson on telling the time into my brain.

So, I read: minutes are called 'pun'. That is, unless they cover multiples of five, in which case, they become 'fun' (ha!). The hour is 'ji', and 10 is called 'ju'. Okay. However, between 10 and 20, the 'ju' comes before the next number, like: 'ju-ichi' = 11, 'ju-ni' = 12. Right. But then, from 20 up to 100, the 'ju' follows the number (ni-ju = 20). I envisaged asking a station guard if the next train from Kanazawa leaves at 12.35: "Sumimasen, ga, er … densha no ju-ni ji, san-ju go-fun ni, kimasuka?" By the time I had got all that out, I reckoned, the damn train would have left.

Senior tutor took the first two classes. On prices. A lesson we had previously only skimmed. She set us in pairs in role-playing exercises. Anjela's note-taking and intelligence immediately made her a star. Soon, it was my turn; I was supposed to be buying a television set. Kamada fixed me with a hopeful smile.

"Hai, Angela-san?"

I forced my brain into gear. Obviously, it was an inanimate object, and it certainly wasn't a long thin thing.

"Kore terebi wa …" I hesitated as Senior Tutor shook her head, more in sorrow than in anger.

"Not 'kore', Angela-san."

I am sure the word for 'this' is 'kore'.

She sighed. "The television set is nearer to me, the assistant, than you, so 'sore' is the right word."

It further transpired that machines are counted 'ichi-dai'. Now she pointed to an imaginary set in the far corner of the room. Because that one was neither nearer to her or me, the 'sore' became an 'are'. Furthermore, when pricing, amounts over 10,000 are translated, I think, as 1 million, 1 thousand. I suffer from virtual innumeracy in my own country, so this was well beyond my poor foggy brain; utterly confused, I got my 'ju's back to front. Helpful suggestions began to come, thick and fast, from the rest of the group: "Ichi-no"… um, ichi-yon, nichi-san …?"

"We say 'issan'," Kamada prompted.

"Sounds like an automobile," remarked the irrepressible Mel. "I crashed mine in New York last fall, and it was then one hell's own ich-mai!"

Kamada's attention was mercifully deflected.

"Not 'ichi-mai' for a motor car, Mel-san."

"Oh yep, it was. One small flat thing!"

The class chortled.

The bell released me out into the corridor. Amazingly, it was not raining. Sunlight glistened on raindrops and the sky had turned a vivid blue.

I stood smoking on the steps, determined to do better next class. I wasn't really that dim. I had learnt French as a teenager in France, and picked up Italian – ungrammatical, but understandable – really fast. It was just a question of staying calm, and concentrating. Right?

Senior Tutor was ready for us, opening a new page in our textbook that required yet more role playing. We stared glumly at a series of cartoons depicting a silly little man with a quiff of hair, reacting firstly to his alarm clock, then jogging, hurrying to his office, and consuming a bowl of noodles etc. All against the clock. Kamada paused beside us.

"Nan-ji desuka?" (What time is it?)

"Nan-ji ..." repeated the Captain, hesitantly.

"Which picture?" I asked.

She pointed to one showing the cheeky little chappie reclining in an armchair, wearing an expression of idiotic bliss.

I tried: "Sore wa ..."

"Iie, Angela-san. Kore wa."

Captain Schulz had another try.

"Angela-san, kore wa nan-ji?"

"...desuka," added Kamada.

The clock face showed 10.15, presumably in the evening, unless he was either unemployed or had been sacked for eating noodles in his employer's time.

I prayed for guidance from above, but none came.

"Ju-ji go ju pun," I muttered.

She despaired of me and turned to another.

Anjela knew the answer. "Yoru no ju-ji ju-go fun desu," she said, fluently.

[42]

The final half hour Kamada devoted to numbers and dates, all thrown at us at breakneck speed and chalked up on the board for us to translate, together with their many exceptions. We were to remember that 800 is not 'hachi-hyaku', becoming 'happy-hyaku'. 4 is 'shi' alright, but, before 100 it becomes 'yon'. Also we were not to forget that under those circumstances, 3 changes the 'h' of 'hyaku' to a 'b'. By now the board was choc-a-block with numbers. Was that 1000, or maybe 1,000,100, or even conceivably 1000 million?

As Mr Pocock began to translate them in his beautiful, plummy Oxford-don voice:

"Ichi man, sanbyaku sen ..." the rows of figures flickered in front of my eyes like some manic kaleidoscope.

I simply cannot do this. The board became a haze as I stared through a shame-making blurr of tears, dimly seeing Kamada holding one fist to her ear, the other on her chin. The young Venezuelan girl called out: "Telephone! You telephone!"

"Hai, Natasha-san!" Kamada was delighted at the success of her mime.

I stared ahead, seeing my teacher like a rabbit might see oncoming headlights.

"So. I am telephone operator in a big Tokyo hotel. Angela-san. What number do you want to call, please?"

"I'm sorry. I can't. I really can't do this. Excuse me ..."

I ran outside and found a bench concealed from the main path, and sat and wept from a sense of utter failure. What on earth had induced me to leave a reliable job, my comfy cottage, my beloved dog, and especially, my country, to come to Japan? Arrogance, that's what. I hadn't listened when people told me that Japanese was a difficult language. Oh, no. I had assumed that my brain, unused to formal study for some forty years, could now spring back with the same sort of elasticity that the young college graduates in our group were now showing. And, patently, it couldn't. As for the other mature students in our class, one had studied Japanese before, and they had all come here for fun – a cultural hobby. I had come with a purpose.

I needed to learn the language to earn my living. But, I couldn't. Too dim. Too thick. Stupid. And, too old. By the time Anjela found me, I was a right maudlin mess.

She missed her next lesson, and came armed with a good supply of tissues.

That young girl was unforgettably kind to me. She regaled me with fascinating stories about the Berlin Wall coming down, and how she and her fiancee were there, on it, on that momentous night, dancing! Finally, she suggested I might like to accompany her and sample my first glass of sake. It was a very good idea.

We returned to class Hana II just as the lesson was finishing. The teacher, Fukiya-san, accepted our apologies with a smile, but just then, Senior Tutor Kamada came hurriedly into the room.

"Aa, Angela-san! Are you better?"

I explained, hesitantly, that I thought I should be in a lower class.

"Flower I?" Kamada gazed at me steadily.

Then, speaking fluent English for the first time, she told me that I was too hard on myself.

"You try too hard. Just think how much more you know now than you did at first, eh? Taniguchi-san and I are impressed by how much you have learned. Really impressed," she insisted. Now she was holding my hand.

"We know that only Tara-san and you had had no knowledge of Japanese before coming on the course. And, of course, it is easier for Tara-san. She is young!"

Yes, I had noticed. Now, other members of the class joined in.

"C'mon, Angie, you're doing great, okay?"

"I think you should continue to study," Frau Schulz told me. "You will improve."

Kamada gave me a lovely, warm smile.

"I know you will," she said.

I will. I will. I will work at learning Japanese, and I will succeed. I have maligned Kamada in my mind. She and the other teachers really want me to succeed, and I will. In a haze of determination and sake, I caught the No. 18 bus. And, it dropped me at Hikarigaoka.

Tonight, I intend to learn those figures, come what may.

Each successive day the humidity has increased. Today is so oppressive that even the teachers raise no objections to us opening the classroom windows as wide as possible. I can only assume that Kamada has instructed the other teachers to let me learn at my own pace, because although I was asked questions, they tactfully only did so when they reckoned I had already grasped the point. All our group are more relaxed now, and there is shared laughter in the students' salon as we exchange information about our host families. Late that afternoon, in sweltering heat, I crammed myself onto the No.18 bus that once more avoided Hikarigaoka completely and ended its journey up the mountain track. The driver called out the name of the final stop, and turned to me, pointing at the building outside. I shook my head, croaking, "Hikarigaoka arimasen!" This driver was a jolly young man, with a friendly grin. He tried opening and closing the doors several times, invitingly, then, when this ruse failed, he got up from his chair and took me by the hand, courteously pointing to the track. I, however, remembering the long walk back, grew obstinate and remained firmly in my seat. He glanced at his watch, strapped over pristine white cotton gloves, and sighed. Obviously, he was now landed not only with an elderly gaijin, but one who was simple, to boot.

"This," I told him firmly, and loudly, in English, " IS a No.18 bus. It should go to Hikarigaoka, and I'm going to stay on it until it does."

Still smiling, he shrugged pointing to a sign beneath the No.18, written, of course in the usual mix of kanji, hiragana, and katakana symbols.

"I don't care," I said. "I can't read it, and I am absolutely not going to walk all the way down this mountain. Right?" Me and my satchel full of schoolwork, and my handbag and lunchbox sat stubbornly in my seat for nearly fifteen more minutes, ignoring his encouraging gestures towards the door until he gave up, shrugged, got back into the driving seat and turned the bus around, dropping me all the way back to Hikarigaoka.

"Arigato!" said I, waving from the pavement.

"Do itashi mashite," he called back, courteously.

The No.18 bus sped away.

I managed to explain what had happened to the Kitamuras.

"Aaa yes," said Naoko, "a few buses do go up there. There is an institution up the mountain for old people, and some who are … well," she touched her forehead with one finger.

Obviously, on both counts, the drivers thought they had got me to the right destination.

This heat! I have never encountered anything like it anywhere. Looking out from my window, the trees look like cut-out transfers. There is no air. Nothing stirs, not a bird, not a cricket. No one is on the street. Over everything hangs a heavy, hot grey sky. I simply cannot study. I am filled with a sort of super-charged expectation and dread. I have now been in Japan for a little more than a week. Everyone here in Hikarigaoka knows what to expect. I do not. They have all experienced typhoons. I have merely watched them on TV. It is a curious sensation, feeling that everything outside seems to be waiting. There is an energy coursing through me, part trepidation, part irrational anger. I wish the wretched typhoon would hurry up and get it over with. Those vague feelings of anxiety before an English thunderstorm are nothing to this emotion. What I feel now is perhaps what primitive man felt; an elemental feeling of suppressed violence, the expectation of some force still unseen, but about to strike – and all nature is utterly still, at its mercy. The Kitamuras' television has been charting the progress of this oncoming typhoon throughout the day. From what I could understand, it has already hit the southern island of Japan with tremendous force, and is now heading straight for Kanazawa. ETA Kanazawa approximately one hour from now.

Whew! A small blast of hot air stirs the curtains, and I look out again in time to see a single bird-sized butterfly flutter past; its wings are black, dotted with yellow spots; dramatic, rather than beautiful. I walk from bed to desk, dripping with sweat, before the next hot whoosh of air. As if in response to it, all the frogs start to croak. They croak, squawk and grunt from the bushes and undergrowth, the smaller ones shrilling from trees in the garden like a grotesque orchestra tuning up before a performance. From a few streets away, a dog starts to howl, and more and more join in. Someone across the street bangs a shutter closed. Something must be about to happen. This last blast of hot air is much stronger, succeeded by a sort of vacuum in the air, as if a monster had breathed out and then sucked in, but there must be some residual movement of air because I can see all the leaves on the maple tree shaking.

Here it comes! The first outrider of the typhoon; a wind so fierce it tosses the maple nearly to the ground, its topmost branches brushing the pavement, and a blue tarpaulin from a car comes whirling down the street, followed by a dustbin lid. Taro, locked in the garage for the night, stops howling and begins a pitiful whimper. I am going to try to record this. I bring my mini tape recorder to the window and hold it outside. But, as I do, the rain starts. Rain, driven by gusts of wind, lashes diagonally against the glass and I cannot hold the machine to the gap. I slide it shut. Just one thing is moving in my room. A large, black, yellow-spotted spider has crawled out from somewhere, and taken up a fixed position on the curtain. He appears to be clinging on for dear life. I don't really mind spiders, but, given a choice, he is not the companion I would have chosen for this night. As darkness fell, the bursts of wind became almost continuous, growing ever stronger. It sounds exactly like feral cats, fighting to the death. This house, normally so quiet, is now creaking and straining. An ashtray falls off my desk, and all the books are slipping from the shelves. I heard Taro whining in relief, his claws clicking up the stairs; Hoshiri must have heard him growing ever more hysterical and taken pity on him. Now, even my heavy bed is heaving and shaking, threatening to slide across the floor. I am scared. It is after midnight. God only knows what velocity the wind is. The screeching noise is deafening. Oh, to be in England, in its season of mellow fruitfulness and harvest festivals … the biggest marrow, the lightest sponge cake … suppose the roof blows off? Suppose the house collapses? I sit in the middle of the floor the floor, clutching one of the books I had brought with me: *The Wind in the Willows*. In my other hand is my friend's Resistance medal she had lent me. I wonder what talisman pagan man carried when the elements threatened him? This is the very copy of Kenneth Grahame's book my husband had read me while our eldest daughter was being born. I am comforted by it. The typhoon raged until 3 am, gradually abating. I fell asleep, still on the floor.

Breakfast television showed the devastation cause by the typhoon. Because Kanazawa is not accustomed to experiencing typhoons of such severity, and also because such as do come seldom arrive so early in the year, no precautions had been taken to avoid damage. Had it come a month later, the trees in Kenrokuen Garden would have had their branches strapped to bamboo poles in a sort of wigwam rope arrangement to save them from snapping under later falls of snow, but now we saw pictures of colossal trees uprooted, and ancient Cedar of Lebanon branches ripped off, lying in jumbled heaps. The Garden has had to be closed.

Kenrokuen is one of the most famous gardens in Japan, one I had planned to visit only the day before, had it not been so hot. If only I had. Amazingly, the maple tree outside in the street is still standing, although practically leafless. Many others have snapped, but, with typical Japanese efficiency, these are already being cleared by a bevy of workers, armed with saws, rakes, brushes, and wicker baskets. They must have begun clearing the streets at 5 am.

It was still pouring with rain when Hoshiri drove me to the Centre, his car crunching over twigs, and swerving to avoid heaps of roof tiles. Everywhere, trucks filled with refuse beetle up and down and housewives are energetically whisking brushes to hoosh mud away from their doorsteps, with total disregard for the rain. Kamada told us that it had been the worst typhoon to strike Kanazawa for forty-five years, and that there had been considerable damage to houses in the old quarter. People had died on Noto peninsula, and many killed in Osaka.

There are advantages in not understanding Japanese. I reckon that had I understood the weather reports, or the half of what the

Kitamuras had been talking about at supper, I would have been far more apprehensive. Luckily, I had assumed typhoons to be a fairly normal occurrence – an experience – and had put on an appearance of seeming nonchalance before going to my room. Perhaps this fitted in with the perceived view of the British stiff upper lip? I do like the Japanese words for weather report: 'tenki-yo-ho'. Imagine it on the BBC: "And here we have Michael Fish with his tenki-yo-ho for the British Isles …"

On Saturday morning, the courier arrived bearing my case, sent on by the inestimable Mr Oki, accompanied by a charming note from him, hoping that my stay in Kanazawa would be the happiest time of my life, and begging me to wrap up warmly when winter came. I cannot conceive of a Western counterpart being so solicitous. I had just started trying to compose a letter of thanks to him, using the dictionary from my case to do a bit in Japanese, when Naoko tapped on my door to invite me to come and watch her Tea Ceremony lesson.

There were three students; two solemn young men in their early twenties with crew-cuts wearing jeans and sweatshirts, and a very beautiful young girl with long, glossy hair tied back with a crimson ribbon that matched her lipstick.

As Naoko ushered me into the sacred room, I recognised that this was an honour. Special slippers on, I knelt on one of the zabuton surrounding a low table in the centre of the room. Two of the others did the same. As if in slow motion, Naoko gestured to the chosen young man that he should leave the room. Through paper panelled walls, I could see his shadow, now kneeling in the corridor. After a few moments he pushed open the panelled door and glided into the room, toe heel, toe heel. He knelt again before us, then repeated his glide towards the small charcoal burner. Naoko watched his every move intently, her head a little to one side, like a robin. And because every single movement apparently has a special symbolic significance, she chided him, gently, for not having placed a ladle and a feather at the correct angle beside the burner. Once he had done this to her satisfaction, she permitted him to lay blocks of charcoal, each placed

[49]

in a particular way, and ceremoniously light the fire. From his belt he extracted a square of silk cloth, specially folded, and dusted the kettle – initially passing the cloth in the wrong direction, causing Naoko to cluck disapprovingly. Then the final cleaning was accomplished, using just the tip of the white feather, replaced, of course, on exactly the correct spot. I noticed that absolutely everything touched in the preparation of this art has first to be minutely inspected on all sides before being put to use. The great moment came when, at last, he was allowed to reach for the tea caddy, pound the tea into powder, and whisk it in the tea bowl. This tiny whisk resembled a shaving brush, though its bristles were made of bamboo. The young man whisked away diligently, forehead wrinkled in concentration, while Naoko kept up a constant stream of admonition and instruction. She has such graceful, pretty little hands. Mentally, I blessed my convent education; nothing else could have prepared my knees so well. Nonetheless, I was starting to feel pins and needles in my feet, just at the precise moment when I was approached by the student, now uncurling himself from the floor, and producing a brocade purse from his belt; from it he selected a postcard-sized piece of coloured silk containing a bent sliver of bamboo, and a miniscule pearl-handled knife, approximately the length of a matchstick. Everyone bowed. I was handed a pink marzipan sweet filled with chestnut that had to be cut into sections with the knife and held carefully on the silk square, using the left hand. It must be eaten with every expression of delight, using the bamboo sliver. Never had I felt quite so inept. So European. So clumsy.

Now, I was instructed how to drink the green tea poured into my bowl; one takes up the bowl using both hands, showing proper humility by turning the most decorated surface towards the giver, and then drains the contents in three gulps, before first turning it, to admire the decoration, then up-ending it, placing both elbows on the ground, to ensure that no harm came to the bowl, no matter how humble it was. Finally, one should up-end the bowl so as to respect its maker. In turn, each student performed the same ceremony, slowly, gracefully, reverentially. By the end of the lesson, my left foot was beginning to execute an involuntary hokey-kokey. I couldn't kneel any more.

"Arigato," I said, twitching slightly. "Totemo omoshiroi desu."

And, so it had been; very interesting. Extraordinary. I had been privileged to be allowed to observe it at close hand.

Back in Naoko's kitchen, I asked the students how long they had been attending these lessons. The girl had come for two years, the two boys for eighteen months.

"Tea Ceremony was created by our Emperor, many centuries ago, for relaxing. And, on happy occasions," Mariko explained.

"It encourages talk, and beautiful things," Ryo said. His tee-shirt bore the inscription: 'Coca Cola! Spiritual Zest!'

"What other things do you enjoy doing," I asked.

Both boys grinned: "Sumo wrestling and American football." The girl liked to read and go shopping with friends. They all left, out into the pouring rain.

Sunday. It has not stopped raining. Kanazawans are very positive about their rainfall, announcing proudly that they have the highest rainfall in all Japan. Hoshiri was collected by a work colleague to go on a firm's outing to some distant shrine. I decided to attend a service at the local Christian church. Losing my way, I arrived late to find the inevitable rows of outdoor shoes ranged below the step, and only a few pigeon holes in the porch still containing slippers; those that remained were for men, much larger than even my broad gaijin feet. The Mass was well under way, an elderly Italian priest officiating before a congregation of devout Japanese ladies wearing dark clothes and mantillas, with a sprinkling of besuited husbands and fathers. The sermon lasted for well over half an hour, given with many a flamboyant gesture and dramatic pauses. I admired the priest's fluent Japanese, and got the impression that his audience, whilst sitting phlegmatically, were enjoying a sermon of the good old-fashioned fire-and-brimstone variety. Unable to understand, I looked around and found the sight of some familiar things reassuring: the sanctuary light twinkling, the altar cloth and vestments, and, of course, the universal presence of the Host and the tabernacle.

After the service, reclaiming my shoes, I met the priest, an Italian from Florence who rarely sees his home town. "Dominus vobiscum," he said in parting, making the sign of the cross on my forehead.

And the peace of the Lord went with me back to study in my room. I looked up the Japanese word for Hell, and recognised it as one much used in the sermon. Hoshiri Kitamura returned later, in time for supper, looking exhausted. I asked if he had enjoyed the firm's outing. He looked surprised.

"I was to my firm's outing," he told me.

"I know," I said, trying to spear a raw shrimp on my chopstick, "and, did you enjoy it?"

His face remained impassive.

"It was the firm's outing," he repeated.

——————

Kanazawa is apparently renowned for many things; apart from its rainfall and Kenrokuen gardens, it makes the best sweets in Japan. All the teachers in the office suggested them as the best present for me to buy Mr Oki, and became very animated in directing me to their favourite sweet shops.

It would have been better had they simply sent me to Daiwa Depato, since I knew where that was. Lost as usual, in a small alley, I asked a group of young Japanese for the correct bus stop to a sweet-making area. They immediately drew closer together.

"Bus stoppu?"

"Hai?" I said, resolutely, giving them the number I wanted. They looked at me nervously, as if I had recently escaped from that building up the mountain. I produced my dictionary.

"Look. 'Bus stoppu', right?"

"Aaa, busu stoppu!" Light dawned, and they burst into a flood of explanations, none of which I could understand.

"Yukkurito, kudasai," I begged … tell me more slowly. They renewed their barrage of directions at the same speed.

"Wakarimasen," I told them. I did not understand.

Impasse. The girls covered their mouths with their hands, the young men looked at each other with raised eyebrows.

"Wakarimasenka?"

Correct. If only they would direct me, slowly, perhaps I could locate that bus stop, but that was not their way. For a crazy moment I wondered whether this was a naughty national sport, ideally designed to be played out in teeming rain with each stage taking approximately five minutes. If this is a recognised strategy for inducing madness in foreigners, it is one well grasped by officials, and must form an integral part of staff training for all managers. Perhaps maximum points are gained by the one who can actually reduce the foreigner to tears of frustration. In the West, we are well accustomed to being waylaid and asked questions such as: "Regent Street, where is?" To us, this is comprehensible. To the Japanese, any grammatical fault renders an enquiry meaningless. After several more attempts to find the sweet-making area in Kanazawa I gave up, and began to ask passers-by directions to Daiwa Depato, the largest, most renowned store in Kanazawa.

"Daiwa Depato wa doko desuka?"

"Ha?"

Enough. I raised my voice, and my umbrella. The two businessmen stepped backwards.

"You," I said, pointing the brolly in the direction of the smaller, "have been learning English in school for six years. So, please listen. "I AM LOOKING FOR DAIWA DEPATO!"

Game over. He directed me to the department store in halting English, and I bought Mr Oki a big box of sweets.

A few days later, I came downstairs to find Hoshiri and Naoko squatting on the floor, talking to a salesman about the installation of a new hot carpet for the winter. We exchanged our usual morning greetings: "Ohayogozaimasu!" The salesman looked at me with an expression of utter disbelief. Had his guard dog greeted him, or his koi carp performed a rumba, he could not have looked more gobsmacked, especially when I picked up my chopsticks and began eating my breakfast hamburger. I could see the three figures reflected in a glass cabinet as I ate, and heard familiar words – 'Igirisu-jin', 'seito' and 'uchi de' – so recognised that they were telling the saleman that they had an English student staying in their home. Although I couldn't understand his response, his tone was unmistakeable:

"Rather you than me!"

They all laughed.

"Iie, iie, yasashii hito desu," Hoshiri assured him.

Later I looked up the definition of the word. 'Yasashii' can mean gentle, kind or easy. 'Yasashii inu desu' means this dog does not bite.

I am getting properly used to early rising. Drinking tea in bed this morning I saw sun shining through the curtains, and tripped downstairs happily, coming into an unusual scene. Hoshiri was not in his usual chair, watching television. He was bumbling round the kitchen, ineffectually laying the table. Naoko had her back to me, at the sink.

"Ohayogozaimasu!" I said, brightly.

The response came from Hoshiri, hunkered down in front of a china cupboard. Naoko, without turning, mumbled something unintelligible. Was I late?

"Otetsudai shimashoka?" I enquired. Could I help?

Naoko turned around slowly, her eyes swollen and red from crying. She had just received the news that her aunt, who had brought her up, had died. My response was instinctive.

"Oh, my dear, I am so sorry."

I moved forward to touch her, to express my sympathy. Naoko's was equally automatic; she instantly stepped back, pulling away from me, stiffly. I helped Hoshiri stack bread on the shelf of what I had thought to be a miniature microwave, but which turned out to be a toaster. Between us we burnt the toast, but for once, Naoko did not notice.

In school, Taniguchi suggested I buy a consolation card, and helped me to write a message of sympathy.

That evening, when I gave Naoko the card, she seemed to have shrunk. She expressed gratitude, but seemed oddly embarrassed and ill at ease with me. It took me half an hour to find out why. Her problem was that she must go away to attend the funeral, but this meant she could not fulfill her duties by cooking for her guest.

[54]

"Naoko-san, no problem," I told her, relieved to discover the problem was so slight.

"Please, do not worry. I have cooked for my family for many years, I can cook for Hoshiri-san for one evening, and make his breakfast. Western style, I'm afraid, but well, he'll survive, I promise."

Still unsure, she gave a faint smile. Apparently, according to their culture, a visitor does not take charge of cooking in the host's house. It was unprecedented. The more I insisted that she should not worry, the more she bowed and thanked me, murmuring:

"But, you are my guest ..."

"But ... in England, we would do this," I told her.

Hoshiri drove Naoko to the station on his way to work the following day. I decided not to go to the Centre, and stood on the step waving her off: "Itte rasshai, Naoko-san!" Dressed entirely in black, she looked smaller than ever, sitting beside her husband, looking straight ahead as I called out the traditional parting.

I had never before been alone in Naoko's house. She rarely left it, except to go shopping once a week with Hoshiri, or to go to her club, the International Lounge, on Wednesday afternoons. Looking around her kitchen, everything spoke of her; the ironed dusters, the gleaming rice bowls, neatly folded linen outside the shower room, the plumped-up cushions, and the scraps of silk and brocade she used to dress her Japanese dolls. Branches of twisted willow were waiting for her to make an ikebana arrangement for the Tea Ceremony room. I felt an intruder in her empty home.

I headed off for the nearest supermercado, armed with a list of ingredients for a simple, satisfying Western meal, Hoshiri being, as far as I could judge, a conservative eater – the Japanese equivalent of a meat-and-two-veg man, except that such an analogy is basically flawed.

My proposed menu was quintessentially plain: boiled sweetcorn with melted butter, followed by roast chicken, roast potatoes, lightly boiled green vegetables with gravy, and my tried and trusted apple-and-banana crumble for pudding.

Japanese supermarkets are wonderful; pristine, with lots of aisles all full of elegantly displayed goods, even here in the suburb of Hikarigaoka. There was an long fish counter, stretching half the length of the store. Then I came across a stand devoted to displays of curious vegetables, and the next aisle devoted to different brands of shampoo. I returned to the fish counter, crowded with shoppers. "Irrasshaimase?" (what would I like?) came at me from all sides. Idiotically, I had forgotten to bring my dictionary.

"Chickenyu desuka?" I tried.

The assistants looked baffled. Well, so they might, from behind a fish counter, I reasoned.

However, Hoshiri would be coming home from work expecting a good meal, and I had promised his wife he would have one.

"CHICKENYU! Cluck, cluck, squark, cluck cluck." I flapped my arms and took little mincing steps. Lord, preserve me from having to demonstrate an egg laying routine.

Fortunately, the mime was enough. A little group of Japanese housewives, laughing, directed me to the right counter.

"Are wa toriniku desu," they announced.

In front of me were tiny little breasts of chicken, looking as if they had come from bantams.

"Ah. Toriniku wa chiisai. En, motto okii ga arimasuka?"

With both hands, I sketched a whole chicken. My helpers melted away, dismayed by my indecent appetite. Seemingly, entire chickens are not sold in Japan. I revised my proposed menu; perhaps, if I slit open the little breasts, I could fill them with a minute amount of stuffing, and, still roast them. Plain, ordinary potatoes were in short supply, but I found them, and located butter for the crumble. Packets of Paxo stuffing and Oxo cubes eluded me, and plain flour was indistinguishable. The packets of sugar looked different, and so did the cooking apples. I blessed the universality of the banana, and returned home. Shopping had taken nearly two hours.

Back in Naoko's kitchen, I unpacked the shopping and started opening cupboards. Where on earth did she keep her roasting tin, or, her pyrex dishes? I even lifted the trap-door in the floor, but it revealed only a crate of beer and some tins of fruit. Time was beginning to run out. Obviously, they must be in the oven. Under the hob I opened the oven door. It wasn't an oven. Just another cupboard. Too late now to faff about.

I boiled the chicken breasts, peeled the spuds with a blunt kitchen knife, quartered them and put them in with the chicken on one of the two rings on the hob, saving the other for the sweetcorn, and subsequently for stewing the apples. However does Naoko manage to serve so many dainty cooked items on two bedsit-type rings?

I heard the front door open, and Hoshiri came in calling out "Tadaima!"

"Okaeri nasai, Hoshiri-san," I returned.

Unfamiliar smells assailed him as, hesitantly, he approached the kitchen.

"Please sit down," I suggested, "I'll have your dinner ready in a few minutes." He sat down obediently, and I switched on the television. This evening he was not watching it. I could feel his eyes on my back, watching my every move in his wife's kitchen. I was now hunting for a gravy jug, and, as I rootled in yet another cupboard there he was, right behind me.

"You want what, Angela-san?"

"Dai jobu, dai jobu, I have it!"

I hadn't, but anything to save him from searching through the dictionary. Everything was boiling away merrily, but there were no strainers, no platters, no vegetable dish … over my shoulder I saw Hoshiri laying the table with little bowls and chopsticks.

"No, no, Hoshiri-san. This is a Western meal," I called out, in my best Joyce Grenfell tones, madly thickening the chicken stew with rice flour. He looked up sadly as I was mashing butter into the spuds with a fork.

"Honto! It will be nice."

I dished up the sweetcorn in two separate bowls, with butter. He looked disappointed at the sparcity of the meal, and when I placed before him the salad I had concocted out of a sort of cabbage, his expression verged on the lugubrious. Rapidly, I brought across a dish

[57]

with the chicken stew and onions, and another containing the mashed potato. Hoshiri beamed and started on the stew, leaving me the mash. I pulled them both away and apportioned out servings of each. He sat, dismayed, staring at the hillock of mashed potato surrounded by a moat of chicken stew on his plate, but observing me covertly, he took up his pair of chopsticks and made a valiant attack on the mashed potato.

"Oishii desu!"he declared, after eating a few mouthfuls. Relief!

The stewed apple, served with ice cream, also went down well, although I know he would have preferred to have been served the whole lot at one fell swoop – sweetcorn, apple and ice cream, salad, and chicken stew with mash. However, he accepted my odd Western ways, and I made him a cup of my Earl Grey tea with lemon to finish the meal. Hoshiri left the table like a lamb and settled in front of the TV quite happily while I, unwatched, did the washing-up.

Flushed with success, I was up with the lark next morning. I had been unable to find porridge in the supermercado, but had got a Kelloggs mini-pack of various cereals, and arranged them around his bowl with milk and sugar. Hoshiri returned from his morning gallop with Taro and sat down to watch TV with barely a glance at the table. The carton of tomato juice I had bought smelt peculiar, despite clearly showing a picture of tomatoes. One sip showed my mistake; Japanese apples apparently are big, and round, and red.

Ah well, not to worry. I broke eggs into a bowl with milk and butter, and put slices of bread into the toaster, pouring his glass of apple juice.

"Breakfast!" I carolled.

His eyes sadly took in the absence of gruel, fish stew, or whitebait. I lit the flame under the kettle, and then moved to the table with his glass of apple juice.

"Dozo," I said, encouragingly, "try some cereal."

I pointed at the little packets around his bowl and went back to start cooking the scrambled eggs. Just then the toaster pinged, and Hoshiri and I made a dash for it.

"No" I told him, "that is for the scrambled egg. Please try the cereal first."

I whipped it away and buttered each slice for the eggs. Deprived of one of his favourite foods, the expression on Hoshiri's face as he shuffled back to the table would have made strong men weep. However, we Brits are made of strong stuff, and I was determined he would experience the delights of a true British breakfast. Delicious scrambled egg nearly ready, I turned to see him still sitting in front of his empty bowl, and suddenly realised he had never seen any of the cereals before.

"Choose, Hoshiri-san." I poured milk into his bowl.

To oblige me, he selected All Bran, which would not have been my first choice, washing the mouthful down with a gulp of apple juice. He ate the solidified scrambled egg without comment. Our drive to school was punctuated by his appalling hiccups.

We drove in silence.

My day at school passed with me feeling guilty. I had let Naoko down. I had given her husband hiccups, and made him miserable.

I dashed back early, and spent two hours concocting a myriad of little dishes; an avocado dip, a bolognaise sauce to cover mince, more mashed potato, a cream of mushroom soup, and three different salads, plus a big fruit salad. And, I resolved, if he wanted to eat the whole lot at once, I was not going to stand in his way. At six o'clock Hoshiri arrived, and as I turned to greet him, wearing Naoko's floral pinny, he announced that we were going out to eat. Right now. We consumed big bowls of soggy rice and he ordered a steak dowsed in soy sauce for me, and a selection of raw fish for himself, before leaving to collect his wife.

Naoko served us both a proper breakfast the following morning, with all the requisite trimmings. Her relatives had sent me presents of tangerines, crisps and cookies for obliging her. Never before had I seen Naoko so warm; touching my cheek she asked, "This Sunday, will you pray for my aunt?"

"Of course I will."

We smiled at each other with genuine affection.

[59]

Her Tea Ceremony students came again the next day, and, after the lesson, she invited them to stay and try some real English food. Out from the freezer came my avocado dips, now an unappetising shade of mud, the dressed salads, now sodden, the cooked mince and spaghetti sauce, etc. The students gazed at it with barely concealed horror. National culinary honour at stake, I reconstituted a shepherd's pie from the mince and sauce, topped it with cheese, and popped it under the grill, forgetting that very many Japanese loathe the taste of cheese. Meanwhile: "Angela-san's cold soup," Naoko announced, doling out the avocado dip. We crunched our way through a few spoonfuls each, the skinny lad taking his chopstick to a knob of green ice. I watched its progress as it slid down his gullet, like that of an optimistic snake consuming its weekly ration. Bravely, under the eye of their tutor, they tried a little of everything, and turned with relief to Naoko's rice balls wrapped in seaweed.

Later in the week I looked for the residual packets of cereal but couldn't find them. However, Naoko does not like to waste food, and Taro has been unusually silent these last few days.

———

Senior Tutor Kamada-san began her class this morning with a stern warning. We were too slow, she informed us, and, unless we worked harder, it seemed likely that we would not complete the book, Japanese For Busy People. This awful threat left us unimpressed. Our class gazed at her phlegmatically.

"So-so-so," murmured someone, mimicking the assent of the Japanese.

"So what?" Mel remarked.

Kamada, lips tightening, attempted a new line of approach, designed to appeal to foreigners' well-known competitive attitude.

"The class below you is in front of you," she declared, eyes flashing. "So! So, today, this morning, we will cover four lessons!"

"WHAT?" I couldn't believe it.

Nor could Frau Schulz. She let out a heavy sigh of exasperation.

"Now this is stupid. In all my years of teaching, back home in Germany ..."

"... in pair work, please. Schulz-san to Mel-san, Cook-san to Tara-san. Yubinkyo de... role playing in the Post Office."

The natives subsided, grumbling under their breath.

"But for you, there is not a problem," Frau Schulz told me. "In five more months you will be laughing – in Japanese!"

Cultural events in the afternoons are now coming thick and fast. Yesterday we were taken to a local cookery school to participate in preparing a Japanese meal. Mel was in his element, immediately wrapping an apron round his ample middle and buttonholing the teachers.

"This is great! Back at home I just love to cook."

The teacher was surprised: "You cook, Mel-san?"

"Sure. I'm a modern man, Sensei."

"But, your American wife not cook for you?"

"Wife ichi tried ... wife ni, couldn't ... wife san..." he sighed dramatically, and looked at Tara: "You keen on cooking, Tara-san?"

"No way, Mel-san!"

"Modern American man," the teacher observed.

One by one the cooking instructors chivvied us into line to watch a demonstration on how to tie little twisted bunches of parsley containing some seven stems into precise shapes before dropping them into seaweed soup. This, bubbling away on a hot plate, had a distinct smell of drains. Under our stubby fingers, we massacred fragile stems, squashed the leaves, and tried to slip them, unnoticed, into the soup, where they disintegrated.

"In Germany, we chop it," said Frau Schulz, inadvertently dropping her bunch. She ground it under sensible brogues. "Ach!"

The lesson was shown that night on local TV and watched by me and the Kitamuras. I was shown struggling to extricate a vein from a raw shrimp, using a tool like a hairpin. Supposedly, the vein should come out in one piece. Mine did not. Both Kitamuras were highly entertained. But now Naoko had a surprise for me.

"Tomorrow, special Kimono Show for you. I arrange it with my friend at the International Lounge. You go at two o'clock. Is good?"

How wonderful. Would there be geishas gliding down a catwalk, each wearing one of those exquisite, hand-painted kimonos? I had seen the material for them spread out in the fast-flowing waters of the Asanagawa river, a process intended to set the vegetable dyes.

Naoko nodded: "Hai, like geisha."

The next day I plodded my way through the inevitable monsoon-like rain to reach the International Lounge, and was greeted by a pretty receptionist. I asked if Naoko had arrived yet. She shook her head. "No, not here, Cook-san. I take you to Howaito-san."

Howaito-san was a massively fat woman, clad in a navy blue kimono, shocking pink obi, and white, divided-toe socks. She bowed, grasped me by the arm, and indicated I should take off my coat. The door closed behind me. Now, my layers of jerseys ...

"Sorry?"

She and her assistant began to haul my jumpers over my head. My skirt slid to the floor and was scrupulously folded. For the next half hour, they slipped white chemises over my head, tied tapes, twirled me round and round, pushing and patting, and tugging at a sort of broad cummerbund that enclosed my chest in a vice-like grip. Then they asked which kimono I would like to wear, making my selection from a wooden trunk, but, rigid in my cotton strait-jacket I could scarcely bend to make an informed choice. Now an obi was tied tightly under my squashed bosom, and a cushion affair attached to my back. The two women turned me slowly round, lips pursed, still patting and adjusting their handiwork until at last they were satisfied with the result.

Howaito-san, Expert Kimono Dresser, had done her best. Not of course a masterpiece, because I was, after all, a gaijin. Too much enbonpoint, too graceless, too tall. Also too cold, too wet, and feeling a complete wally. They escorted me down the stairs to receive the admiration of the secretaries. Seated in the office was a reticent, middle-aged American student, Mr Stanley. He was reputed to be an advanced student, who had already mastered both the hirogana and katakana alphabets and was well on the way to learning the Japanese pictorial alphabet, kanji. Only some 3500 symbols to acquire. Before long he would be able to read a newspaper, the phone directory, road signs – and of course, the front of the No. 18 bus! Whenever I had seen him, he had always been engrossed in some book of Japanese text.

Now, Mr Stanley, disturbed from his studies by the clapping of secretaries, raised his eyes and stared at me, transfixed.

"Good God!"

"Say no more," I growled.

Howaito-san was crouching on the floor, pointing a camera.

"Smile, Cook-san!"

"Beeyutiful," chorused the secretaries. Guiding was never like this. Daring Mr Stanley to express a glimmer of amusement, I smiled at the camera, and made to effect a deep curtsey, foolishly forgetting that kimonos are not designed for Queen Charlotte's Ball; anxious hands caught me as I staggered back against a typewriter. Had I ripped the kimono? No, thank God. I mounted the stairs again, taking careful tiny steps, disrobed, and got back into my own clothes.

"We send you photograph," Howaito called. I rather doubt it.

Naoko explained that Howaito-san was the best kimono dresser, always very busy, dressing brides. Had I enjoyed the kimono show? I assured her it had been a memorable experience.

Our class is due for another cultural experience tomorrow. We have been booked in to see a performance of Noh Theatre. We took our seats, a long line of foreigners, amid a sea of dark heads and muted, anticipatory chatter. The theatre was huge but by comparison, the bare stage appeared tiny. There were no props; one looked out at gleaming cypress boards backed by an oil-painted mural of pine trees. Leading from the stage was a sort of wooden trellis bridge, approximately fifteen feet long. As the lights dimmed, the orchestra and singers took their places on stage, all wearing black kimonos to indicate to the audience that they were not really there, and their presence should therefore be disregarded. We had also been told that if an actor turns his back and stands motionless, this means that he

[63]

too is no longer present. The orchestra consisted of four men: three timpanists, each with a different-sized hide drum, and a flautist. These sat at the back of the stage. Then all the male singers knelt, stage left, wearing tall pointed black hats reminiscent of a Bishop's mitre.

At first, softly, growing ever more insistent, came the whimper and keening of the Japanese flute, soon followed by muffled drum beats. Before the drum was actually struck, the drummer extended his stick and uttered a little yelp. It was an eerie sound. I thought of a wolf pack, or werewolves gathering in a forest.

At last, down the connecting bridge appeared a gorgeous spectre, with hair piled rigidly high, face concealed behind a dead white mask, wearing a kimono in shades of turquoise, gold, and silver, bound by a crimson obi. As it advanced, gliding, almost seeming to float towards the stage, it sang in a curious falsetto, a lament that criss-crossed the notes of the flute. Now the drum beats and wolf sounds increased in volume as another even more magnificent creature emerged behind the first, his tall hat out-rivalling those of the chorus, an imperious white hand fluttering a fan. His was the voice that resonated against the drums, but it had an unearthly quality; it did not seem to issue from the mouth. His chant, varying in tone from deep bass to a choking moan, seemed to emanate from out of his whole body. The voice took over the person.

This particular story, like most of Noh Theatre, described the Underworld; a tale of a mother's search for her dead son throughout the world of the spirits. Action was minimal. To progress down the bridge and attain the stage proper wearing ornate, stiffened kimonos could, and often did, take anything up to fifteen minutes (ie. a foot per minute). However, each fractional movement had a special significance. Noh Theatre cognoscenti will sit, enthralled, to watch their hero extend a little finger at a particular juncture, so indicating that a butterfly had just alighted on his hand. Even to me, the exquisite simplicity of mime made the invisible clear – I too could envisage that butterfly, and I could have sworn their faces were expressing emotion, though this was impossible, since all we could see were their white masks.

The actors control both orchestra and singers, like a conductor his orchestra; it is their movements that dictate the pace of the performance, and these very precise movements, and tales, have been performed here in Japan for hundreds of years, probably before early mummers travelled round Britain.

We saw three plays. The first and final ones were tragedies; lost, or damned humans, seeking revenge or looking for loved ones. The central play gave us light relief. A pompous and foolish lord was making his way through deep forest so as to deliver a sword to the Emperor. The action began as he rebuked his servant for causing him to lose his way, but, once asleep, the sword is stolen by the Fox God, and only redeemed when the servant – a marvellously comic yokel – manages to trick the God into relinquishing the sword. The action was very funny, and although unable to understand a word, I laughed a lot.

The performance lasted for about four hours, always to a background of timpani and flute, with sporadic chanting. During it the audience chewed nuts and sweets, slept, or left with shopping bags, returning an hour or so later, bowing, to resume their seats and eat more goodies. Mel and most of our group left in search of a sushi bar after the first couple of hours, but I couldn't leave, utterly entranced by the beauty of these sexless beings performing their timeless rituals, uttering such inhuman sounds; it was mesmeric, even if the duration of chanted dialogue reduced Will Shakespeare's longer monologues to a virtual text message. There were others who had been deeply moved, too. The devotees of the theatre who sat on either corner nearest to the stage, some following each line of the chant from their own scripts. In the hurly-burly of the departing audience, they sat on, gazing at the empty stage, in a world of their own. Hoshiri Kitamura collected me from the theatre. He was delighted that I had enjoyed the performance, and suggested, diffidently, that perhaps I might care to attend the next time his Noh singing instructor came to the house to give him a lesson?

"I would be honoured," I told him.

———

With the imminent ending of our course the college continues to privide cultural events.

"This Thursday afternoon, you have all been invited to observe the rite of the Tea Ceremony, held especially for the Class of Hana II here in Kanazawa," Taniguchi told us, excitedly. I explained that I had already experienced several such ceremonies in the house of my host family, and so, therefore, I sort of thought … But no, Taniguchi clapped her hands in delight at my good fortune.

"You are SO lucky! Now, today, you will understand so much more than the other students. Do you not find yourself growing more deeply into the cultural significance of our Tea Ceremony each time you attend?" Her eyes shone.

"Hai, so desu," I agreed, weakly.

Intrigued by her enthusiasm, and determined to absorb this quintessential part of Japanese historic culture, practically the entire class turned up: Bertram Pocock, Frau Schulz with her seventy-two-year-old husband in tow, Mel, ("Tea and sympathy? Geishas? This I need to see"), Anjela, Andrea from Argentina, and Tara ("This is gonna be kinda interesting, but give me a mug of Nescafé, every time").

We knelt on minute foam rubber cushions set around a small stage. Next, two vestal virgins wearing red kimonos flitted across the bare boards, taking tiny steps on their wooden geta, their whitened faces impasssive, rosebud lips smiling. The Master of the Tea Ceremony made his impressive entrance, sweeping across the stage, his dark blue kimono brushing past us. He scanned his European audience with eyes like dark pebbles. This was a histrionic performance, not remotely like that of little Naoko conducting her tea ceremony. His interpreter explained how the origins of the ceremony dated back to a bygone Emperor, who, having enjoyed the taste and beneficial properties of tea, had decreed that his people should also enjoy its beneficial properties, and should make of its sampling a happy, relaxed occasion.

In true Japanese fashion, this explanation took some forty-five minutes. During it, the scarlet-clad acolytes remain kneeling in front of the central brazier, unmoving. Round the stage, his audience fidgeted, shifting uneasily from haunch to haunch, surreptitiously massaging feet, wiggling toes. At last, at a signal from the Master, the *electric* brazier was switched on, the kettle received its final buff up with the tip of a feather before being set to boil, and one of the young women began to pound and whisk the green tea into a powder. The other was assisting Captain Schulz to a chair. His bones could be heard cracking like dry twigs in the silent room. Finally came the ultimate moment when, like zombies, we all received our tea bowl, the cha wan, from the hands of the young geishas, and fingertip to fingertip, forearms resting on the floor as we had been instructed, we bowed our foreheads to touch the mat in respect (For the tea? The deceased Emperor? Or maybe for the teacher?) before reverentially picking up the bowl with both hands, turning it twice as required in order to ensure that the best pattern faced our host, and then slurping up the contents in three gulps. Elbows yet again on the mat, I remembered that we must upend the bowl in order to gaze, awestruck, at a squiggle on its base, because this represented the painter's or manufacturer's name.

"In your countries," tinkled the interpreter, "some of you probably do not know about tea, no?"

"I guess they never heard of Boston, no?" Tara giggled.

In the background, Captain Schulz shifted uneasily in his chair. "Ach so!" His knee sounded like a pistol shot.

TV pictures of Black and White Minstrels danced before my eyes, singing their famous jingle. Within my memory, comfortable-sized women in floral war-time pinnies had dished out mugs to all in trouble: "Come on now, love, get this down you and you'll feel better"... Vicarage teas in Buckinghamshire, thermos flasks on the beach ... Not for the first time since coming to Japan, I was experiencing a sense of the surreal. Now, it had the effect of releasing a sense of nostalgic chauvinism, as I determined to inform them about our love affair with the great British cuppa.

"Well, actually," I heard my voice say, "we do drink tea several times a day, every day, where I come from, in Britain."

The interpreter translated, and I warmed to my theme: "Indeed, we are renowned for our enjoyment of tea, over many centuries."

"Aaa, so desuka?"

"Yes, absolutely. But, there is a difference in how we, er, well, we don't follow any set ritual when we share this, er, relaxing occasion with friends. And, we certainly would never upturn a teacup when in company, as this would be regarded as exceedingly bad manners."

"It would?"

From the rest of the class came a sort of collective sigh. Had I just held my peace, we might now not be kneeling here, but have time for a long cool beer before catching our buses.

"So! No one in your country ever looks to see the name of the maker?" enquired the Master, gazing at me as a Greek might an infidel.

I blundered on. "Well, yes, I suppose they might, but, you know, not obviously. I mean, not in front of the hostess … I suppose if one really wanted to know if the teacup was genuine Dresden, or whatever, one would wait until her attention was distracted…" From the stage, four pairs of eyes were riveted on me, absorbing these curious cultural mores.

The Master was attending carefully to the interpreter, who was doing her best. From time to time, he nodded earnestly.

"How you distract please?" she asked at last.

I shrugged, unable to carry on with this scenario I had conjured up. I mean, honestly, forget the whole thing. I was getting acute pins and needles. Then, for no good reason, I remembered the pack of animal snap cards Naoko had just bought to amuse her grandchild.

"Well, something like: 'Hora! Are wa hepi, desuka?'"

Pointing dramatically to the furthest corner of the room, I hastily reversed the tea bowl, glimpsed its base, and then righted it, wearing an idiotic simper of innocence. The interpreter again conferred with the Master.

"Sensei say, do you have many troubles with snake in England?" she asked.

"It was only a joke snake," Frau Schulz said, helpfully.

"And I guess that, in her country, it would be reckoned rude even to point at a snake during a tea party," came from Mel.

"Like, the snake would not be relaxed," Tara drawled.

The Tea Ceremony team were listening to the interpreter, while their heads followed the dialogue as if it were a ping-pong match.

"Who invented the idea, back in Britain? Some merry old monarch?" Mel again.

"Nah," I told him, getting the giggles: "Hepi In Wonderland!"

Mel was well up for this. There was developing a naughty sense of the last day at school atmosphere, mildly anarchic.

"OK, OK, Howzabout, The Mad Hatter's Tea Party – organised by St Patrick?"

"But we must not forget that it should be a cultural occasion," Anjela observed, with mock solemnity.

"Exactly!" Bertram Pocock agreed. "But, well … Edward Lear comes to mind." He spoke sonorously. "As in: 'The snake and the pussycat went to sea,' he paused, 'in a beeyutiful Tea Green boat'!"

The entire class of Hana II lost it entirely, hooting with laughter, rocking to and fro, self-control thrown to the winds, stretching their legs and chortling. Even those who had not fully understood the literary allusions were laughing; "I mean, that's just so ridiculous …"

"Gee, Bertram, old man, you put the tin lid on that goddamned snake of Angic's …"

On stage, virtually unnoticed, the Master of the Tea Ceremony gathered his robes around him, bowed distantly, and left, followed by the two assistants. Our laughter subsided.

It had only been a bit of silly fun, shared by people with very little in common, except that we were all far from home; not an intentional insult.

The interpreter spoke. "You should go now. The Tea Ceremony lesson is finish."

Slipping back into our shoes in the porch, Tara said:

"I wish I didn't feel so darn guilty. I didn't want to hurt the guy's feelings."

I agreed. "I know. I know. I feel bad. I mean, I started the whole thing off, but I really didn't mean to insult him."

Frau Schulz heard me. "Do not worry about it, Angela. It is just the cultural difference. They are not used to mature students talking, and making questions."

I remarked that I did not feel I had been particularly mature that afternoon.

Mel was more robust. "Ah, the heck with it! All of us have knelt there for an hour and a half!"

"An hour and thirty-five minutes," Frau Schulz corrected.

"… bowing and scraping at a few scoops of mushy green peas. Me, right now, I intend to head off to the nearest sushi bar for my own personal relaxing experience. Any takers?"

"I think," said Bertram Pocock in his usual beautifully modulated tones, "Yes, I think I shall seek the comfort of a chair, before returning to the bosom of my host family. I propose to go and play pachinko in the nearest arcade." (A popular amusement with Japanese men of all ages; a sort of sophisticated fruit machine.)

Captain Schulz looked at his wife. "We will return to our room to study," she said. Anjela and Andrea went off together to the public baths, and Tara decided to join Mel. She promised they would buy the Master a glass of sake if they met him. But tonight was the night when Hoshi Kitamura was expecting his Noh Theatre tutor, so I had to decline all invitations.

Naoko was waiting for me, very intrigued to know who had been our Tea Ceremony Master. I showed her the college brochure, and she was greatly impressed.

"Truly, he is a most renowned Master! Did you enjoy?"

I explained that it had been interesting, but added, with truth, that I enjoyed hers much more. She shook her head and made tut-tutting noises, but, swift as the twitch of a curtain, I spotted a tiny complacent smile flicker briefly across her face. Observing that Naoko was dressed formally, I too, changed into a long summer skirt, determined, on this occasion, to do everything correctly. As a great honour, I was permitted to bring in the tray of o'cha to the Tea Ceremony room, where Hoshiri knelt, facing his tutor across the low, carved cedar table. I attempted to emulate Naoko's students, gliding toe heel, toe heel, in stockinged feet, knees wobbling, willing the tea not to spill, and serving the two men with due deference. As we all slurped the finest green tea, I observed the tutor from under lowered lids. He was a broad man with a great barrel chest and a jowly face, its skin hanging in pendulous folds like a bloodhound. He had deep-set, blackcurrant eyes. His stubby hands encompassed the delicate cha-wan. No one spoke. At last, he took the final third slurp, reversed the bowl, bowed, and addressed his pupil.

"Now we begin."

He began to chant; those same extraordinary sounds I had heard in the theatre. After a few minutes, he gestured to Hoshiri to continue. I watched, amazed by the sounds emanating from my host; this skinny, emaciated little man, whose ribs I could practically have counted through his shirt, was producing a confident deep bass that would not have disgraced Paul Robeson. The tutor, eyes closed, was beating a rhythm in the air. Then suddenly, he too began to chant, his voice counterpoint to Hoshiri's. His was a voice of enquiry, and, in response the sounds changed colour, becoming plaintive, in a minor key, as in and out, together, they wove a pattern of song; yet, song is the wrong word. In this ricepaper room, Gods and humans were communicating in primeval verse, and earth spirits, those bygone spirits of the lower earth called out at, or to, each other. Hoshiri, as in a trance, was swaying to and fro.

The spell was suddenly broken.

"No, no," boomed the tutor. "Like this. Listen ..." His voice yelped and caressed to an unheard beat which I could not comprehend. His pupil, however, understood, and began once more. Apparently he did better, for the teacher, eyes closed, opened his fingers like the petals of a waterlily flower opening. "Yes ... yes ..."

After an hour I slipped silently away, and rejoined Naoko in their living room, where she was crouched on the floor, sewing with minute silk stitches, making a dress for her grand-daughter's doll. I asked her if she would like to hear a cassette of a Western song, and played Alud Jones singing 'O For The Wings Of A Dove'. I made cooing sounds, and mimed a bird flying. Naoko listened intently, her head to one side.

"Suteki na," beautiful, she murmured.

Her husband, lesson over, listened for a moment or two before leaving the room. I recognised that his taste in music, as in food, was conservative. I heard the front door close as he left the house and then yet again I heard the familiar sound as Hoshiri went down the drive: click-clack, clack-clack, click-click-clack …

"Naoko-san? Why does husband-san make that noise with those wooden chair leg things every night?" She seemed surprised by my ignorance.

"Why, for fire, or course. And, for the night. Tradition for the night."

Suddenly, I understood. Here, the ancient tradition of the curfew, these sticks clashing as a warning to citizens to damp down their fires before retiring, was still being enacted, night after night, just as once it was in medieval Britain. Although the British used a bell, rather than sticks of wood. When Hoshiri returned, Naoko actually suggested that I might make a cup of my English Earl Grey tea. The three of us slurped it with relish.

Lying in bed, I thought again about the coming weeks. Only one more week to go now before the end of EuroCentre course for foreign students until it re-opened next spring. Just one more week before all my class return to their own homes in Europe, Argentina, America, and Australia. Only the young Canadian girl, Tara, would be remaining in Kanazawa.

Should I stay on for five more months, as planned, taking private lessons, and trying to pay for them by teaching English? If I did, where would I stay? And, what about the problem of renewing my visa? No one had yet addressed that. Over the past four weeks, by studying desperately hard, I had achieved a modicum of Japanese, but much of what we had been taught I had not properly digested, even though the class had, at Kamada's insistence, nearly reached the end of Japanese For Busy People. Did I really think that, if I stayed, I could achieve the fluency I needed?

Perhaps the sensible thing to do would be to recognise my limitations, stop wasting more of my limited funds, and go home to get on with a normal life for someone of my age. But, which was the voice of cowardice, and which the voice of reason?

Overhead, in the night sky, the elements seemed to suffer from violent indigestion; rumbles of thunderbolts came nearer and nearer, harbingers of snow that would soon descend. Not the sound of an ordinary approaching thunderstorm in England. Not a sudden crack, just monstrous crunching rumbles grumbling overhead. I remembered, back in Ireland, one small daughter pleading: "Mummy, Mummy, I don't like it. I'm scared. Make it go away!" And me, soothing, "It's alright, darling, it's just God, scolding His angels." But, they all had their own lives to live now. Decisions about my life were for me to take, alone.

If I counted up to twenty, slowly, without hearing another rumble, I would stay. If not, I would leave.

I fell asleep.

After class, and before going to an Ikebana flower-arranging class that had been arranged for us, I hunted out Saito-san, the chief liaison official between the students and their hosts. I found her in her office, incongruously humming a tune that sounded very much like 'My Bonnie Lies Over The Ocean'. She and the other teachers were busily sorting out invitations for host families due to attend the end of term performance given by all students. She listened, distractedly, to my request.

"Please tell me, Saito-san. You know I arranged with the college to stay on. I do need to know which family I will be staying with after I leave the Kitamuras. This Friday?"

She looked flustered, running her hands through her hair, blinking at me through horn-rimmed glasses.

"But, surely, Angela-san, you do not really intend to stay on after your course finishes? Does your husband not need you to be at home?"

I improvised rapidly.

"No. I think he is actually in Australia at the moment. And, probably has to go on to New Zealand. So, I am able to continue my studies here. I just need a nice Japanese family, like the Kitamuras, to have me to stay."

I knew that here a woman without a husband loses respect, even dignity, and I couldn't afford to become useless in their eyes. Saito frowned, sighing.

"Very well, I try for you, but it will not be easy, not now that the courses are over. Host families stop, and, of course, the price of accomodation with them goes up …"

"Perhaps if I come back and see you when you are less busy?" She nodded, vaguely, and I left. Maybe the decision was destined to be taken out of my hands, after all?

The demonstration of Ikebana flower arranging was something I had been looking forward to. Another florist, Carlos, a Spaniard from Class Hana I, had joined our group and we watched as the Ikebana expert showed us examples of Japanese flower arranging as it had emerged according to different formal school throughout the ages. Like all professionals, he made it look so easy, artlessly bending a willow branch, blowing open the petals of a flower, placed just so, and then standing back to observe his finished creation.

I do not understand Ikebana. As a once-busy florist, it had seemed ridiculous to spend practically one hour in placing a mere three or five branches and flowers. The ultimate effect broke every rule of Western flower arranging. Therefore, at first, in my ignorance, I trivialised it, only gazing briefly at the arrangements shown in many of Kanazawa's shop windows. But, it seemed, Carlos and I had begun to recognise the subtlety and balance between plant material and container, both of us joining with other passers-by in admiring each new arrangement.

It was a pity that Watanabe Sensei could speak no English. He had with him a female interpreter whose sole superlative was 'gargeous'. Watanabe-san would now show us a gargeous Ikebana arrangement from the oldest school of gargeous Ikebana, using only traditional bamboo, pine, and gargeous chrysanthemums.

Watching him place each branch, I was constantly convinced

that this arrangement was about to be a failure, in that nothing radiated from the centre, branches criss-crossed untidily, the tallest twig not necessarily at the apex of the arrangement, the colour scheme seemed not to blend, and at no time did any variety of flower or leaf 'come through' the design. Yet, every time, when he had finished the arrangement, he had created a mood in miniature to delight the eye. Carlos caught my eye: "Gargeous," we breathed in unison.

Finally, we were invited to try our hands at making our own Ikebana from a selection of containers, and some buckets of branches and flowers. Frau Schulz was first to reach the bucket, commandeering most of the red carnations, and the only budding camellia branch.

"Ikebana old-Dutch-master style?" queried Carlos, noticing that his share of their conjoint table had shrunk considerably. Tara advised him to keep his elbows in, and think minimalist. Frau Schulz ignored them, busy disciplining her red carnations, cutting them down to a uniform length.

The rest of us settled down to flower arranging. No one spoke, except to utter an occasional wail as a whole, carefully constructed edifice collapsed. It was hard to work without that regular stand-by, the oasis block. Not even a few strands of chicken wire to support the stems. Try as I might, I could not dismiss all the past years of tuition and experience. Connie Spry's was never like this. After half an hour of attempting to create a design remotely resembling any of the ancient schools of Ikebana, I stopped trying and just had fun, juxtaposing bent twigs and long spiky iris leaves with one fluffy carnation as its focal point, set in a pattern of irregular pebbles. Frau Schulz had achieved a solid hedgehog of crimson carnations, the camellia waving above it like a distress signal.

"Gargeous," murmured the interpreter, passing it by with Watanabe-san.

They paused by my table, and I prayed that no one would breathe too heavily, or the whole lot would collapse. The Master spoke:

"He say that is a modern school arrangement. It is gargeous, but,

[75]

it is not Ikebana!" (C'est magnifique, mais ce n'est pas la guerre). I nodded agreement. But I had to know.

"Excuse me, sensei. But would you please explain how it is that none of us have been able to capture the spirit of Ikebana? I mean, even when I tried to copy one of your arrangement, it simply did not look right."

Through his interpreter, he tried to explain.

"All of you are too concerned with the shape of your materials – the leaves, the branches, the flowers …"

"But of course," came from Carlos, standing beside his very pretty, perforce miniature, arrangement.

"For a flower arrangement, what else?"

"Why, the space!" came the answer, "It is the space between the objects that creates the arrangement."

Is this a subtle, or a simplistic outlook? Personally, I think it epitomises the bewildering essence of things Japanese. He went on to explain that we should not imprison living materials; that each item must present itself, and be itself. Carlos and I gazed at him, struggling to comprehend the concept, so very different from our own. Then, motioning to his interpreter, he produced from his briefcase two beautifully illustrated books on the art of Ikebana, and presented one each to Carlos and me. The interpreter was greatly impressed:

"Watanabe sensei himself has made many of the gargeous arrangements pictured in these books!" she told us. We each bowed as gratefully as we could, chorusing our well-trained: "Domo arigato gozaimasu." It was extraordinarily kind of him, and a great honour.

For the EuroCentre party, we all gathered in the canteen; host families, teachers and all pupils. All ninety-four pupils, whose expertise in Japanese ranged from third-year students down to the Class of Hana I. The Principal, a slight, serious young man I had never seen before, made an enthusiastic speech in which he praised the generosity and kindness of the host families who had so nobly opened up their homes to the gaijin. We all applauded vigorously. It was then the turn of each and every student to read their own laudatory speeches. By the time it came to the turn of our group, the content was minimal, our range of adjectives being limited to 'kind', 'interesting' and 'good'. Nevertheless, the volume of applause that greeted each laboured offering never waned, and all the teachers and host families listened intently, nodding approval at each compliment. I was at a disadvantage when it came to each student introducing their particular host family, since neither Naoko nor Hoshiri had been able to come; she having her Tea Ceremony students, he at yet another business outing.

Finally, as the host families resumed their places, all students and teachers joined hands and sang the EuroCentre theme song, accompanied by a stolid child on the keyboard, and set to the tune of 'My Bonnie Lies Over the Ocean', with words that included all those newly learned adjectives, liberally transposed.

Bereft of my very own host family, I wandered over to where Bertram Pocock was standing beside a host father holding a guitar. Smiling, the man offered us both a cigarette.

"Me, I smoke, like – like chimneys, English style," he remarked, grinning.

We both introduced ourselves, Japanese-style.

"English person, guide, Cook, Angela."

"Australian person, retired, Pocock, Bertram."

"And I am Joji Uno. I work for the local government, and I am licenced ski instructor, and volunteer nature explorer. I self-study English."

"You speak it remarkably well," said Bertram Pocock.

"Yes," agreed Joji Uno. "But, trouble is, Japanese-style is not to talk English like Queen. Japanese people afraid to talk English. Me, I like to talk. I tell my daughter, you hear her on the keyboard, that make mistakes does not matter. You must talk, talk, talk, so you learn." He pulled a face, comically. "But, the ladies, they do not like that. They do not learn. My wife, she not talk a word of English. She is shy Japanese lady. I am modern father, and I want my daughter to be modern, too, to travel, talk English proper, and maybe be an Olympic skier."

By popular demand the proud father was then called upon to give the assembly a song, and, obligingly, Joji Uno jumped onto the dais, grasped the mike, and launched into a keening lament. Two songs later, the proceedings officially came to an end.

The following morning, I again presented myself at Saito's desk. She shook her head, sighing:

"I am sorry, Angela-san, but, no, there is no one."

"You mean to say that out of a population of 432,000 there is not one single family willing to have me as a paying guest?"

We looked at each other in mutual irritation. I recognised that the long season must have been hard for her, dealing with all the problems incurred by foreign students; those who, unused to handling money, had run out of it, the inevitable clashes between teenagers fresh from campus living entering the ultra-conservative world of a Japanese family, omissions relating to bathwater, or slippers, overdoing the saki, or staying out all night. Now should have been the time when she could justifiably draw breath – except for this troublesome English woman who was pestering her. Suddenly, I had a flash of inspiration.

"What about that man at the party? You know, the cheery one who played the guitar?"

She shook her head.

"I don't think so. He doesn't live in Kanazawa. He lives far out, in Mattoh."

"I don't care," I said. "He can speak English, he wants his daughter to learn, he likes people, and," I added, "he smokes!" Saito laughed.

"Well, I try for you," she said.

And, two days later, Saito announced that the Uno family were prepared to receive me for the next month, after the weekend.

"I have arranged with the Kitamuras that they will drive you there, to make sure you are alright."

"No, really, I wouldn't want to trouble them …"

"It has been arranged," Saito said, firmly.

In the students' salon, classmates exchanged addresses and snaps, made plans to meet again, somewhere, some time, hugged friends, and posed for photos with the teachers.

Goodbye, dear Anjela, you have been a good friend to me … cheerio Mel, good luck … Bertram Pocock, it has been a pleasure …' bye Carlos, maybe we'll meet again at a flower show … Frau Schulz, and Captain Schulz, yes, most certainly, should I come to Germany …

The Class of Hana II went their separate ways, leaving me setting out for Daiwa Depato, seeking presents for the Kitamuras.

I got back at six. Naoko and Hoshiri were waiting for me, beaming.

"Tonight we have a goodbye surprise for you! First we go to a Japanese restaurant to eat, and then … then, we take you to a concert! A European pianist is come to Kanazawa, and we take you to listen!" I felt that Hoshiri was making a supreme sacrifice on my behalf. I know he does not care for foreign music.

After a delicious meal, eaten kneeling at a low table, we went to the concert hall, to discover that the pianist had been unable to come, and that the programme had been changed.

First, the orchestra would play some Strauss, and then we would hear the world premiere of a concerto written for the yokobui. Hoshiri brightened.

After the Strauss, performed with regimental accuracy, but with none of the swirling sounds I was accustomed to, a very tall, very thin old man took centre stage. He wore a thick blue kimono and wooden shoes, and had a long wispy grey beard and shoulder-length grey hair. In his hands he carried a Japanese wooden flute, the yokobui. For a few moments he stood, immobile, staring out at some spot far away from the audience. I imagined him like Gandulf.

The concerto began with an introduction from the violins. These kept up a rapid pianissimo buzzing, sometimes growing more insistent, sometimes subsiding to a faint murmur. It was as if we were near a swarm of summer bees. Then, the old man lifted the yokobui to his lips and began to play. At first, the notes only punctured the background buzz. Now came a few questioning trills. Swaying to the music, the yokobui seemed to haunt the bees, and they grew still. He was indeed a magician! The notes, at first plaintive, slid into the air, culminating in joyous arpeggios, reaching higher and higher. I had a sense of freedom, a glorious release from earthly things! It could not last … almost imperceptibly, the bees returned to their humdrum buzzing, and the yokobui notes quietened, momentarily joining them in a faint vestige of a tune. The sounds came together for a few instants, and it was over.

Once again, the lonely figure stood still, seemingly entranced. Then, he glanced down at his audience, as if surprised by their presence, bowed deeply, and left the stage. It had been a mesmerising performance. Pure magic. I shall never forget it.

The last day at the Kitamuras! I am packing up my belongings. Incongruously, a silly old doggerel we used to sing at school is running through my head: 'This time tomorrow, where will we be. Out of the gates of miseree …' This is certainly not the case for me. I have been so well looked after by my two kindly hosts. Nothing has ever been too much trouble for them, although, from time to time, I must have been quite a trial to them, interrupting the smooth routine of their lives. It seems incredible to realise that, four weeks ago, we hadn't met. Now, we have got used to each other, built bridges, and become friends. And I shall miss them. Tonight, Naoko has cooked a sayonara supper for me, and invited her daughter and son-in-law to share the delicious tsui-yaki. I presented her with two cassettes I found in Daiwa Depato – another Alud Jones, and a Pavarotti, a singer I discovered she had not heard of. For Hoshiri, I bought a bottle of Baileys Irish Cream – with an attached note explaining that it was not a normal part of a Western breakfast. Kojira, the son-in-law, was intrigued by the note. Hearing about the Western breakfast fiasco he roared with laughter and, even as they left, he was still muttering "lovely, lovely scramble egg" with a broad grin on his face.

Naoko also had a very special gift for me. She came up to my room and unpacked three exquisite kimonos. "You choose, Angela-san. Which one you like?" She was adamant that I must accept this present in memory of my stay.

The two of us carried on drinking mugs of instant coffee, squatting on the floor until long after Hoshiri had retired, only saying goodnight shortly before midnight. It was much later, when, packing all done, I crept down to take a hot shower, my big Western bath towel over my arm. Eyes shut under the shower, I basked, totally forgetting that the twin tub washing machine in the anteroom had a drain serving both the washing machine and the shower. Too late, I discovered soapy water gushing out over polished floorboards, lapping the vegetable rack. Root vegetables were bobbing up and down in the bubbles.

Dear Lord, I prayed, don't let Naoko wake!

For nearly one hour I swabbed the floor with my bath towel, and rinsed the veg, finally dripping quietly upstairs on slippered feet in the wee small hours, glad to hear basso profundo snores coming from the Kitamuras' room. I gave the washing machine room a hasty once over the following morning, having listened to 'Für Elise' for the last time. All, thank God, appeared to be in order. One last look around my room; at the row of Japanese dolls, at my coffee-stained desk, and the floor where I had sat and shivered during the typhoon. I went down to meet Naoko, dressed smartly in her International Lounge outfit, navy skirt and frilly blouse, and a smartly besuited Hoshiri, and then we were off, to meet Joji Uno, as arranged, in a lay-by. Once there, I was transferred to his van, in a symbolic gesture that reminded me of a father giving his daughter away.

"We follow," Naoko told me. She gave me a quick hug.

I got out of their car, and walked towards the white van where my next host waited.

CHAPTER THREE

With the Uno Family

THE OLD WHITE VAN racketed along the road at speed, Joji Uno driving fast, with a sort of devil-may-care expertise, one hand on the wheel, the other holding a cigarette. He passed me a packet of Salem cigarettes.

"Remember, Cook-san? You and me, smoke like chimneys!"

Japanese pop music blared from the radio as he wove through the traffic. Looking back, I could see Hoshiri crouched tensely over the wheel, Naoko with one hand pressed to her mouth.

"Er, the Kitamuras drive quite slowly," I told him.

"Ha? Nearly there," Joji said.

Half an hour later, we reached his house. It was the last one, at the end of a rutted side-track in the middle of rice stubblefields; a modern grey cement building with a covered area beside it that housed the van. I got out, and Joji's wife Mieko appeared at the door. She was a small woman, wearing a navy tracksuit. As the Kitamuras and I approached, she fell on her knees on the doorstep, murmuring the traditional greeting. Hoshiri and Naoko bowed, formally, and I did my usual embarrassed bob and duck. Chained to a kennel, a brown husky-type dog bounded, barking.

The Unos entertained their guests in a large kitchen where a kettle bounced up and down on top of a kerosene stove, filling the air with steam. Joji Uno was a jovial host, showing Hoshiri an album of photographs and proffering cigarettes, while his wife padded silently round the kitchen table, serving us small iced cakes and bowls of green tea.

Fumiko, their daughter, came clattering noisily down the stairs and stood, staring. Her father put an arm round her shoulder, addressing Naoko.

"You remember my little girl? It was she play the keyboard at the EuroCentre party?" It was explained that Naoko had been unable to attend because of her Tea Ceremony commitment, and both Unos were tremendously impressed. Mieko Uno's head shrank even further between her shoulders as she continued to shuffle round the table presenting us with more nuts and sweetmeats. Fumiko was despatched to the piano, and played a Chopin piece, rapidly, without inflection.

At last, when the heat had achieved rainforest humidity, and the air was blue with Joji and Mieko's cigarettes, Naoko glanced at her watch.

"Perhaps, before we leave, we take Angela-san's cases to her room?" she suggested.

Joji led the way, sliding open a door.

"Fine Western bedroom for English lady, eh?"

I looked round at my new room; at a big double bed with a flouncy duvet, a red plastic hat stand for my clothes, and a 1950s style dressing table with a swing mirror. There was also a black desk complete with anglepoise lamp, and my very own kerosene stove, with a kettle on top. Surveying the room from within a glass case, a china doll stood. She had blonde curly hair, and bright blue eyes that matched her crinoline and parasol. Naoko let out a little gasp of pleasure:

"Oh, Angela-san! I think you will be very happy here," she said.

The Kitamuras reversed, cautiously, down the narrow track, narrowly avoiding a two-foot muddy drop into the rice field, and, with a final wave, they drove away.

I was surprised that Joji cooked the lunch. He was tossing slivers of fish in oil as Mieko, his commis chef, handed him tiny fungi and squares of meat from the big, free standing fridge, whilst also laying the table, gliding to and fro from a red 'utility' glass reeded cabinet, selecting bowls and saucers. Fumiko sat on the floor, eating crisps, watching her parents, but making no attempt to help. I remembered a phrase from my textbook, and offered to help Mieko, but she, blinking behind thick horn-rimmed glasses, shook her head violently. I must rest myself after my journey. In the afternoon, Joji Uno insisted on driving me back to Kanazawa to show me the route to the college and back to his house. His van was not like the cherished conveyance of the Kitamuras. This was an aged vehicle with an old car seat bouncing from side to side in the back, rattling against his tool box. It had a rusty step, and the passenger door had no outer handle.

He drove with one hand on the wheel, pointing out places of interest:

"Very good shoe-mender that. When your shoes need mending, you go there and say you a friend of Joji Uno. I was at school with him, so, no problem."

He swerved in front of two cyclists and a taxi, driving down a narrow street of wooden houses and shops, many displaying linen banners.

"Old quarter. Here they sell the silk for kimonos, and hand-made paper. Also they make our special famous Kanazawa sweets." Ah.

I looked out at the passers-by, many wearing traditional long blue cotton robes and wooden shoes. From behind beaded curtains, delicious spicy smells filtered into the van. "I was born here. See? Just down that street."

We came to the bridge over the Asinagawa river, and, abruptly, he stopped the van. Behind us, cars braked sharply, but, no one hooted, no one shouted insults, as Joji Uno got out, telling me to follow. Together, we peered down at the fast-flowing river.

"Here, my brother and I used to fish for salmon. Sometimes, big fish we caught. I took them back to my father and brothers, and it was I cooked for them. We were so hungry then, after the war, and we had no money." He explained that his mother had died shortly after the war, from lack of food and medicine.

"Many ordinary folk were like that, then. But, of course, not the rich ones, oh no. In Tokyo they still had money, and did not care what happened to the likes of us."

I asked who had brought them up.

"My father. He was a schoolteacher. All of us boys went to school, and, we worked. I was eight years old. My job was to cook for the family."

I remembered VJ Day in London … the cheering crowds I had been a part of in Trafalgar Square. But, back in Mattoh, a little boy of eight saw his mother die from malnourishment, and was cooking for his family.

We went on to O'Micho market, heaving with people, fingering the fruit and vegetables, and bargaining shrilly with the stallholders. On display were pyramids of mangoes; persimmons and tangerines gleamed beside luscious plums, there were rush baskets full of figs, and platters of nuts placed on fig leaves.

Joji seemed to know every seller, cheerfully helping himself to grapes while bargaining for daikon, the long white radish served with most meals.

"American?" queried the grape owner, leaning across his display, jerking his head at me.

"No, no. From England," Joji told him, leaving the grapes and sinking his teeth into a large apple priced at 200 yen (nearly £1). "Aaa, Joji-san! Ni-hyaku yen desu!"

Joji ignored him.

"A Shakespeare lady, this! She speak Queen's English," said Joji, with pride.

It rang no bells. The stallholder glinted gold teeth at me, and the two men resumed bargaining. We returned, laden, to the van. I refused to carry the sack of live crabs.

There was still about half an hour before dark. I wandered out to explore the neighbourhood, giving the Unos' dog a wide berth.

Beyond the paddy fields, now crunchy with yellow rice stubble, blue ragged mountains stretched to the sky. Kestrels hovered, keening at each other, sometimes settling in groups on telegraph wires along the track. I walked along narrow tracks that bisected the paddy fields, to a small, curly-roofed temple standing among trees, surrounded by groups of strange carved wooden and granite gods, some with beaks. Like on a totem pole. Nearby were a cluster of wooden houses, their gardens full of persimmon trees, their fruit branches laden to the ground, buzzing with dozy, feasting wasps. An old man approached, riding a bike. He skidded to a halt beside me, his feet out-stretched like a water bird coming in to land, and looked me up and down. Finally he asked: "Do you like Japan?"

That much, at least, I could say: "Hai. Nihon de, daisuki desu!"

Satisfied, he smiled, and rode away down the track. It was growing chilly, and dark. The distant mountains were nearly invisible; bats flickered round the temple as I walked back towards the lights of the Unos house. I agree with Naoko. I think I shall be happy here.

The morning sun is shining through the window. I have unpacked, and hung as many clothes as possible on the hat stand. My textbooks and notes are piled on the black desk. Time to start studying.

"Angela-san?"

Joji had returned from his night shift, looking remarkably wide awake. He showed me a photo of himself, wearing a blue kimono, standing in macho profile, feet outstretched, holding a bow and arrow. Would I like to see Kyudo, the art of Japanese archery? Of course I would.

"Yes please, Joji-san. Kyudo de, daisuki desu."

Like Sumo wrestling, only seen on the Kitamuras' TV, Kyudo has a ceremonial, almost sacred atmosphere about it. Joji and I knelt on cushions, looking across to a wooden gallery, where a line of archers stood, facing targets set at the end of a grass sward. There were about fifteen archers, all wearing long robes and white divided-toed socks, the 'tabi' that Howaito-san had worn. In the front line stood a man who must have been at least seventy. He was bare-chested, an animal skin across one shoulder. Behind him stood a very beautiful young girl in a white cotton robe; she couldn't have been more than eighteen. On command, a trio of archers stepped forward; all bowed, raised their bows in unison, and extended the strings of their bows as far as possible. In total silence, they waited, tense, and motionless. Another staccato order, and three silver-tipped arrows flashed through the air. Only one hit the target: that of the old man. The others, expressionless, retired. Next, it was the turn of the young woman. She took her stand with two others, and stood like a beautiful statue, her lips tight. They strode three paces, waiting for the order. 'Fire!'

This time, only she hit the target, her arrow trembling, dead centre, on the bullseye.

"Photo OK?" I whispered to Joji.

"Sure. No problem."

As others lined up once more, I took my flash photo. And, then another, as they raised their bows. The aged umpire glanced at us impassively, before issuing another order. All the archers lowered their bows. We were approached by an official, also wearing a white kimono. He knelt beside Joji, whispering. Joji nodded. He turned to me.

"I think we go now, Angela-san."

We left, hurriedly.

"Joji-san! I'm so sorry … did my flash?"

Joji Uno, clambering back into his van, looked unrepentant.

" Yeah, yeah … flash disturb archers, but, no problem. You have your photos!"

Lunch was a slice of cold meat and fruit, because, apparently, Joji's older brother and wife are coming to supper tonight. I retired to my room, determined to get on with as much work as possible. It was not to be.

"Angela-san! Come and meet my friend."

The Rabbit Man was sitting at the kitchen table, drinking green tea, a large white rabbit on his lap. He bowed to me, whilst continuing to fondle the ears of the rabbit. Mieko, ever attentive, poured me a bowl of green tea. I sat and tried to catch a word or two of the conversation, but I think it was largely in local dialect. From the little I could make out, I thought they were talking about music.

Two more bowls of green tea. I was wondering if it would be considered rude for me to slip away quietly, when Joji suddenly bounded to his feet, announcing, "We go now, Angela-san."

We all, except Mieko, went outside. The Rabbit Man mounted his old sit-up-and-beg bicycle, his rabbit placed tenderly in its bicycle basket, and Joji and Fumiko swung onto theirs. I was handed Mieko's bike, as the others set off down the track at speed.

I had not ridden a bicycle since childhood. Was it true that, once ridden, never forgotten?

"Come on, Angela-san," Joji shouted, from halfway down the lane.

One foot on a pedal, I scooted for a few lengths, and then mounted, wobbling from side to side. Whenever we came to a side road, I dismounted, crossed it, and got on again, careering in pursuit of the others, my front wheel veering manically from right to left as I attempted to steer. Mieko's old bike had a mind of its own. However, the breeze was refreshing, and I was making progress. Bumping over the railway lines at Mattoh railway station, and remembering the distance from the Unos' house to it, I contemplated hiring a bike. It would be far quicker than walking to the station each morning, I reasoned. We were now coming into the little town of Mattoh. The others, cycling unconcernedly some fifty yards further on, mounted a pavement and carried on cycling, past a parade of shops.

That kerb was my undoing. Teeth clenched, I sped my bike up over the edge of the pavement, swerved to avoid a shop placard, and fell off, collapsing onto a lamp-post. A couple of shopkeepers came running out, and Joji, Fumiko, and the Rabbit Man (still clutching his rabbit) dashed to my side.

"Are you alright, Angela-san?"

"O'genki desu!" I assured them, breathlessly, still sprawled on the pavement. Only two bruises: my knee and my dignity.

"But you should have told me you couldn't ride a bicycle," Joji said, reproachfully. He helped me up, watched by assembled by-standers.

I scooted most of the rest of the way.

Our host's house was a small wooden building, down a cobbled alley. He pushed open the sliding door and led the way into a room with ricepaper walls. All around them were rabbits. Rabbits of all colours, brown, albino, black, grey, and brindled. Some were in cages, munching lettuce, others hopping round the floor.

We left our shoes in the straw and were offered house slippers by his wife who greeted us on her knees inside the living-room step. Now we entered a dark room, built of some sort of baked mud. There was tatami on the floor, and the end wall appeared to be made of ricepaper. Our hostess saw that we were all kneeling comfortably on zabuton, served us the inevitable green tea, and made a great fuss of Fumiko, bringing her biscuits and chocolate bars. Rabbit Man brought in a brindled rabbit and sat, peacefully smoking, with it on his knee. Joji attempted to pet it, but, without warning, the small creature sank its teeth into his hand.

"Wah! That animal is dangerous!" Joji said, sucking his wrist.

Its owner continued caressing his rabbit, and Joji turned to me, grimacing.

"He say it is shy," he told me.

Now, Mrs Rabbit Man slid back the ricepaper wall, revealing a large screen. Her husband, cigarette dangling from his lip, and shy rabbit tucked securely under one arm, was fumbling on a shelf.

"Bartok?" he queried.

"No," Fumiko said. "Ballet, please."

From all corners of the room, Tchaikovsky flooded out from a stereo, and, onto the screen, danced the little swans. Later, there was Debussy. Rabbit Man was undecided. Which conductor would he favour? Finally:

"I think, today, we will enjoy George Sholti conduction," he declared.

Every shelf in that tiny room was crowded with audio-visual discs, others were filled with classical CDs. Behind the screen, his cabinets were filled with long-playing records. I marvelled.

"It is my hobby," he said, simply.

Joji Uno's brother came, as promised, to dine with us that night, and Mieko had prepared a mighty feast. More and more dishes kept arriving at the table for us to sample. Older brother was much interested in the status of my husband. What was his job? Why had he permitted me to come, alone, to Japan? I transformed my spouse into a jet-setting executive, and oriented him primarily in Australia, that being the furthest place I could think of, but stated that his services might well be required in many cities throughout America, and possibly Canada …

"So, you see," I explained, "there would be no point in my staying at home, alone."

Joji nodded, knowingly, and turned to older brother.

"Angela-san married to big business man," he informed him.

Four hours later, we still knelt at the dining table. But, at last, older brother couldn't manage another mouthful, despite Mieko's entreaties. As the men left, I insisted on helping Mieko wash up. This entails first soaking each item before individually swabbing it with a soapy sponge under a cold running tap, and finally rinsing it under another tap. The process takes forever before every bowl and container can be dried, and replaced in the green kitchen cabinet. I retire to bed, stupified with exhaustion, my tummy bulging from a surfeit of food.

What an amazing day! Back to college tomorrow.

I caught the train from Mattoh to Kanazawa the folowing morning, looking like a bag lady. Mieko had made me place short welly boots in one plastic bag, the sandwiches she had sweetly provided in another, and my handbag and spare cardigan ('in case you feel cold, Angela-san,') in a third. Plus my school satchel.

The train arrived spot on time. As usual, the carriage was filled with people of all ages, all eating. Young businesswomen, dressed in trouser suits, sat staring out in a dreamy kind of a way, their busy fingers extracting tiny chocolate sticks, rather like twiglets, and popping them, one after the other, between perfectly painted lips. Many of them had slightly buck teeth, but this is considered 'cute' in Japan. Schoolgirls, giggling, exchanged little cakes, and broke off pieces of waffle. Older couples tucked into their wooden boxes of bento, using chopsticks. Schoolboys, feet on seats, devoured whatever their mothers have provided: crisps, cans of cola, sweets, and bento. My carriage reeked of food. Once sated, they all fall into a sort of trance, apparently sleeping, drooped over their neighbour until their station is reached. Then, miraculously, as if by a sixth sense, they bound to their feet, and exit the train.

My first one-on-one lesson, with Taniguchi.

Today, the problem set was conjugating adjectives. Vaguely, I remember that both verbs and adjectives are declined according to which group they accord to. I have a ghastly recollection of reading that they conjugate thirteen different ways. Also, there are, seemingly, at least three ways of negativising a verb – or, of course, an adjective. Why does Japanese have to be so deliberately complicated? Taniguchi was being very patient. Regrettably, I was becoming exasperated.

"Now, look, Taniguchi-san … I thought you told me that the word 'mo' meant 'also'?"

"Hai, so desu."

"Then," I said, "how come it now means 'already'?"

"Because that is its meaning within the sentence, Angela-san."

I took a deep breath. "Right. Okay. What about 'kara'? You said it translated as 'because', didn't you?"

"Hai, so desu."

"So. I don't get this sentence, Taniguchi-san: 'the train because Tokyo finished Osaka'?"

"Of course not. This would not make sense, would it, Angela-san? You must observe the positioning of the word within the sentence."

My voice was getting shrill.

"What about 'ni'? You told me, I know you did, that it meant 'from'. Yes?"

"But, sometimes," she said, gently, "we may use it as in your 'on', or maybe, 'at', or 'to'. It could be as in your 'from', you see."

"Taniguchi-san," I said, "let's have a cup of coffee!"

We went down to the staff room together, and spoke of other things.

I am at the local bank in Kanazawa. I desperately need to be able to withdraw the money sent to it by my own bank. This has become urgent, because no one here will accept my Access card, and my fallback float of yen is rapidly coming to an end. Faxes to the Kanazawa bank from the British bank had proved fruitless, although they had sent me copies of documentation, plus my introductory letter to the Kanazawa bank. "You just need to go in with your passport," their letter advised. That is what I am doing. Officials conferred. I was asked to wait. Minutes passed. A quarter of an hour. Half an hour. More time, until a young man approached and said they needed to telephone Tokyo, because they had never received forms like this before. Then, the bank closed.

"You come back tomorrow," said the young man, courteously escorting me to the door.

"But…" the doors closed behind me. The following day, I had a word with Sara, from the college. She spoke fluent Japanese, and rang the bank on my behalf.

"It will be alright, Angela. Go in, and – be patient."

I went in, and smiled sweetly at the official.

"I have come to collect my money," I told him, showing my passport.

The time was 1.35 pm.

At 2.30 pm I was asked for all other documents in my possession, so as to photocopy them.

3 pm, and all other customers were leaving, umbrellas now at the ready. Obviously, the day has gone off.

A bevy of cleaners arrived, hoovers began to hum, and the bank staff lit up cigarettes. All except one charming young woman who asked if I would like to open an account with their branch.

"Yes!" I gasped. "No problem!"

But I would need a stamp.

"Sure. I'll buy one. Where?"

"No, no. You must have one made. A special one."

The bank, once again, closed.

I had no money left. I trudged back up the hill. Sara had left, but Saito was still in the office. She lent me my train fare, and a spare umbrella. I dripped all over her desk, and relieved my feelings about their banking system.

"Tomorrow will be better," she promised.

The following day, I went into that bank, steel in my eyes.

"I want my money," I announced. "Now, please!"

The same official took up three or four well-fingered documents and approached another, who opened up a drawer, counted out the money, and placed it on a little tray.

"Just sign here, please, Cook-san."

I signed, and with deferential smiles and bows they gave me my money, neatly clipped in tidy bundles. I returned Saito's loan, and umbrella. She was looking perplexed.

"Why did you not tell me about the other bank, Angela-san?"

Gradually, I remembered ensuring that I would always be solvent in Japan. If you cannot make contact with X bank, for any reason, please send the money to Y bank, I had said. And they had. Sent money to two banks. Saito assured me I would have no more problems, as she had an account at Y bank, and in future, I could use her personal stamp for an unused account, to withdraw money.

Wonderful though it was to have money once more, I knew I must start to earn some. Tara had got a job working at a local nightclub. She is nineteen years old, pretty, and well capable of staying up half the night. I know my limitations. It was time to advertise my services as an English conversation teacher.

Next day, I looked at the notice-board in the Centre that advertised English lessons. Most of these were of the: 'Hi there, I'm Mike from Idaho, and I'd just love to meet with you Japanese students, and get to know you thru English. Call me, any time on ...'
Or, 'Karen calling. Anyone want to hear about our culture? I come

[93]

from the great Australian outback. Give me a shout on …' variety.

I was surprised by the ingenuousness of the Japanese students posting their own advertisements. These read: 'My name is Yasuko. I am 22 years old. I am a graduate from X University. I would like to meet and talk with an English teacher to discuss the Beatles, and fashion …'. Or, 'rock and roll, and film stars'. These were mostly printed in coloured biro on message slips. I shrink from putting up my own. What on earth could I say to encourage prospective students? 'Middle-aged English female who left school early and has absolutely no experience of teaching or imparting grammar, minimal knowledge of pop stars, seeks students'? Hardly a riveting inducement. I decide to leave it for another day, although recognising that this part of Japan exists in a timewarp, often MY timewarp! Restaurants, hotels, shops, and, of course, Kanazawa Mr Do-Nuts are still blaring out music by the Beatles, and Madonna's songs remain popular, interspersed with Japanese pop songs. I have even hears popular songs from 'The Sound of Music' played as background music in genteel hotels and banks.

However, I will get some practice. Joji Uno has asked me to help him in his capacity as Volunteer Teacher of English Language to a group of local children, aged between seven and twelve. I agree at once, because I owe him so much. Were it not for his generosity, I could not continue daily classes at the centre. He has insisted that I pay him a reduced rent because his house is far out and my rail fares considerable. I protested that it had been my decision to ask his family to be my hosts, but he refused to listen.

"I will not accept the full rent from you, because now we are friends," he told me. I too, am starting to feel that he, and his quiet, caring little wife, are indeed good friends.

Today, I have no lessons. Mieko has ridden her bike off to her sandwich-making job, leaving me a sample sandwich on the kitchen table. All morning I have sat at my desk, working. It is the season of chilly autumn days, sunshine occasionally breaking through the clouds, shining onto the rice stubble. Fumiko is back from school, playing ball with her friends, driving Koro to a frenzy of barking. He strains at his leash, ignored by the children. Cautiously, I approach the kennel, and am met with a wagging tail and wet tongue, licking my hand. I stayed, petting him, remembering my own Serena, back home in Ireland, loved, walked twice a day, a part of our lives. That evening, I asked Joji's permission to take Koro for a walk.

"Why you want?" Joji asked, drinking his glass of beer, poured as usual, by Mieko.

Mieko was worried.

"You will tire yourself, Angela-san. Dog too strong."

They both stood in the porch, watching, as we set off at a gallop, tacking across the uneven rice paddy fields, Koro wildly excited, me hanging onto his leash with both hands. For a split second we halted at a gully, as Koro paused to savour an intriguing scent, and then careered on, Koro dragging me in his wake with a shoulder-dragging wrench. Put Koro as lead dog on a sleigh, and early explorers would have reached North, or South Pole in record time. Maybe both. We arrived back at the house, panting. Joji took the leash from me and shouted at the dog, who instantly cowered.

"Ladies cannot control dogs," he laughed.

"But some can," I protested. I launched into a bit of propaganda on Koro's behalf, explaining how much exercise people in Europe gave their pet dogs.

"Even our Royal Family are renowned for exercising their corgi dogs," I told them. Joji was interested: "Ha?"

I waxed lyrical, explaining that, as children, our Queen, and her sister used to take the dogs for long, long walks every day, after their lessons.

"In the West, we believe it is good for the character of children to be kind to animals."

"You hear that, Fumiko? Angela-san say that the Queen take dog for walk every day!"

Fumiko, toasting a sweet potato at the stove, looked singularly unimpressed.

The following weekend, Joji asked if I would like to see the sea of Japan, and I suggested we take Koro. We drove to a pebbly beach,

Koro tied up in the boot. I had somehow imagined that the sea in the East would look different, but it didn't; same sort of shingle, same shells. However, the water was still much warmer than at home, and I took off my shoes and paddled in the shallows. Fumiko and her father did not, shivering and uttering cries of "Waaah! Samui desu!"

"Suppose," I suggested, "we let Koro off the lead … what would he do?"

"He go," replied Joji, simply.

"Really?"

He humoured me, unclipping the lead. Koro ran in ecstatic circles around us. We ran, and, he ran. We separated and called him, and he bounded between us. Success! Then, suddenly, he spotted some animal in the distance, and took off. All of us chased after him until he disappeared over far-off sand dunes. Twenty minutes later, Joji Uno went back to his van to pursue Koro on wheels. Fumiko and I, red-faced and out of breath, made our way back to the car park. It did not take much imagination to decypher her thoughts: British Royal Family doggy preferences bedamned, her family had been saddled with an old English woman who was, patently, daft as a brush. We did not speak.

Ten minutes later Joji's van drove into the car park, with, thank God, Koro on board, tied up once again. I apologised, profusely.

"No problem, no problem," Joji said.

Oh, Koro! If you could have only known! But I can do no more for you from now on, except walk you on the lead. Later, after we had eaten supper, perhaps to show his forgiveness, Joji suggested that I might like to accompany him to the pub. I hesitated, looking at Mieko.

"But … wouldn't you and Mieko-san like to go together? " I asked. "I mean, I can stay and be with Fumiko?"

They both shook their heads.

"No, no, Angela-san! It is like I told you, she is shy Japanese wife. She don't go to pubs."

We two set off on foot through a light drizzle. Ten minutes later, Joji pushed open the door of what seemed to be an ordinary modern house and led me into a long, dark room with a bar on one side. There were pictures of a beach in Taiwan with wafting palm trees, and shelves of dummy bottles of VSOP surrounding the bar. Joji hoisted himself onto a bar stool, and began a jolly conversation with the owner, a flirtatious forty-something-year-old with scarlet lipstick and a low-cut black blouse. He bought me a Kirin beer, and, after the daughter of the house had produced the usual rolled hot towel to wash our hands, a bowl of cuttlefish and salad. Mr Michelin would have been proud of that cuttlefish.

Gradually, the bar began to fill up with local businessmen, now wearing their uniform casual wear, open neck shirts, or polo necks, and jeans; they smelt of newly applied aftershave. Most seemed to know Joji, all stared at me. I finished my beer, and Joji ordered me another.

"Karaoke?" he enquired.

Anything rather than more cuttlefish.

"Hai, arigato," I said.

The woman behind the bar flashed me a broad smile, and clapped her hands.

"So! 'Yesterday'?" she asked me.

"Sorry?"

A TV monitor was pushed at me, showing a video, and the words of the song, written in English. A microphone was thrust into my hands.

"Hai! Now, you sing!" Joji said.

He had to be joking. There was absolutely no way I was capable of singing 'Yesterday'. Or anything else, for that matter. I mean, I can't sing! Honestly, I can't. A group in the far corner began to clap: 'Uta! Uta!" they shouted. And the music began. I tried.

That music seemed to go on forever. I could not have believed a pop song to have so many deceptive changes of key, so many ups and downs of harmony. I finished, crimson in the face, wishing myself invisible. Everyone applauded, kindly, and more beer circulated. Joji and the owner performed a spontaneous free-style rumba to great acclaim, and I was then grasped in the arms of a very small man who whirled me round and round, using steps somewhere between a waltz and a samba. The bar was now jam-packed with people and cigarette smoke. Someone sang 'Que Sera, Sera', and a group of Thais standing wedged at the far end of the bar sang a national lament, quite beautifully. Joji now claimed me for a dance; a cross between 'The Birdie Dance', and possibly the hokey-kokey. This was greeted with much friendly mirth. I too, was feeling happy; I was on my fourth beer, and second plate of cuttlefish, when Joji suddenly bounded from his stool, and clapped his hands, calling for silence.

"Listen, everybody!" he shouted. "Tonight, we have with us my English guest. I ask you all to stand up, and she will sing 'God Save The Queen'."

There was a scraping of chairs, and everyone got to their feet, standing, silent and reverential, many with one hand placed over their hearts. I looked round the room, taking in some sixty or so mainly Japanese patrons, all standing with lowered eyes. What had I – or, for that matter, Her Majesty – ever done to deserve this?

I slid from my stool, grasped the mike, and gave the assembly the only verse I knew, in my wavering soprano. Dame Kiri Te Kanawa and I, noticeably, have nothing in common.

Joji followed this up with a long lamenting pop song, accompanying a video. It seemed to relate to a father's emotions as he watched his small daughter growing up from a toddler to a young bride. The owner took a flash photo of Joji and me, and we walked home to where Mieko was dutifully waiting up for us.

"O'cha, Angela-san?"

Dear Mieko! "No, thank you, Mieko-san. I think I'll just go to bed."

She smiled sweetly at me. Joji's voice boomed up the stairs after me:

"Are you happy, Angela-san?"

"Yes, thank you! It was a … an unforgettable evening," I said, truthfully.

"I make party go well, and I have good voice, eh?"

"Absolutely, Joji-san. Hyaku pacento! One hundred per cent."

Climbing into bed I reflected that I would probably never understand Mieko. I had now lived in her house for more than two weeks, and I knew no more about her than I had the first day we met. She was dutiful, gentle, and always kind to me – but what did she really think of me? Of having this foreign woman in her home, entertained by her husband? In common with many wives, she was always referred to, not by name, but as 'Okasan', which means 'mother'. Before giving birth to Fumiko she was called 'Okusan', meaning wife. The suffix 'san' has no gender, it is merely a polite way of referring to a person. For children, this is changed to an affectionate 'chan'.

The following evening, I saw another side of the Unos' domestic life. We had eaten supper in unusual silence. Joji was unaccountably brooding, sitting at table with lowered brow. I tried to exercise a new tense I had learnt at college, and asked Fumiko what she had done that day, at school. Fumiko gave me a brief glance:

"Lessons," she muttered.

It was too much for Joji. His hand shot out, and quick as a flash, he slapped his daughter across the face, hard.

"Of course you do lessons at school," he snarled. "Angela-san is not stupid, she know that. Now, you tell her just what lessons you learned today, you hear me?"

Fumiko was crying, great hiccupping, noisy sobs, one hand pressed against her cheek.

"Look," I protested, "it really isn't important."

I noticed Mieko slide from her stool to stand beside her daughter, stroking her head, making soothing noises. Now, Joji Uno's temper erupted; picking up his beer glass, he threw the contents all over Fumiko. The glass shattered against the wall. Mieko moved like lightening; hardly had the broken glass reached the floor before she had pushed Fumiko, now screaming at the top of her voice, out of the room, shut the door, and returned to attempt to placate her husband. Joji, however was giving full vent to his temper; veins standing out in his forehead, he was thumping the table with his fists, as his voice rose to a crescendo of fury. I sat, amazed that such a trivial, if insolent answer could have evoked such a response.

Gradually, the storm abated, from a roar to a grumble, punctuated by Mieko's soft tones cooing rhythmically in the background. She remained acutely alert, I noticed, and when Joji lunged for the door to go after Fumiko, she was only inches behind him. Joining us for supper was Joji's younger brother, a baker. He and I attempted stilted conversation, he trying to explain how he made waffles, against a background of muted roars, screeches, and clucks coming from an upstairs room. The three returned a little later, Fumiko snuffling loudly. Her father made her sit beside me once more.

"Now you will tell Angela-san what lessons you learned today," he said, menacingly.

"History," she gasped.

"And?" growled her father.

"And kanji, and … arithmetic."

"That's interesting," I said. "Thank you, Fumiko."

Joji helped me to a beer, and Mieko poured a replacement for him. She had a cloth in hand and was busily mopping the beer off me, the table, and the wall.

"She is only twelve years old. Very young."

I gathered that Joji was apologising for his daughter. I agreed that at twelve years a child was still a child, but still? Joji leant back in his chair, and prepared to pontificate:

"Here in Japan, nowadays, there is not enough discipline for young people. When the Americans conquer us, they bring their ideas with them, and so now, many parents spoil their children. They think this is modern way. They let them do as they want. I do not like this. This is not the right way to bring up children."

I have seen quite a few children here who conform to his assessment; children who pushed and shoved their way to bus seats, and were rude and noisy, but privately I found it curious that he could ignore Fumiko's frequent refusal to obey her mother, answer her, or pick up a coat from the floor, let alone help round the kitchen.

The sheltered environment provided for all Japanese children I met was in stark contrast to their Western counterparts: here, girls would never be allowed out at any hour of the day unless their parents knew where they would be. Little girls I came to know in other families still played with dolls, fluffy toys and skipping ropes, and spent hours with colouring books, or painting pictures, when aged thirteen or even fourteen, while boys of similar age played ball games, and flew kites at the weekend. Their time is controlled and constantly supervised by parents, teachers, and local youth organisations. Life, for a child in Japan, is one of integration, within the family, school activities, and in the community. All are expected to work hard, and, play hard. Even in a small town such as Mattoh, the sports facilities are, by our standards, extensive.

Every weekend, after her piano lesson, Fumiko goes to a local fencing club for two hours. This club is full of other young people all doing aerobics, or teams practising basketball, and there are also swimming pools, tennis courts, and different hobby classes. The young are encouraged to be intensely competitive in whatever they do. I cannot ever recall seeing groups of children, or teenagers, just hanging out, doing nothing. I note that their children, and young people, are controlled; are governed, and I wonder if we are, perhaps, missing out on some basic, essential element in the bringing up of our next generation?

I bumped into Mr Stanley, the old American student, a few days later, and mentioned the apparent latent violence that could exist. He agreed, telling me domestic violence was widespread. He quoted a friend who had shown him a much-prized carriage clock that was badly dented. His friend explained the damage with a little laugh: "Pity about that mark, but ... well, I was angry with the wife."

He also told me that a politician was recently questioned by a Western journalist about his alleged violence towards his wife. The politician turned to the local press gathered at the interview, saying cheerily: "Look here, boys, how many of you have ever smacked your wives?" The majority happily agreed that they also had been guilty of 'minor' domestic violence.

I woke the following morning with a dry tickle to my throat, and a thick head.

"Please, God! not one of my notorious head colds," I pleaded to the Almighty, preparing to set out on the walk to college.

The temperature variation here is incredible, alternating between the stifling heat of Mieko's kitchen, where the kerosene stove is flaring on three flames, kettle on top, snorting steam, to the long road to the station where an icy wind threatens imminent snow. The train is a moist fug of cigarette smoke, the Centre – because the Authorities will not allow central heating until December – is freezing. Teachers run down corridors, clutching skimpy cotton cardigans to themselves, crying: "Aaa, samui! Samui, desu, neh?"

"So. Get the heating switched on," I suggested to Senior Tutor Kamada.

I sneezed, loudly, three times. She looked surprised.

"But no! It is never switched on before December 1st! I could not, Angela-san."

"Well," I told her, reaching in my pocket for another sodden tissue, "sorry, Kamada-san, but, I am leaving. I am cold. I think I am getting a head cold, and I can't study. I want to go to bed."

She looked concerned, patting my arm, and begging me to take care of my health. I spent the night dipping into my store of Beechams pills. Perhaps they do not work so well if taken in cold water, but my kettle was out of water, and I dared not go down to the kitchen to boil one there, because Joji had elected to sleep that night in the kitchen.

This family varies its sleeping habits from night to night; Fumiko often sleeps in her own room, beside mine, under a Mickey Mouse duvet, and Mieko usually slips up and sleeps on the floor beside her daughter. Sometimes Joji will join them. Other times the couple will retire to a room off the living room, but, occasionally, as tonight, he is sleeping on the floor of the kitchen, in front of the TV. When Joji is on night shift at work, mother and daughter sleep downstairs. In the morning, I go downstairs to cancel today's lessons. Mieko is worried:

"Are you catching a 'kaze'?" she queried. This is a word that can mean either a strong wind, or a head cold.

"No, no," tell her, flexing my biceps in true Japanese mode. "O'genki desu!"

I sneezed, thunderously, twice. The Uno family look appalled. Apparently it is an A1 social gaffe to sneeze in company, and I apologised. Joji launches into an explanation of the word 'kaze'.

"Once, when our country was about to be invaded, Angela-san, a great wind suddenly sprang up, sinking the invaders' fleet. Ever afterwards, exceptionally brave young Samurai were allowed to adopt the name of that saviour wind. Like, 'kamikaze pilots'."

Mieko cycled off to her sandwich-making factory, and I retired to bed to nurse my kaze, not feeling particularly brave. She had brought a pizza to sustain me.

I turned off my kerosene stove, opened my window, and slept intermittently throughout the day, waking every few minutes to sneeze some more. That evening, I crept downstairs, red-eyed, and told Mieko that I wouldn't want any supper that night, thank you. She looked as if I had stabbed her to the heart, following me upstairs, to beg me, on her knees, to eat a little something.

"Thank you, Mieko-san, but, truly, I couldn't. I'm fine … tomorrow, I'll be better, and, I'll eat then, OK?" I slid my door shut, to avoid sneezing at her, and reached for more tissues.

Five minutes later Mieko came in, bringing me a plate of biscuits, closing the window, and turning up the stove to full volume. I turned it off.

Twenty minutes passed before I heard a soft shuffling, and Mieko crept in bearing a bowl of ice cream. She closed the window, and, once more, lit the stove. Next, it was a plate of chocolate cookies, placed tenderly on the desk. Then she came with a bag of sweets. Mieko would put the stereotypical Jewish Mama to shame. I resolve to be extra nice to her next day to make it up to her, but, when she entered to bring me a jug of boiling rice water just as I had fallen asleep, my resolve went out the window.

"GO AWAY!" I growled.

She placed the jug by my bedside, stroked my forehead with a cool hand, and slipped away. I felt ill – and ashamed.

Joji and Fumiko had already left when I came down to breakfast. Mieko was preparing a special, nourishing one for me; on the hotplate, bubbling in stock, and flavoured with chopped chives, lay a plump goldfish, eyeing me with a glazed milky stare. I remembered my dentist's aquarium, and averted my gaze. It was placed in front of me, in a turquoise blue bowl.

"Um … I'd rather not eat the head, Mieko-san?"

She looked disappointed, but ultimately ate it herself.

"Oishii desu, neh?"

Absolutely. "Taihen oishii desu, Mieko-san. Domo Arigato Gozaimasu."

She was now sliding busily round her kitchen, darting to her gas ring, slippers off as she gets to the square of carpet in front of the kerosene stove, slippers on again as she opens the fridge door, and discarded once more as she reaches the table to present me with a cold fried egg. Kneeling on her stool, cigarette in hand, she watches me, benignly.

"Eat, Angela-san. Good for your body condition."

I pick up my chopsticks to dissect the fried egg, while she is pushing a little barricade of goodies around my plate; a tub of marge, salad, a bun, pickle, and, of course, a big bowl of rice. As I start to eat, she kindly spoons powdered milk into my coffee mug, stirring it to save me the trouble.

A flabby morsel of egg slip from my chopsticks just before I make contact with it. Mieko makes good the smear with a handy damp cloth. Her smile never wavers. Noticing a breach in her fortifications, she fills it with a jar of salad cream:

"Kore wa oishii, Angela-san!"

I am not allowed to help with the washing up, because 'my body condition has not been good', so I go to the washbasin beside the twin tub washing machine where yesterday's washing is soaking in cold water, brush my teeth, and leave her to her favourite moment of the day: those few precious moments when, mug of Nescafé in one hand, cigarette in the other, she can close her eyes to the world.

Joji's shift finished early today. He bounded into the house asking after my 'body condition'.

I told him I was fine now, especially after Mieko's wonderful breakfast.

"Good, good. Then, we go to Kanazawa. I take you to see Kenrokuen Park."

Kenrokuen, the famous park, was delightful: stately, green, and charming. Joji explained the relevance of many of the shrines. One story related to the two stone, dog-like creatures, whose significance has to do with our human passage through life and through death. Some shrines can only be approached under a tall arch, called 'tori' – the word for 'birds'. All these had a heavy, looped rope with tassels for the faithful to shake, so as to attract the attention of the gods.

Often, outside many of these tori, two trees stood, festooned with white paper strips. I was reminded of the curling papers I used to use on my straight hair, before going on a date. But these were intercessions, placed by students hoping for favourable results.

In our Western world, they light candles.

I remembered another occasion, talking to Naoko's students. They had all bowed their heads before eating, uttering an invocation. And, I had said that, we too, had been taught to pray:

"For what we are about to receive, may the Lord make us truly thankful."

They looked at me in astonishment: "In the West, you pray?"

I realised then that the understanding of my European world was rooted basically by American television films. Many of these showed violent scenes, watched contentedly by the Japanese people, all, or most, happily secure in the knowledge that their government would not permit such disturbance.

Joji led me past the Marriage Tree – an ancient, colossal tree that had once fused with its neighbour, great roots stretching out from its trunk; more an object of sculptural curiosity than a thing of beauty. Hopping and scuttering round it, two pigeons were courting; the male with chest fully plumped out pursuing his more dowdy mate who was playing a coy Chase-me-Charlie in and out of the roots. Groups of Japanese day-trippers produced cameras, and when finally the male claimed his connubial rights, the happy couple and the Marriage Tree were captured for posterity on a few hundred Nikons.

The typhoon had wrecked terrible damage; ancient trees lay uprooted on the ground, now surrounded by park workers swarming up bamboo ladders, erecting wigwams of bamboo with ropes to secure tree branches against winter snowfall.

We walked to a lake, autumn trees mirrored on its surface, and crossed a narrow wooden bridge leading to a crimson café also reflected on the water. Koi carp surrounded the bridge. These koi had become thoroughly clued up about visitors; every footstep on the wooden bridge to the tea house caused a flurry below, and there they all were, apricot ones, spotty ones, silver and white ones, tails thrashing the water, beady eyes fixed on the person above, and all with round pouting mouths, prepared to vacuum up any dropped crumb, ululating silently, but looking like a chorus of operatic divas.

We sat in the tea house, drinking bowls of green tea, gazing out at the the cypress, sumac and maples reflected in the waters of the lake. Kenrokuen was so beautiful. I would have liked to have gone back to bed, and just reflected on it; gone to bed and dreamed of the beauty of that place. But it was not to be.

I had promised Joji that I would teach local children conversational English, and he had recruited a group in the nearby schoolhouse. This would show me if I was any good at teaching! I had never taught before, and had grave doubts about my ability to actually teach English.

The schoolroom had about twenty children, all sitting behind desks, awaiting our arrival. Fumiko sat in the middle of the front row, looking glum.

Joji and I mounted the podium, facing them. Behind us, a blackboard.

"Hallo, children!"

I beamed at them. Mieko, recruited to record the event, had her camera poised. No child spoke.

"You answer the Teacher!" Joji roared, from beside me. "You hear me?"

A small boy in the back row began to cry. Fumiko, mesmerised by her father, muttered, "Hallo, teacher," and Joji smiled.

I did my best. Still with a fixed smile, I wrote up the verb 'To be' on the blackboard, and had them chant it after me. I pointed at myself. "I am the teacher. Okay?" I pointed at them: " You are the students. Shall we try to say it?" "I am the teacher, you are the students." Dutifully, they repeated the words, understanding nothing. On the board I drew a dog. "It is a dog!" I announced. "A dog." I drew another. "Two dogs, right? Dogsssss we say. Woof woof! A cat, two catsssss … miauw! A bird, two, three, four birdsss, tweet-tweet …" I sounded like Golum, in Lord of the Rings.

"Attend to the teacher" Joji instructed, menacingly.

Desperately, I drew a smiley face on the blackboard:

"I am happy!" I announced. Then, I drew a sad face, with down-turned mouth.

"I am sad. Shall we all say that?"

Silence.

I can't do this.

"Shall we all sing a special English song all children like to sing?"

I decided against giving them 'Baa-baa Black Sheep' since a) all sheep in Japan are kept in sheds, and never seen by children, b) they apparently bleat 'Maa', not 'Baa', if heard at all, and the concept of explaining 'a dame' through Joji was well beyond my capabilities. We had a wavering attempt at 'Twinkle, Twinkle', led by me, and illustrated on the board.

At no time did any child look at me. Apparently, eye contact is considered rude. At the end of the hour, I gave out little bags of sweets to every child, and watched them clatter out onto the laneway, newly animated, chattering, relieved to be released. How on earth am I going to to earn money for my lessons? Born teacher, I ain't. Joji and Mieko, however, seem content.

"You teach, English-style," Joji said. "This is good. I like English-style teach. Modern, this is."

Fumiko, trudging beside her father, linking arms, said nothing.

—◊—

The Centre seems almost deserted without its foreign students. Our old students' salon is shut up, and our teachers take their few pupils into their own staff salon for coffee. After my private lesson, I popped my head round the door of the admin office to see if any mail had come for me. Only three staff were there, huddled round a one-bar electric heater; Miyazaki, who was now in charge of the few remaining students, Mari, the secretary, and Saito. They were eating cake. Even when relaxing, Saito, wearing her usual tweeds, managed to look like a frenetic journalist trying to meet a deadline, her hair sticking up where she ran her hands through it. She was talking, rapidly, on the phone. Mari, in her usual immaculate white shirt and navy skirt, looked up at me and smiled.

"Cake, Angela-san?" Miyazaki had a closed pussycat face, and a penchant for fluffy pink or lavender jumpers. "We were just talking about you," she added.

"Me? Why?"

Outside the wind lashed rain against the windows; leafless branches tossed and thrashed. It was going to be a long, wet journey back to the Unos.

Saito put the phone down.

"As you know, Angela-san, this Saturday, EuroCentre will give an end-of-season party for all our host families," she remarked, conversationally.

"That's nice," I said, my mouth full of cake.

"And," she continued, "because most of the students have now left, we have decided that you should represent them, and give a little speech. In Japanese, of course."

I swallowed. "Saito-san … I mean, I, well, I am of course honoured to be asked, but I do not think my Japanese is good enough. Seriously, I couldn't. They wouldn't understand what I was saying."

"Some would," Saito, ever the realist.

"And the teachers would all help you write it," added Miyazaki, helpfully.

"It will make our host families very happy to hear you," Mari said, clapping her hands.

"And, it should be you, Angela-san. You are our oldest student."

Thank you for pointing that out, Saito.

Some considerable time later, I gave up. With the proviso that I alone would write my own speech, and deliver it, warts and all.

"And now, if you will excuse me, I had better get off and catch my train. I'll make a start on the speech after I've done my homework, tonight. Lovely cake, Miyazaki-san, thank you."

I, my bags and dripping brolly made for the door, but Saito called me back.

"Just tell me, Angela-san ... when would you prefer to make your speech? Before you do the dance, or, after?"

"DANCE?"

"Hai, hai," they chorused. "Did Tara-san not tell you?"

I plonked my baggage back on the floor, and prepared to do battle. Saito, undeterred by my expression, continued cheerily.

"It is arranged. You and Tara-san will dance traditional Japanese dance at our party, wearing true Japanese kimono."

"Absolutely not. No way. I am not prepared to perform a Japanese dance, or a Highland Fling, or any other dance. For heaven's sake, Saito-san! I don't know any Japanese dances!"

"This is no problem. We have made the arrangements. Two Japanese Dance instructors are going to teach you and Tara, and dress you in kimono, right?"

"No."

Mari looked about to cry. "Please, Angela-san?"

"I'm sorry, Mari," I told her.

Saito carried on, blithely: "And, all our host families will enjoy it so much, and Tara-san will enjoy it so much, and you, Angela-san, will enjoy it so much. It will be such a happy experience for all of us."

They must have laced that cake with something mind-blowing. Ultimately, I gave in.

Battling against the blizzard along the long road from the railway station at Mattoh, it was now too dark to make out the potholes.

Unseen schoolboys pedalled past me at high speed on unlit bikes, swerving to avoid me at the last minute, bells tinging. I was thoroughly cross with myself, and Saito, and Tara, for not having warned me.

Why hadn't I stuck to that wonderful little Saxon word, NO, I grumbled, swearing as a very small car zoomed past, soaking me in muddy water.

It was nearly midnight before I got down to preparing the speech, determined to try and achieve the correct degree of politeness for the occasion, and, if possible, the right tense. At least my dictionary was supplying me with a few novel superlatives. But was that phrase an 'if' clause, or, should it refer to the previous sentence, whereby, it became a 'when'? Again, there was the possibility that it was more like the suffix 'because'? And, what about the important little word 'no'? In Japanese it can mean 'apertaining to', or 'belonging to', depending on whether one is referring to the subject, or the object.

Mieko crept into my room to close my window against the dangers of the night air, and to bring me a sweet potato for my body condition. She tutted that I had only one bar of the heater on, turned it up, and crept noislessly out again. Just for her, I would like to get my speech right; she is so gentle and sweet, and I have come to learn that the more one gets right, the greater appreciation one shows for the kindness of the host families.

Saturday, at midday, I arrived at the International Lounge, suitably attired, I hoped, to deliver a speech on behalf of all the six or seven hundred foreign students who had been to the Centre for their one-month course over the past year. I wore a business-like navy suit, a blouse with a Thatcher-type bow at the neck, court shoes, and unobtrusive pearl earrings, as befitted one who was, after all, the oldest remaining foreign student. I had timed my speech; spoken slowly, it lasted approximately five minutes. I was slightly bothered by its brevity, knowing that all Japanese dignitaries spoke for a minimum of twenty minutes, but hoped that this possible breach of good manners would be excused.

Tara raised an eyebrow: "Wow! Power dressing, eh?"

"My new public persona," I explained.

"Okay. So, now, bring on the dancing girls."

There were indeed two dancing instructors. Senior coach was a squat, middle-aged lady with highly suspect coal-black hair piled high, a la Madame Pompadour, and scarlet lipstick. Her assistant was Kato-san, a gawky young woman with buck teeth. I remembered seeing similar young women involved in Folk dance, and Morris dance, and Square dance, the world over – ardent enthusiasts all, much given to bossily pushing other dancers into place, whilst tapping, or clapping to the rhythm. Neither teacher had more than a few sketchy words of English.

Under direction, we slipped on the divided-toe tabi, and picked up coolie straw hats, each adorned with circlets of paper flowers and little bells.

"We call dance: 'Japanese hat with paper flowers dance'," explained Kato.

She switched on the ghetto blaster on the floor. It gave out tinkly music.

"JAAAAAA, hai!"

Madame Pompadour glided onto the floor, elegantly twirling her hat from side to side. Her assistant, smiling eagerly, pushed us into line behind her. We four sallied forth in a crocodile, fixed smiles in place, swaying slightly in time to the music. Now the line faced front, and began the steps of the dance: glide right, 1-2-3, whilst turning the hat from hand to hand. Stamp twice, then glide left, 1-2-3, holding hat flat against tummy. Then jiggle it, to make the little bells ring. Next, step forward and reverse hat so that paper flowers face audience. Another single stamp. Right foot extended, jingle. Left foot forward, another jingle. Raise blasted hat over head with both hands, and curtsey, simpering. Simper right. Simper left, and finally execute a slow, decorous pirouette whilst alternating hat on the inner elbow.

"Repeat, AGAIN!"

Had the teachers allowed us to stand behind them and copy their actions, we might have got it. But no, traditionally we had to learn in line, Madame in the lead, Kato, alias Bossy Boots, bringing up the rear. Tara and I, trying to watch our instructors out of the corner of our eyes, constantly glided the wrong way, causing minor damage to the paper roses, and BB considerable distress:

"No, no, Angela-san! Oh, no … left, left, left, and stamp, hai?"

Madame, however, continued to dance, seemingly oblivious of her pupils. She was patently enjoying herself, beginning to sing along in a high-pitched, little girl voice:

"Haaa-eee-aaa-ai-eee, aaa-ai-eee, aaa aa," The bells on her hat jingled in time to the music, whilst to her left, the two stooges essayed a confused Eastern version of the hokey-kokey, punctuated by snuffled murmers of: "Ooops!" "Sorry, Tara"… "Oh God, sorry, Angela …"

Beside me, Kato attempted to rectify my pirouette: "Like SO, Angela-san."

"Scuse me, Angela, but, your roses are getting up my nose," Tara murmured, circling in the opposite direction. We stopped dancing, shaking with barely suppressed laughter.

Mindful of the Tea Ceremony fiasco, I attempted to pull myself together.

"Seriously, I do think it would be easier for us to follow if we danced a little behind you," I told Bossy Boots. She was indignant.

"Not the way we do it!"

The music finally stopped.

Tara said a big, smiling "Arigato," and I joined her.

"We'll do our best," I promised, looking at my watch. "Sayonara!"

Madame was changing the tape. She flashed us a brilliant smile. "Now, we teach Harvest Dance!"

Tara's mouth fell open: "You gotta be joking!"

New music blared out, and this time, although still distinctly Oriental, it had a more robust, Country and Western flavour. Once again, we were chivvied into line, positioned as before. This dance seemed to be conducted in a crouching position; knees bent, our shuffling conga wound its way round the floor. By peering round Tara's jeans, I made out Madame gesturing sharply to the right, hand held taut:

"Cut, cut right," came the accompanying chant from the rear. Madame repeated the gesture on the other side.

"Cut, cut left."

No problem.

Still stooping, we copied two 'dig, digs' with relative success.

With a graceful gesture, Madame now straightened up, languidly running her hand across her forehead, thereby stepping back into the residue of Tara's stooping 'dig' (even in stockinged feet, young Tara must be all of 5'6" of shapely Canadian womanhood). Not a hair of Madame's helmet came adrift, and her wistful smile stayed in place.

"Gee, I'm so sorry, Madame ..."

"Wipe sweat, wipe sweat," intoned Kato, keeping strictly to the beat.

Leaning slightly back, Madame appeared to shake herself, and then turn.

"Jiggle breasts, jiggle breasts, and turn," explained good old Bossy Boots.

As one, Tara and I stopped.

"WHAT DID YOU SAY?" Tara demanded.

The music played on, as BB, ever willing to instruct, repeated the movement, suiting action to word: "Jiggle breasts, jiggle breasts, and turn, OK?"

"Now, just you listen to me" I said, so loudly that even Madame stopped dancing.

"There is absolutely NO WAY that either Tara or I intend to jiggle our breasts for the entertainment of the host families in Kanazawa. Right? Understand?"

They didn't, but they recognised something was seriously wrong. They consulted.

"Dig, dig?" Madame queried, hesitantly.

"That's fine by me."

"Cut, cut?"

"No problem."

"Wipe sweat, wipe sweat?" put in BB, looking anxious.

"OK."

"Jiggle breasts, jiggle breasts?"

"NO WAY!" we chorused.

Both teachers were looking crestfallen. I looked at my watch; in about half an hour, all host families would be arriving at the Centre, across the road. Saito would be shamed if we didn't turn up.

"Tell you what I am prepared to do," I told them, "when it comes to that bit, I'll do a little wiggle – a sort of throwback to the days of Rock and Roll." I demonstrated. They looked bewildered, but relieved.

"Groovy!" Tara said.

I looked at her austerely, over my silk bow, and spoke in mock plummy tones:

"A bum wiggle does not offend my culture, Tara-san. A breast jiggle does."

We managed a mouthful of delicious lunch laid on by the International Lounge before an agitated figure appeared, dragging us off to a taxi.

"But why?" I asked, "I mean, the Centre is only over the road …"

The taxi took us through traffic to Kanazawa's most prestigious hotel. Commissionaires approached on either side, escorting us through an immense foyer dripping with chandeliers and floral arrangements, past a long table laden with platters of exquisitely displayed food. Upstairs, we came to an enormous room with a stage at the far end, filled with hundreds of people in formal suits and silk dresses, all clutching glasses of waeen, and chatting. The host families. And, their relations.

Tara and I looked at each other in horror. "Oh, my God!" we breathed.

Naoko spotted me from afar, and came running across to greet me.

"Angela-san! Ogenki deshitaka?"

"Genki desu, taihen genki desu, arigato, Naoko-san," I lied, feeling distinctly unwell.

"Hoshiri-san wa?" She shook her head sadly. Hoshiri had to work.

Across the room, Joji raised his glass of beer to me, mouthing "Kampai!" I couldn't see Mieko. Somebody tapped me on the elbow. Saito-san, almost unrecognisable in a smart green silk suit. She looked tense.

"You stand here, beside the platform, and watch me. You are to give your speech after Watanabe-san, the Chairman. When he has finished, I shall nod, and introduce you. Then, you climb the steps, thank the Chairman on behalf of the foreign students, and make your speech. Right?"

I extracted my speech from my school satchel, realising I had not prefaced it with any thanks to the Chairman (and, how on earth did one say 'on behalf of' in Japanese?).

The crowd hushed. On stage, a booming voice was testing the mike. The movers and shakers of the Centre took their places, and Saito, public smile well to the fore, introduced them. Each spoke for many minutes, and were much applauded. Finally, it was the turn of the Chairman, that genial young man wearing horn-rimmed glasses, to address his audience. Saito fixed me with an unblinking stare. I began to sweat. The Chairman sat down, crossing an elegant silk-socked ankle, as Saito reclaimed the mike and launched into her final address. Dimly I caught the words:

"Igirisu-jin ... Shakespeare no guidu ... Cook, Angela-san!"

All I remember about that speech was looking out at the sea of expectant faces lifted towards me; beginning it, nervously, and then hearing a gentle wave of quiet laughter as I made a mild joke about 'us foreigners – and our curious ways'. Blow me, I thought, they do actually understand what I am trying to say! I risked a glance at the row of teachers and saw that Kamada and Taniguchi were smiling. End of speech. Bow deeply, acknowledge applause, and get off platform.

A nice glass of wine, or beer, and a cigarette, would be just ...

Bossy Boots grabbed me as I left the stage:

"Angela-san! You come quick! Tara-san in kimono now."

In a small room backstage, Tara's jeans and tee-shirt lay over a chair. She was wearing a very thin white kimono, gasping, as

Madame tightened her obi, in a scene reminiscent of an Edwardian drama; the lady clinging to a bedpost, whilst her maid tugs at her corset strings.

I was given a similar white kimono, and reflected on the happy chance that had stopped me from wearing black underwear that morning. Round us, Madame circled, like a tugboat approaching an ocean liner. Bossy Boots was now in a frenzy of apprehension, giving us our paper hats, and ushering us down the passage to the stage. Even in the dim light, I noticed that every stitch and label on our bra and pants was clearly visible through the thin stuff of the kimonos, and remarked to Tara that we could make our names as the famous duo 'Marko & Sparko'. She gave a nervous giggle.

The amplifiers burst forth with the tinkly music, Pompadour gave a little introductory jingle of bells, Kato gave me a sharp push, and we were onstage, all giving our versions of 'The Japanese Hat with Paper Flowers Dance'. It went quite well until Tara, (until my dying day I will swear it was her) pirouetted the wrong way. For a moment our hats seemed locked in mortal combat. A pink paper rose fell from mine.

"Is this the War of the Roses, or what?" I grunted.

Her stamp and mine narrowly missed collision.

Our efforts were rewarded with considerable applause. Breathless, we bowed to our audience, the chairman and teachers in the front row, and to each other. A click, and on came that well remembered 'Harvest Dance'. Tara and I, scarcely able to breathe, let alone crouch, encased in our obis, went into the routine. Snaking round the stage, we 'dug' twice, 'cut' twice, 'wiped sweat' twice, and I gave my promised little shimmy. In the auditorium, a murmur was heard; a chuckle, quickly suppressed. Second time round, the movement evoked more audible mirth, and, as we continued to dig, cut, and wipe, it became apparent that the audience was waiting for the next step. Regrettably, the latent exhibitionist in me took over. Next time around, one eyebrow raised, I gave a slow, very deliberate bum wiggle on the beat. This evoked a roar of laughter, and from then on some of the host fathers began to clap in time as we reached that point. Madame, leading from the front, was smiling delightedly at the success of her dance, Tara was squealing with laughter, I was enjoying myself, and fortunately could not see the effect on Kato-san, still presumably digging and cutting to my rear.

The dance ended to tumultuous applause. Well, noisy, anyway. Immediately afterwards, as a special reward, we four were given permission to bathe in the hotel's ultra-modern bath. We were whisked away to a small locker room where four remarkably small fluffy towels had been laid out for us, and left to enjoy. The two ladies stripped off within seconds, carefully folded their kimonos, showered, and ran, giggling, across the mosaic tiles. Naked they sat, side by side, on the edge of the pool, dangling their legs in the hot water, uttering shrill squeaks of delight.

"You know," I said to Tara, "I think that nakedness and water react on the Japanese like alcohol does on Westerners. They immediately lose all their inhibitions."

"Yeah … it just takes us longer to get our clothes off."

By the time we got into the scorching water, Madame was swimming, using a jerky breast-stroke, holding her hair well clear of the water. Kato was splashing herself, eyes shut, humming happily. They patently had no intention of denying themselves the delights of this furoba, still playing in it as we dried ourselves on the fluffy dishcloths and got dressed.

"Look, they're perfectly happy," Tara said, "and, I think we've earned a drink."

I agreed. I could murder a Kirin beer, right now. We waved our goodbyes and thank-yous, and the ladies waved back, merrily.

It was not to be. The tables were empty of food – and drink. Everywhere, waitresses were stacking bowls and platters. A few families still mingled, and Joji, and Tara's family, had kindly got us cups of coffee. Saito hurried over:

"Angela-san! The chairman has asked me to speak with you."

I braced myself. Had I lowered the tone of the gathering? She pressed on, earnestly:

"He wants me to thank you for making the party so very happy for all our guests."

"Really? Oh. Well, thank you Saito-san. I mean, I know there were mistakes in my speech, but …"

"Yes, indeed, there were many, many mistakes, but, we understood what you tried to say, and it was kind, and funny."

She was joined by Miyazaki, Taniguchi, and Kamada.

"We not forget your dance, Angela-san. It was high spot!"

"Harvest Dance was your high spot," Saito agreed. Elegant in her silk suit, she winked at me, and imitated my boogie. Everyone laughed.

"Sexy dance," observed Joji, quaffing the last of his beer.

Miyazaki had news for me.

"When you leave the house of Uno-san, Miss Homma has found you a room with a friend of hers. You are so lucky! You will be living in an old geisha house!" She beamed.

I hoped that my Harvest Dance had not been misinterpreted.

We drove back through the gathering dusk. It had become bitterly cold. Looking out across the rice paddies, a thought came to me. I recalled seeing lines of workers, mostly women, bent double, making their way along the lines of rice, first with a sickle, then a hoe. Nearing the end of a row, labouring under the burning sun, sweat poured off them; stretching up, the peasants would rub their sleeves across their foreheads. Then, hands on backs, they shook their shoulders to ease the strain … Oh, well.

———

Joji and Mieko have planned on a treat for me tonight, to celebrate the party. We are, he told me, proudly, to have waeen with our supper.

"And after, you have the first bath!" Mieko added.

All I can say about Japanese wine is that it is sometimes pink, sometimes white, but always with a taste like decaying rose water. Mieko sipped her half glass, before declaring it made her head go 'kura-kura'. Were she to sniff the dregs of Scotch from my tooth glass, I reckoned, she would probably fall insensible for the week.

Supper over, Mieko began to entreat me to take my bath.

"Tonight, Angela-san, you take bath first! Before Oto-san!"

Despite the rare privilege of taking the bath water before Joji, I felt that my swim at the hotel should have sufficed for the day. But it would have been rude to refuse her. Resignedly, I collected my own Irish bath towel (brought with me) and trundled off to their tiled shower room, where the bath had been prepared for me, filled to the brim under its slatted wooden bath cover. As at the Kitamuras, the shower hangs on the wall, hand held. All clothes must be left in the anteroom, draped over the washing machine before entering the shower room, and turning on the shower. No matter how carefully I play with the gauge on this shower, the result is always either icy or scorching, and, as I leap aside to avoid its vagaries, I always manage to knock over the array of shampoos, bath gels and whatnots lined up on a tiled shelf. Pumice stones, nail brushes and plastic bottles start to float. The solution is to kneel precariously on the edge of the bath whilst stretching out to adjust the temperature of the shower. Next, retrieve shower head from the drain, and standing beside it, work up a good, all-over lather. It is essential to re-check the shower before rinsing, because, by this time, the wretched machine has built up a head of steam, ready to pickle the unwary. Now, one has to perch on a tiny plastic stool, like Miss Muffet on her tuffet, and apply shampoo. After this, eyes tight shut against the foam, it is necessary to relocate gauge and shower head, blindly, usually receiving an icy deluge down the back of one's neck. Only now may one slide back the bath cover and clamber, warily, into chin-high, scorching water. One can only *sit* in a Japanese bath, because they are not made long enough to stretch out in.

I normally spent approximately one and a half minutes enduring this poaching before replacing the cover, and creeping out into the chilly ante-room to reclaim my towel, but most Japanese people love the entire process, and will happily spend half an hour after washing, soaking. And singing, in the bath. One fill of bath water is intended for the use of the entire family, by rote, and it is a cardinal sin to empty it after use.

[119]

I had bought a book called Guide to Some Customs in Japan. With regard to bathing, it read:

'One of the things a foreigner will most miss when he leaves Japan is the Japanese bath.' I make no comment. In my home in Ireland, our bathroom, as opposed to the kids', had a thick red carpet, a long deep bath with an old-fashioned brass plunger, and a heated towel rail. Now there I could have what the Emperor might call 'a relaxing occasion'.

———

Only a few more days before I shall be leaving the Unos, and going to stay with a woman called Keiko, living in the Old Quarter of Kanaza, in the geisha house.

One of the many things I will miss, oddly enough, is the train journey. Along the road to the station, someone's camellia hedge is just bursting into pink flower, and most houses have pots of deep blue gentians on their steps. What I thought was a plastic crane, standing beside a pond, turned its head and flew off, trailing its legs inelegantly, a beautiful white bird framed against a clear blue sky.

This morning, I arrived at the station unusually early, and sat watching the life of Mattoh flow past in unhurried fashion. Elderly men rode aged bicycles with plants or vegetables in their baskets, wizened old ladies pattered past me on their wooden geta, occasionally pausing to raise their faces to the sun, while others awaited the train, kneeling on a bench, gobbling peanuts; they look so tiny, seemingly without legs, their kimonos foreshortened. On another bench sat three very pretty young girls, chattering; their faces reminiscent of a pert pekinese, with round little faces, flirty eyes, and beautiful glossy hair, topped by a Minnie-Mouse-type bow in varying colours.

The train was, as usual, crowded with schoolchildren, clamouring like groups of children all over the world; but I wonder why they are not already in class?

Outside, as the train rushes past, housewives are out in force on their balconies, beating futons with what look like long plastic shoe horns. Builders clamber up bamboo ladders, swarming over the timber scaffolding of these new houses. I have been told that some seventy-five per cent of modern houses near Mattoh still have a timber-frame construction, but that now the lathe and plaster (once bamboo and daub) has been replaced by cement blocks. These, however are much thinner than ours, and must let out a lot of heat in winter. Like all aspects of Japanese commerce, the building industry is labour intensive. Traditionally, until most recent times there has been very little unemployment in this land, very little homelessness, and still today the workers take a pride in their work, never apearing resentful, or bored. Thinking about it, I have never heard a Japanese person say, "Oh God! Another Monday!" Or, "Thank the Lord, it's Friday!"

In my carriage, young women sat, staring out into infinity in a dreamy sort of way; older couples plonked themselves squarely down and consumed the contents of their bento, before falling asleep. Youths at college wore the ubiquitous jeans, and tee-shirts bearing slogans that are unintelligible to us, but apparently make positive sense to them: today, opposite me, sit two teenagers, one wearing a tee-shirt inscribed 'Universal Concrete – Happiness & Spiritual' The other boy's read 'Try Zest in the Sky'.

I am beginning to recognise many of my daily fellow travellers and and to notice the height difference relative to their ages.

When I was guiding in Stratford-upon-Avon, I assumed that all Japanese people were small, but now realise this generalisation applies mainly to the older generation.

Senior Tutor Kamada explained that young people now ate a richer diet and more dairy products.

"Although some people attribute their growth to the modern habit of Western furniture," she added, eyes twinkling behind her glasses.

Kanazawa station is pristine. Great pots of chrysanthemums, the big, in-curved white and yellow variety, line the exit on a little stage. Delicious smells come from stalls selling tempting selections of waffles, all cooked in front of their customers. I think, over the weeks, I have tried out most of them, but they are never filled with what I expect; when convinced I saw them put jam in mine, it turns out to be a sort of marzipan: if marzipan, I am intrigued to find my mouth filled with a peanut and soy mix; but, no matter, they are always delicious.

I met Tara walking along the main street in Kanazawa, carrying a flowering pot plant. She told me she had rented her very own apartment, and had bought the plant to make it seem more homely. She is still working in the nightclub, and has taken on many teaching jobs.

"But, Tara, when will you find the time to take classes? Or do homework?"

"Yeah ... well, I'm not going to worry about all that right now," she said. She suggested that I might like to double up with her, taking on some classes. I thanked her, and said I'd think about it. I do not have her confidence.

Only a few more days before I move again. Poor Koro will miss me and his walks and I shall miss this family that has done so much to include me in their lives.

Joji was not working today, and I had no classes. He had another of his ideas; would I like to see where he worked? He was in tremendous form this morning, and, unusually, was dressed in his best suit.

"And, later, Angela-san, I have decided to, well, maybe ..." he paused to give dramatic emphasis to his words, "to buy myself a new car!"

Perhaps I would like to accompany him?

Joji worked at an immense modern building situated in the centre of Kanazawa city. There were several buildings, all linked by great horizontal silver pipes; towering over them, chimneys emitted columns of pure white smoke into a clear blue sky.

The first room we entered was obviously a workshop, with work benches, welding irons and tool boxes. On the wall hung neat coils of tubing and an assortment of gleaming hammers, screwdrivers, pincers, etc. – plus of course, girlie calendars. The two workmen there were wearing immaculate white boiler suits, white gumboots, and hard hats. Joji introduced me to them, and gained their permission to show me round:

"To see the first and best garbage reclaim in the world!" Joji explained. "And built here, in Kanazawa!"

We walked along white tiled corridors, passed hissing cylinders, and climbed an iron spiral staircase to a viewing platform that surrounded several pits. Lorries queued on an outer weighbridge, and deposited their loads. Overhead, a remote-control grab slid along on runners, picked up a load, and was electronically directed to deposit the rubbish in one or other pit beneath us, depending on which furnace was now ready to receive a new load. There were five furnaces.

We watched as the giant grab hovered momentarily over the five pits, and then dumped its contents, delving deep into the mess – jagged pieces of rusty metal, industrial and domestic waste, bulging bin liners, and bits of old cars. There was absolutely no smell at all. Slowly, it rose again, metal jaws dripping waste, and travelled to the chosen furnace, depositing the lot into the flames. I was mesmerised. I could have stayed for ages, just watching this process, but Joji was getting restless.

"This is just the first part of making electricity," he explained. "Now we go to the television furnace room."

In front of two men, five TV screens showed the heat of each furnace and its capacity to absorb the next load. The men chatted briefly to Joji, drinking cans of Coca Cola, but never taking their eyes from the screens. We visited the computer rooms next, Joji's pride and joy. Here, every stage of rubbish conversion is regulated, from weighbridge to washed smoke. There were two computer rooms, one as a fall-back, in case of generator failure. These two rooms required regulated heating to ensure constant temperature. All around us, little red and green lights winked and flashed, multimillion tiny clicks clicked, and Joji surveyed his kingdom with pride.

"Do you actually understand all these?" I asked him, awestruck.

"But of course I do. I am engineer. One goes wrong, I fix."

Before we left, Joji explained that the smoke from the furnaces has to be washed several times before being released into the air, so that no pollution at all escapes. All that remains of the miscellaneous muck is ash; totally clean ash that is taken away. Even sewage is burned to a powder and transported.

"Maybe soon we make it into fertiliser," Joji told me.

I asked the purpose of the steel pipes that linked the buildings. They bring water down from the mountains and local rivers, and are converted here into electricity, sufficient to serve the entire population of Kanazawa, all 432,000 of them.

We went to thank Joji's boss for letting me visit this amazing place. He smiled, and asked how we disposed of our rubbish in England.

"Um, landfill, actually," I told him, feeling ashamed.

Involuntarily, one eyebrow quirked, but he remained courteous. "Aaa, so, so, so."

The car showroom was like any other in the world; gleaming cars, and gleaming young salesmen accompanying Joji as he toured the area, pausing from time to stroke a bonnet, or pat a bumper, attended at all times by an attractive young woman who attentively lit his cigarettes. Twenty minutes later, we were seated in an elaborate office, and served tea by the same young woman. Brochures were set out, fan-shaped, before Joji, and the salesman launched into rapid speech, whilst his female colleague turned pages on the various brochures, She was wearing a strong, flowery perfume, leaning helpfully over Joji's shoulder.

Finally, after much laughter, we left.

"So, are you going to buy a car from them?" I asked as his van, previously parked two streets away, rocketed back to Mattoh.

"Maybe." Joji said, enigmatically. He began to sing.

The same two sales staff came to his house the following evening. Mieko served them green tea, and they sat at the kitchen table as Joji showed them his photo album – the one containing pictures of him skiing.

"Eeh, Uno-san suki ga jozu desu, neh?" breathed the young woman.

Joji gave a deprecating shrug.

The talk moved on to football. By now, cigarette smoke hung dense on the air, but no one had mentioned the two words I knew meant car: 'jidosha' or 'kuruma'. The kitchen clock ticked on, and Koro carried on barking.

At last, with much bowing, they stood up to leave.

"And … the cigarette lighter?" Joji enquired.

"Optional extra," the woman said, regretfully.

"Rajio?" Fumiko burst out.

She regretted that also.

"How about a roof-rack, for skis?" Joji was obviously chancing his arm.

"More optional extra … I am so sorry."

Joji told me that he might not buy the car.

"White cars are very common in Japan. Not my style. I like silver cars best."

They returned, two days later, and Joji bought himself a car. A silver car.

"How about the optional extras?" I asked.

He grinned, wickedly. "Cigarette lighter, radio, AND ski-rack. Now, not optional extras."

Mieko was despatched to produce Joji's hanko. His special hanko, made from a narwhal whale tusk, with Joji's name beautifully carved on it in kanji script. This is only used to stamp large purchases, and has to be dipped in ink that is contained in a specially embossed gold leaf horn container. The ink itself was solid, rather like the stuff I once used in brass rubbings, but this is precious ink, all the way from China, and, unbelievably expensive. It is made from the smoke from innumerable candles, I was told. The ink block is rubbed in its container, with a speck of water to dampen it, and then the hanko is pressed onto it, to sign the deed of sale.

However, it seemed that the ski rack would require some

modification, so the new car would not actually arrive for a few weeks.

"But," explained Joji, over supper, "when you come to visit us, I shall have it, and I will take you for a drive in my new silver car!"

We toasted it, and me, over a farewell supper that night.

CHAPTER FOUR

At the Geisha House

J OJI UNO DROVE ME, my wheels and my baggage to the
Centre. "You have problems, you call me," he said.

Waving, one hand on the wheel of the van, he drove off.

How many people in Ireland, or Britain, would have welcomed
a foreigner, made them feel so at home, and shared so much of their
lives?

Miyazaki agreed to let me park my luggage in the staff room.
Some of my clothes, headed by Humphrey, the hot-water bottle with
the teddy bear head and tartan jacket, fell off, tumbling down the
steps. She shook her head.

" No bus! You need a taxi," she said.

The taxi drove up a narrow, cobbled street. On each side were
wooden-fronted houses. They had no obvious windows, no sign of
life. This was a secretive street; no evidence of neighbourhood watch,
no neighbours. Just one elderly woman in a kimono pattered past,
taking no notice of the taxi.

Typically, the driver accepted his fare and waited while I unloaded
all my luggage onto the street. Then the taxi reversed, and left.

Still nothing stirred on the street. No welcoming door opened, as

I stood before one of the oldest house on the street: a famous geisha house.

I could not see any bell. I lugged my possessions through the door, into a cement-floored lobby filled with boxes of vegetables and a big canister of kerosene, and sat on the wooden step, adding my outdoor shoes to the row, making sure they were facing in the right direction.

"Er… Konnichi wa! Cook, Angela desu!"

Takahashi-san materialised through a sliding door.

"Hallo," she said. "Welcome. I am Keiko Takahashi." She spoke in English.

Keiko Takahashi was one of the thinnest women I had ever seen. Aged late thirties, I reckoned, height about 5'4" – slightly taller than me. Her hair appeared to have been crimped, falling in a bush, just brushing her shoulders, her lips narrow, painted crimson. She wore a turquoise velvet jumpsuit.

"Hallo," I said. "Sorry if I am late, I had to wait for the taxi to come." I also spoke in English.

Her eyes narrowed, taking in my luggage. She clicked her tongue, impatiently:

"NOT on the floor, Angela! Never put things on the concrete floor. It is one of the rules of the house."

"I'm so sorry," I said. "I didn't know."

Together, we picked up the two cases, dusted them off, and placed them on the step.

I was given a pair of house slippers, and she led me through a windowless inner room, sliding the porch door behind us. We entered the dining room, also without windows. There was a teak dining table, and four upright chairs set round it. The kitchen stretched out from here. This was a long, narrow room, with linoleum on the floor. On the left-hand wall stood a fridge, a toaster on a small shelf, and glass-fronted cupboards containing a vast assortment of bowls, saucers, mugs, and plates. An electric light burned overhead, because, yet again, this was an inner room, without natural light.

Keiko moved back to the two-ring cooker beside a double sink unit and work surface. She took up her cooking chopsticks, and carried on stirring something.

"We will eat first, and then, I will show you to your room," she said. "Usually, I eat much later, but tonight I have to go out. I hope you will be alright?"

"Yes, Of course."

"Good. Plates in that cupboard, bowls beside them. Would you lay the table, please?"

Obviously, in this house, we are going to share the day-to-day tasks. This will be good for my Japanese. Perhaps our relationship will become like that of students, sharing digs?

Mieko-san would be appalled.

After a good meal, and a cup of peppermint tea, we washed up, and then Keiko led the way up the first set of stairs, insisting that I change into another set of slippers before mounting them, leaving the ground floor set placed neatly at their foot.

I was allowed to retain them before climbing up the ladder-like second set of steps that led to my bedroom. I was walking blindly, until Keiko pulled a string, hanging somewhere against a ricepaper wall, and an electric bulb came on. At the top of the house she slid open another panel, and we came to my room. It had a window! Actually, two windows, because, if one slid open a dividing panel, there was a second room beyond it.

We entered the bedroom. I saw a quilt spread on the tatami mats, over which was zipped a cover. There was also a fluffy fun-fur tigerskin blanket, and two eiderdowns, clipped together with what looked like giant paper clips.

"Lovely," I said. "Thank you, Keiko-san. I'll be fine now, so, if you want to get off?"

"We will make your bed first." she told me, firmly.

Under her strict guidance, I squeezed a blanket into the cover, and fitted a minute electric blanket between the two eiderdowns. Each of these had to be clipped, and pinned precisely.

"If you do not move too much, Angela, the electric blanket will not crease. But you must be careful, because a creased electric blanket is dangerous."

I said that I could not guarantee my movements when asleep, and that I thought I would turn it off when I got into bed.

"Perhaps that would be better. If you think your feet will move in the night," Keiko said. She showed me how to light my kerosene stove, and left. I heard her pull the string on the stairs to turn off the light.

I looked around my room. There was a screen to hang my towel on, an empty chest of drawers, and a delightful dressing table, complete with oval mirror, two jewellery compartments, and two small drawers, presumably for make-up. It stood two foot from the floor. The other room had a desk with an anglepoise lamp on it, and a bentwood chair. There was also a fitted hanging cupboard for clothes, and empty plank shelves. I unpacked my bottle of milk powder, called 'Creep', the jar of Nescafé, and the books brought from England, plus my little tape recorder, dictionary, and photographs, and stood back to survey the result. The room looked slightly more personal.

The last of the daylight was fading, fast, and I remembered that the lavatory and washbasins were on the ground floor, down a corridor. The stairs were in total darkness. I fumbled about for the string, but couldn't find it. Armed with my cigarette lighter, I got to the foot of the second staircase, where my ground-floor house slippers awaited me. The corridor led off the living room, beyond which, in an alcove, a faint light glimmered. I crept past the shrine – bless you, Buddha – and clacked onto wooden duckboards spread over a concrete floor. Plastic slippers on, loo located. Three of them, actually; a Western-type lavatory, boasting a heated seat and a sort of dashboard of little knobs, a gents' urinal, and the traditional Japanese squatting variety.

Returning, I blundered into two more featureless rooms with tatami on the floors. This is a deceptively huge house. I wonder will I ever find my way around it?

Back upstairs again, still clicking the lighter, I resolved not to drink Nescafé before going to bed.

It was cold back in the room. Time to try lighting the stove. As I struck the first match, a solitary drum began to beat, softly, somewhere down the street. The match flame burnt my fingers, and I blew it out. 'Boom … boom … boom.' I lit another, trying to remember how to light the stove. The match went out, and I cupped it, hastily. Wearing slippers on tatami was considered bad form, so a blackened matchstick discovered on it would probably count as desecration, quite apart from the danger of flames spreading from rush mats to wood, and ricepaper walls.

More drum beats now joined the first. These were quicker; 'boom-boom, boom-boom …' I slid open the window and peered out at the other wooden houses across the street. From a few, a faint radiance could just be made out, but the street itself was in darkness, and there was no drummer to be seen. The sounds were issuing from those dark houses. The beats grew faster and faster, joined by the thin note of a flute wailing, the noise reaching a frantic crescendo – and then, suddenly, they stopped.

My imagination began to run riot: perhaps the drums were a background to some religious ceremony, held by monks in the nearby temples? Not unless every second house was devoted to the worship of some god or other. They started agains, insistently: 'BOOM. Boom-boom. Boom.' Such an eerie, alien sound in this ancient geisha quarter of town. Perhaps those drum beats accompanied some sexual rites of Eastern decadence? Concealed deep within these great secretive houses, flower-like maidens were … were what? The increasingly hectic tempo didn't suggest the mere serving of tea.

Just then, a taxi whirled down the street and parked below my window, its light beams briefly illuminating the room. A group of men got out and stood, laughing and talking as they paid the driver.

I stretched up my hand and found the little tasselled cord hanging from an overhead lamp. Let there be light … and there was!

I remembered my dear Aunt Roma, telling me, as a child, that I had too vivid an imagination.

Perhaps she was right.

Half a box of matches later, I even managed to light the stove. It gave off rather a lot of black smoke, but its warmth was cosy. I read a chapter from The Wind in the Willows, the one where Mole and Ratty return to Mole's home and entertain the field mice, and then crawled, very carefully, under the cover, having disconnected the electric blanket. My pillow appears to have been stuffed with dried rice. If I turn my head, it rustles.

This ancient house creaks and sighs in the darkness. And, outside, somewhere along the street, drift faint notes of a flute trilling in a minor key. Beside me, within reach, are my rediscovered pencil torch, and a box of matches.

I fell asleep.

—⁓—

Everything feels different next morning. Pale sunlight shines through the window. I attempt to light the stove, and fail. I kneel beside it, slipperless, twiddling the knob and adjusting the wick, but it either flares up, puffing out clouds of acrid black smoke, or else the wavering flame fails to run round the wick, falters, and dies.

Keiko Takahashi is still in her dressing-gown. Tight-lipped, she is making coffee and frying eggs. I lay the table, and make thick toast. We ate in silence.

Helping to dry the breakfast bowls, I explained my difficulties with the stove.

"I'm sorry, but I don't think I quite understand how it works?"

"But why? I explained it to you last night," she said, sighing.

Looking at my room in the clear daylight, I can see that even the desk has a layer of black dust on it, and the whole room smells horribly of burnt kerosene. Keiko gave me some sheets of newspaper, and some little brushes with which to clean the stove. The wretched thing took nearly an hour to clean, and longer to wipe smuts off all surfaces. She came up again and showed me how to light it, and how to raise and lower the wick. She also brought me a small hoover, with which to clean the tatami.

"And then, you had perhaps better have a bath. I will fill it for you."

The room containing the covered bath is beside the row of lavatories, at the end of a gallery. One side of this gallery has windows overlooking an enclosed garden; as in traditional Roman gardens, these old Japanese houses have gardens at their centre. This one is not well tended. There are two scruffy trees straggling up to the light, a cluster of dried-up bamboo, unhealthy looking moss, and a stone lantern. It looks dank and forlorn.

The bathroom was full of steam.

Keiko warned me not to let the bathwater run out, since she would use it the following day.

"We must always save water," she told me seriously, showing me an old iron contraption that apparently reheats pipes around the bath.

Why? Here in Kanazawa, as its inhabitants proudly point out, it rains nearly every day.

Keiko walked me to the local market, Hachi-bacho, where she shops. We passed by the foot of Utatsuyama mountain on one side, and on the other, the river Asanagawa, where I had seen wondrous silks and cottons, all brightly coloured, streeling out in the fast-flowing current to wash away any surplus dye. A man in thigh boot waders pegs them out just below the water, each morning, and collects them each night. Keiko shows me the bus stops to take me to the Centre, but warns me that, at some hours, some buses take a different route. Right!

One of these days, I will climb Utatsuyama, I resolve, but today, the autumn weather is so glorious, I am going to revisit Kenrokuen Park, and glory in the autumn colours, before winter sets in. Me, and three quarters of the population of Kanazawa apparently had the same idea. I found a hidden cascade of mountain water, away from the guides with their red brollies and shrill voices, and spent a peaceful time going over my next Japanese lesson, trying to fix another few irregular verbs into my head. I hope Keiko will speak Japanese to me tonight.

We sat long at supper, drinking beer and sake. Keiko was talking about this house. She had been born in it, as had her mother. Her grandmother ran a flourishing geisha restaurant here, and her own mother had carried on the tradition. Apparently, her mother was renowned for the beauty of her dancing, and her aunt for her skill at playing the shamisen, and mastery of the art of the Tea Ceremony. As a small child, Keiko's mother had been petted and pampered by all the geishas, and encouraged to dance with them. Keiko laughed:

"I'll tell you a story about my mother," she said. "Takahashi-chan. When she was nine or ten years old, the geishas composed a dance that had a part in it for a little monkey that was supposed to leap and bound between the other dancers. They gave the part to little Takahashi-chan, but didn't tell her what she was supposed to be, so as not to hurt her feelings. The geishas were all told to hide their mirrors, never let her actually see her monkey mask, or tail. The first performances were a tremendous success, and the little girl lept and sprang as she had been taught. But, just before the final performance, she caught sight of herself reflected in a piece of glass, and suddenly realised she had been playing a monkey!"

" But, did she really mind?"

"Well, of course she did. She tore off the costume, and rushed away, crying. No one, not even her own mother, could comfort her. She had lost dignity, you see, Angela; and been seen, by everyone, not looking pretty."

I envisaged that child, growing up in this house where everything was devoted to the cult of pleasing men by artifice, and surrounded by beautiful young women whose every gesture was designed to attract – how betrayed she must have felt by the people she loved. Keiko curled her lip, derisively:

"I told her she was a right fool not to have guessed in the first place."

Keiko Takahashi is evidently not a sentimentalist.

The sake flowed, and we talked on.

"And what about when you were a little girl, growing up here?' I asked.

She told me her mother had wanted another life for her daughter.

She had closed the restaurant. Her three sons had their own businesses, and lived far from Kanazawa.

For owners of geisha houses, invariably women, arranged marriages could not happen. But of course, these beautiful young women fell in love. For many years, they might live together as partners, and she would bear children. However, the man would be obliged to marry a suitable wife, and, as the years went on, he saw less and less of his first family. They were, after all, illegitimate.

Keiko's mother and father continued to see each other until he retired. Then, all contact had to cease. Her father is now a very old man, in the care of his legitimate elder son, and living many miles from Kanazawa. That is just the way things are. Acceptable, but sad.

I learned something else that evening. Apparently those companies that visit all schools when senior students are about to leave are very reluctant to employ an illegitimate child. Such a young person could be an unstable employee; one who might upset the natural balance of the others, all working in a perfectly well-moulded team. Therefore, such children, no matter how excellent their grades, were obliged to set up their own businesses, sometimes helped by their own natural fathers.

Keiko's alcohol tolerance is remarkable. She poured me another glass of sake, and explained that, were it known that a young unmarried employee was living with a woman not his wife, his own prospects of advancement would be severely impeded. But, once married, what he elects to do in his free time is his own business.

A fascinating evening. Another time, I must remember to ask about those drums. Another time, I will insist we speak in Japanese. After all, it is what I came here to do. But, I think, weaving my way back along the duckboards (hopefully wearing the correct slippers), and climbing the polished ladder to my room, not tonight. Definitely, not tonight.

Neither of us spoke at breakfast. I had seen the sun shining brightly through my window, but, of course, downstairs all was dim, lit by flickering light. A weekend stretched before me. Maybe I would climb Utatsuyama mountain today, before winter set in. Maybe take in the autumn colours?

The outer door slid open, and a good-looking, forty-ish man came into the room.

"Keiko-san! I'm hungry!"

He gave her a packet of unbaked buns, and lit up a lethal Japanese cigarette.

"You want?"

"No, thank you."

Keiko got up, looking at him quizzically.

"So… I cook you breakfast, while you make Angela-san a butterfly, right?"

He grinned. From his pocket, he produced a tiny kit of nail scissors and an envelope full of coloured paper. Meticulously, he began to snip, until he had created a butterfly.

"Oh! That's beautiful!" I told him.

Keiko shouted from the kitchen:

"Now you make her a moving crab."

"Eeeeh, you want the crab, Keiko?"

"Hai. Then, breakfast."

Making the crab seemed much harder. He snipped away, concentrating intensely, and then crumpled up the paper, suddenly throwing it on the floor.

"Eyebrow tweezers, Keiko?"

Clicking her tongue, she fetches them, and he uses them to curl tiny wisps of paper. On the table in front of me sits a perfect little crab, some two inches in diameter.

" Angela-san, you blow," he instructed.

Very gently, I bent my head and blew on it, watching, as the tiny creature, pincers waving, sidled across the table.

"Subarashii!" And it was, astonishing.

He shrugged, smiling: "Iie. Yasashii desu."

It hadn't been easy, but the end result was fantastic. I left them.

Upstairs, the sun still shone. I sat at the desk and tried to concentrate on the complexities of the 'te' form and all its different usages, but my mind wandered to the other side of the world. This Sunday in England – right now, people are still sleeping, but later, church bells will ring out over quiet Cotswold villages …

And here, in Japan, there is a world waiting to be explored.

Walking shoes in hand, I made my way downstairs once again. Keiko and her friend were still sitting at the table, which was now covered with snippets of coloured paper. She glanced up: "Are you going out?"

"Yes. Just for a bit."

"But. Where are you going?"

"Oh, just out."

I felt like a rebellious teenager.

This insistance on knowing where exactly anyone living in the house is going to, at all hours of the day, can be maddening.

I felt like shouting:

"Look! I'm nearly old enough to be your mother, right? I got myself to England, and here to Kanazawa (just)! And anyway, I don't need to tell you where I'm going if I go out to buy a pack of cigarettes, right?"

But, of course I didn't. I slid the outer door shut, calling out the traditional: "Itte kimasu," and slipped away. I remembered listening to a young American girl, railing against her host family, when I first went to the students' salon.

"I mean, for God's sake! She's not my goddamned mother! So, why the hell can't she mind her own goddamned business?" At the time, I had suggested that maybe her host mother felt responsible, and was only trying to be kind. Now, I knew what she meant. I badly needed a little bit of freedom.

Asanagawa river flowed to my left, sparkling in the sun. To my right, the maze of narrow winding streets of the oldest part of Kanazawa where temples and shrines lie, concealed behind arches, or carved in streets that have no name. Ahead are the foothills of Utatsuyama.

I began to climb up a little road that grew steeper by the minute. At the end, beside steps cut into the foothills of Utatsuyama, a temple stood, guarded by a huge granite statue. Two white cats blinked at me, one stretched in the lap of the god; the other perched superciliously on its head, giving an incongruous impression of Davy Crockett's headgear. Next to the temple was a little shop, the window filled with what looked like grey stone snowmen in varying sizes, all wearing red cloth head coverings and red bibs. Its door was shuttered.

The autumn sun was surprisingly hot. The shallow steps curved up and up, growing ever steeper, and the bushes more dense. In a clearing, I suddenly came across a massive statue, half concealed by undergrowth: it was of a man wearing a frock coat, and, of all unlikely objects, carrying a bowler hat.

The steps came to an end. Now, acacia, sumac, and maples hung thickly over a dirt track; giant Spanish chestnuts glowed yellow and milk chocolate, and rowan trees were spangled with Smartie berries, all set against against a glorious tapestry of crimson and purple; spiders had spun webs, glistening in the sunlight, soft against my face. This is wild country. I felt as though I was the first Westerner ever to penetrate it. Further along, I came to a wooden finger post, written in English. It pointed down through dark pine trees, and it read: 'Site of the Christian Martyrs'.

The pines made a shushing sound far above my head. Their needles deadened my footsteps. The sun had been extinguished.

The actual memorial is very simple; a large stone cross etched with the figure of a dove.

I wonder, when did they die? How many Christians perished here, deep in this alien forest? What agonising deaths had they endured? I stood in front of the cross, feeling a chill of dread, and prayed for those unknown souls. As I stood there, a twig cracked, and a pigeon took fright, blundering past my head. I heard quiet footfalls approaching, and had an irrational desire to run and hide.

I spun round, to see a young couple, running, hand in hand; the girl was holding a small bunch of flowers. I drew a long breath, and she smiled, shyly. As I climbed back up the track, I saw her place her flowers at the foot of the cross.

Later, hidden in a dense thicket of rhododendrons and dry

windswept leaves I remembered seeing a sign further down the mountain path: 'BEWARE BEARS' it read. I had this uncomfortable mental picture ... There was this bear, see, this big brown furry bear, minding her own business, when all of a sudden, her Japanese Bear Rights were grossly infringed. She rises in wrath: "Who's a-peein' on My bed?" And then this pink yellow-haired alien takes off at speed, heading for a slot of sunlight in the distance....

The actual summit of Utatsuyama was rather an anti-climax. It can be reached by road on the far side, and there was a carpark on one side, and a cemetery on the other; bleak, and full of hideous stone and marble headstones, unrelieved by any growing plants. I did discover the purpose of the little snowmen. They stand as guardians, marking the graves of children.

I decided to take the boring way back by road, meeting a little girl on her ceremonial outing to celebrate one of the special-occasion birthdays, held at three, five, and seven. She was wearing a turquoise silk kimono patterned with cherry blossom, banded with a crimson obi. Her hair was dressed traditionally and hung with trinkets, her mouth painted fuschia pink.

"Camera mo ii desu ka?" I asked.

Her proud father beamed his approval, and pushed the child nearer to me.

"Taihen kirei desu," I told her. And she was, very pretty.

She lowered her gaze modestly, but a tiny smile twitched the corners of her mouth.

I took my photo, and she bowed with instinctive grace. She was five years old.

It was late in the afternoon when I got back to the geisha house. My feet ached. I had been walking for four and a half hours.

"Tadaima!" I called.

"Okaeri nasai," Keiko answered from an upstairs room.

I found her kneeling on the tatami, working an old Singer sewing machine, purple silk spread around her, plus dressmaker's chalk, and a little flat iron. Beside her lay an intricate Vogue pattern.

"Wherever have you been, Angela?" I thought you had got lost."

"I climbed Utatsuyama," I told her, triumphantly.

"Well, you should have told me," she retorted.

"I'm sorry if you were worried, Keiko. I didn't know I was going to, until I actually started climbing, you know?"

She made no response, concentrating on the pattern.

That night she served supper at nine o'clock. The meal consisted of a thick white soup, a hamburger, minus bun, and some lettuce. And as many tangerines as I could eat, since her friend from Shikokku island had sent her a box of them. She counted them out: "One for Buddha, one for me, one for Angela – one for Buddha …"

There was no rice. She had already warned me that if I woke during the night and needed to go to the kitchen for a drink, I must first check my watch to see if it was after midnight, because then first water from the tap must be poured into a tiny chalice by the sink; the first water drawn each day had to be for Buddha, to be placed before his shrine.

Keiko explained that her eighty-four-year-old mother would be coming to stay tomorrow, leaving the institution she lives in. She is trying to persuade one of her brothers to come and see her during this visit, but, if his visit extends the old lady's stay by one day, her bed at the home will no longer be available.

"But surely, if you explain the circumstances, since she has not seen her son for more than a year, they would understand?"

Apparently not. Japanese bureaucracy is inflexible.

Mother Takahashi-san must have been absolutely beautiful in her day. Even now, she was an exceptionally fine-looking woman, with a high forehead, pronounced cheekbones, and small dark hazel eyes that twinkled wickedly. She was kneeling at a low table, writing, using a fine brush no thicker than an eye-liner, wearing a thick grey and blue kimono, banded with a cream obi. Her hair was coiled into a perfect chignon. We bowed, and exchanged traditional greetings. I was aware that, had I been Japanese, courtesy would have required my bow to be deeper, but a) she was already on the floor, and b) as a European, the gesture would resemble gymnastics, rather than deference.

"Igirisu jin desuka?"

Yes, I had come from England.

"Aa, so hoka." This, apparently was a Kanazawan expression.

"Well, Angela-san," Keiko remarked, using the 'san' form of address to me for the first time, " I must go and do some shopping for our meal. My mother loves to eat. Please talk to her. It will be good for your Japanese." She collected her shopping basket and went out.

Takahashi-san raised her eyebrows, minimally, indicating that I sit on a cushion at her side.

"How do you like Kanazawa?" she enunciated, carefully.

That was an easy one.

"Very interesting," I responded, as per my lessons.

"And the Japanese people?"

"They are all kind, and good, and helpful."

"Do you enjoy Japanese food?"

"Japanese food is always delicious."

I was reminded of learning the catechism as a small child.

Had I been to Kenrokuen park?

"Yes, indeed, it is very beautiful."

A pause ensued.

"Terebi omimasuka?"

Yes, I like watching television.

With relief, her hand reached out for the remote-control button, and we knelt in companionable silence, watching pig-tailed Samurai approach their leader, the Daimio, swear allegiance, and go out to slaughter other Samurai, watched by weeping geishas who would obviously have preferred to keep their menfolk close. The music of the flute and drum swelled and fell. Women sobbed and fluttered fans as youths grabbed swords, and bodyguards leapt into the fray. Takahashi-san watched, entranced. I reflected that *Coronation Street* was a bit different.

Keiko returned after forty-five minutes with brimming shopping bags.

"Have you homework to do, Angela-san? Supper will be in half an hour."

"I am learning Japanese, thank you, Keiko-san."

Her mother and I continued to watch the screen.

The old lady finds my name very funny, and impossible to pronounce. We have settled on An-san. She watches each mouthful of food as it progresses from my chopsticks to my mouth with apparent fascination, carrying on a rapid dialogue with her daughter.

"My mother thinks you are quite good at using chopsticks," Keiko said.

A small nugget of cuttlefish promptly dropped on the tablecloth.

"Sumimasen, gomen nasai," I apologised.

I now know what animals in a zoo must feel like.

Keiko has a small device, resembling a Dinky car, to pick off any crumb that falls. I pushed it round my place, every move absorbed by those bright eyes.

— ᜒ —

Each day, the room is filled with elderly friends, come to visit. Most of them are ex-geishas who had either worked here, or in the neighbourhood. Skinny old ladies, jolly old ladies, plump old ladies with glinting gold teeth; all kneel in the front room, all wearing kimonos, nibbling prawn crackers, reminiscing, and cackling with laughter.

One evening, a local TV station showed a programme featuring this district as it had been. It showed old photographs of the geishas who had worked and lived in this very street, many of whom I had met here in this room. There were several of Takahashi-san herself, in her teens, at the height of her beauty. She was indeed exquisite; hair fully primped out in traditional style with dangling ornaments, her eyes accentuated in a dead white face, mouth painted in a scarlet crimson bow. She was shown wearing a variety of highly ornate brocade kimonos. Takahashi-san was delighted:

"Omoimasuka, Keiko-chan?"

Keiko remembered them well. They were all still folded away in chests throughout the house, probably worth a fortune.

I find Takahashi-san gentle and charming, but can understand that her daughter finds the responsibility of caring for her, and responding to her incessant calls, trying. Old Mrs Takahashi will not let Keiko out of her sight.

"Keiko? Where are you?" she demands, querulously, as many old people do, the world over.

"What are you doing?" "Have you moved the … I cannot find it!" or "Have you remembered to …"

And I am struggling to remember all the rules of this house. I still have not mastered either the doors, or the lights. This old house has no electric light switches, merely bits of string, about six inches long, hanging on walls at intervals. Some of these, when pulled, illuminate an unexpected room behind ricepaper walls; some, if one is lucky, light up a corridor, others simply flash, briefly. I have taken to walking round the house armed with my torch, which Keiko finds funny.

"My mother will laugh at you," she warns.

Personally, so long as I don't fall downstairs and break a leg or offend Mother Takahashi, I don't care. But, groping my way along a corridor towards Keiko's sewing room, I invariably push the wrong panel and bump into a pile of magazines, or a box.

"NOT that one, Angela! Can you not remember?"

Soon after her mother leaves, Keiko is going to go to Europe for two weeks, acting as courier for a group of Japanese tourists. She asked would I like to stay on and mind the house? I was grateful, but couldn't imagine staying here, all alone, this secretive old house creaking and whispering round me, in the dark. I explained that I felt ill-prepared to look after it as she, and her mother, would expect, and I felt her relief.

"I will try to find you another host," she said, "though it may be difficult."

She tapped on a wall in my room that night, after supper.

"May I come in, Angela? I think I shall go mad."

We sat on the tatami which I had swept that morning – thank God – and I opened a bottle of beer.

"You see, my mother will not accept change. Any change to this house. But I must do something. I know I could. I have made plans. I want to sell European teas, and maybe, European bric-a-brac. There is a market for it, here. Maybe I make this house a little Tea House." She stopped, her fingers clenching and unclenching. "But no. It is my mother's house, my brother's house, my ancestors' house. I may change nothing."

We finished the beer, and I gave her a whisky. She talked more. I gathered it was disrespectful to one's forebears to sell a house where they had lived, and, of course, where the ancestral tablets were kept. I had already noticed that if even an item of furniture was moved slightly, an atmosphere of disquiet prevailed. Old Mrs Takahashi would observe it quietly, sighing; not actually looking at the offending vase, chest, or table, but managing to look even more frail, dabbing at her lips with a napkin. Silent reproach emanates from her. Keiko's movements, in response, become jerky as she clears the table, clattering cutlery. Sometimes, from the kitchen, she shouts. Her mother drifts, silently, from the table, and, within minutes, the house is filled with the scent of incense; at the shrine, old Takahashi-san is seeking help from Buddha.

"This house will never belong to me. I can do nothing with it. I cannot change my life. Of course I respect my mother, but, she doesn't understand."

I sat and listened, and made suggestions. Perhaps she should call a family conference with her brothers, and tell them how she felt?

She snorted. "They would not come. After all, I am only a daughter. I live here, but, I am not married. They, and their wives, would say it is my duty to care for our mother. And our house."

"You could at least try," I suggested. " Come on, Keiko, I think you should talk about this within your own family. You might be surprised. They might even agree with your ideas?"

She looked unconvinced. "Things are different here, in Japan".

She left at about midnight, looking happier. I opened my Japanese textbook, and closed it again. Actually, I know what I need. I need a chance to practice my Japanese. Oh well, perhaps tomorrow

Keiko would give me an opportunity. So far, conversation lessons had been decidedly one-way. I crawled into the covers, clutching Humphrey hot-water bottle, and ate half a packet of biscuits from home, falling fast asleep to the faint sound of drum beats.

—∿∿—

Monday morning. I had three jobs to do before class. Collect several reels of developed film, collect my shoes from Joji's shoe mender, and go once more to the travel agency from where I had booked a plane ticket for Tokyo to spend a weekend with an old friend from London who was on a business trip there. Keiko had been surprised I had arranged to travel from an airport in another prefecture, when there was actually a local airport. But I had not been told about it.

At the camera shop, an old man with gold teeth presented me with twenty-four blank sheets.

"You have bad camera," he told me.

Could he fix it?

"No, no, Bad camera. Made in China."

He nonetheless charged me the equivalent of £4 in development charges.

I had left in a pair of court shoes that needed tips on their soles. Barely worn. I had shown him what I wanted, and he had seemed to understand. Now, however, he presented them to me, soles untouched, heels horridly tipped in metal. I re-explained, and left them. Hopefully he will not remove the heels from my Italian shoes altogether. The travel agency maintained I had specifically asked for the other airport. How could I have, since I hadn't known of it?

A dapper young man spread his hands, and shook his head. If I wanted to change now, there would, of course, be cancellation charges. It was regrettable, but there was nothing he could do. Today was not turning out to be a good Monday morning. I had had enough.

"Nonsense," I told him, briskly. "I am obviously a foreigner. I should have been told of this other airport, and I wasn't. And, I am not paying any cancellation charges. I want to fly out of Komatsu, and I want you to fix it, right now." I took a seat at the counter, and sat down.

The young man made despairing, batting motions with his hands, and his superior approached. He burst into a torrent of Japanese. The two turned to gaze at me. I gazed back, resolutely.

"One minute, please," the superior murmured.

Twenty minutes passed, and I sat on. Occasionally, a door would open and the superior peered out, perhaps hoping that this irritating foreigner was a figment of his imagination.

At last, the young man returned:

"You are a lucky lady! We have a cancellation on Komatsu flight."

"Thank you," I said, collecting my new ticket.

I arrived at my lesson ten minutes late, and was greeted with reproach. The teacher had thought I must be ill, and had phoned Keiko Takahashi.

"Well I'm sorry," I told Taniguchi. "I had to …" I looked at her worried face. "It won't happen again, Taniguchi-san, I promise, but look, if I were ill, I would telephone the college and let you know." She looked unconvinced.

After eating a bun at Daiwa Depato, I had arranged to meet Tara. She arrived, pushing her bike. I was immediately struck by how thin she looked. All her old bounce had gone. She said she was sick of Kanazawa, and hated her apartment. Would I like to see it, before going to one of the classes she hoped I would take on for her? We walked back to it, going through a distinctly depressing part of Kanazawa. Her apartment was up three flights of grey concrete stairs that, had they been in England, would have undoubtedly have been decorated with graffiti. On a dim landing, she opened one of three identical wooden doors to display her home.

It was easily viewed. Two small square rooms, divided by a step, and grubby, sliding paper doors. The walls had once been painted a yellowy cream. A strip of faded tatami lay across them, and a single light bulb hung in the centre of each, suspended from wires. One room contained a sink and a curtained recess with a picnic gas stove, and two shelves covered in greasy oilcloth. The same room also had a minute walk-in cupboard with a shower head and an unpleasant squat-type loo. The other room had her rucksack, a futon quilt she had had to buy, and the plant she had bought. There was only one small window facing the well of another tall building, half frosted.

"Oh, Tara!" I said.

"I know. I know. It's ghastly. I can't take it any more. I gotta get out."

We left, so I could watch her take the class she had offered to me. This class was to be held on the top storey of a local clinic. Tara began to unstack plastic chairs and place them round the room. The centre of the room was filled with lines of small wooden desks.

Soon, mothers began to arrive with their offspring. They settled themselves down for a good gossip, dandling infants, ignoring their older kids. Tara was now attempting to cajole fifteen small boys into sitting behind the desks, with no success. They unplugged a TV set, hid behind curtains, leap-frogged over desks, and started a series of mini-punch-ups.

"C'mon now, kids," Tara said, trying to disengage a seven-year-old from behind a curtain. He clung on, and the curtain tore. Another small boy, seizing his chance, jumped from a desk, landing on Tara's back: "Waaaaa ... Batman!" he yelled.

The mothers chatted on, oblivious.

At the end of the hour, Tara, red in the face, had broken up a fight, and persuaded a couple of more timid children to chant "Monday, Tuesday, Wednesday ...."

A bell rang: the children wrenched open the door and disappeared, whooping, down the corridor. Not one mother said goodbye. I looked at Tara. Her shirt had come adrift from her jeans, and her ponytail was loose.

"No way! Sorry, Tara, but no way am I going to try to teach that lot."

I remembered things Joji had told me about the new permissive method of bringing up Japanese children. Because the Americans had 'conquered' Japan, it was believed that this could only have come about because their victors' lifestyle must be superior. Therefore, everything American had been slavishly copied; liberal upbringing was democratic, and seemingly successful; hamburgers, dairy products, ice cream and Coca Cola: baseball caps, sofas, chairs, and rock and roll were all adopted by the young. Also a reduction in family size. It is, of course, much easier to cope with, and adapt to, only one or two small uncontrolled egos, rather than the old traditional-sized Japanese family. And so, despite schools imposing discipline, and grandparents grumbling, many Japanese parents indulge their children, believing this to be the modern, magic formula for success.

"Who are you scheduled to teach next?" I asked Tara.

"Their mothers," she replied.

I thought back to that gossiping gaggle of women, and shook my head.

"No. I wouldn't know where to start. Absolutely not."

Her face fell. "But," she wailed, "I told them you would. Like, I told the organiser I was off, and she was like, livid, and so I told her I had found someone to teach instead, and she wants to meet you, and me ..." her voice tailed off.

I was losing patience. It had been a long day.

"Well, you shouldn't have. All I said was that I'd come and see how you taught. I never commited myself to take on this lot. So, Tara, you agreed to do it for an absolute pittance. Right? And now, you are having a horrible time, and I think you should simply explain to the organiser that you can't do it any more. I'm sure she'll understand. I'm off now. If I'm late again once more, today, God alone knows what my host will think ..."

Her eyes filled with tears.

"My Dad always told me never quit, Tara, and I know I'm quitting, and I know I've done everything wrong, and ..."

I said I'd stay, just until she'd spoken to the organiser.

Nakamura-san came in like an Eastern icicle. Her small black eyes bored into mine.

"Er, Angela-san, an English friend," Tara said, nervously.

"So. Are you going to teach us, instead of Tara-san?"

I regretted that my schedule did not permit it.

She turned her gaze on Tara, speaking in perfect English.

"Did I understand you on the telephone, telling me that you are not going to teach us any more, Tara-san?"

Tara wriggled.

"Yeah, well, look, I'm very sorry, but …"

"But? But? How can this be, Tara-san, when you promised me to teach for three months?"

"I know, and, I feel awful, but …"

"I trusted you, Tara-san. I made a commitment, like you made to me. I spoke to my friends and told them you would be teaching them. Me, they believed. But now, you let me down, when I have done this for you."

Tara began to cry, as Nakamura looked over at her, impassively. I got cross. Suddenly, Tara had shrunk to the size of one of my own children, aged about ten.

"Excuse me, Nakamura-san," I said, quietly. "I am sure that you, as an older woman, can recognise that Tara is a young girl, far from her home. The rate you agreed for her to teach these groups is very low, and she is unable to live on this money. She needs to move on, and be paid properly for her teaching. Perhaps, if you try hard, you will be able to replace her with another – unfortunate – young foreigner. Tara, I'll wait for you for five minutes, and then we are both leaving."

I paced up and down the corridor like a father-to-be as Nakamura's voice rose and fell endlessly. Tara was now sobbing.

I pushed open the door again.

"Stop all this at once! How dare you be such a bully? Come along, Tara, we're going."

We left. Back in her horrible flat, Tara picked up her potted plant and threw it at a wall. It broke the light bulb, and sprayed potting compost over the tatami. We went out and had a beer, and then I left her.

I never saw her again. According to the teachers at the college she left Ishikawa prefecture, and there was a rumour she had married a

Japanese in Tokyo. I hoped not, not within eight weeks of leaving Kanazawa.

~~~

The Centre, like my room, is incredibly cold. There are a few young Australian backpackers, a couple of New Zealanders, and a sprinkling of Americans. They stick together in the library, discussing the vagaries of the Japanese. Occasionally, one of them will answer my greeting with a nonchalant 'Oh, hi there!" but, they don't actually see me. They are not intentionally unfriendly, it is just that someone who could give them approximately forty years doesn't really exist.

I have, however, established a good rapport with my teachers, and we laugh a lot in the staff salon. However, my new teacher, Shinchi-san, and I, have a problem. She has been trained to teach through mime, and the showing of those wretched cartoon cards. At the end of a two-hour class, we have usually only covered a couple of pages of a given lesson. I do like her, but this is a waste of time: hers, and mine. She is becoming progressively more worried, and I am getting frustrated. Our lessons are now embarrassing. Only over coffee are we able to communicate. I remember discussing Western homes, describing a rotary clothes dryer. She clasped her hands ecstatically:

"How I would love one of those wonderful things!"

I suggested, privately, to Kamada-san that maybe I could change teachers: she was horrified.

"Well, how about changing my schedule, so Shinchi-san's feeling are not hurt?" I asked.

This too was vetoed: it was against the rules. Okay. I'll give it a couple more weeks.

I have now been in Japan for nearly three months. I think I am suffering from a slight ET complex. Oh! I do want to go home! Instead, I went to an art exhibition in the Museum of Art beside Shakyo Centre. I met a New Zealander gazing morosely at a huge picture of a Victorian young woman, posed in front of a piano. The painter had meticulously picked out every detail of her ball gown; the taffeta shone, her royal blue velvet jacket gleamed richly, and the lace collar was intricately painted. But her face showed no expression.

She was a cardboard character. Further along, both of us stopped before an oil painting of three geishas. Again, their robes were exquisite, but they themselves had blank features.

"One-dimensional," he growled. "Typical. All their bloody women, one dimensional!"

He bought me a carton of take-away coffee and told me how he had fallen in love with a married woman. How she wanted to be with him, but that his visa would soon expire, and her husband had taken her passport.

"And she just accepts it! Says there's nothing she can do. Says it is so sad, but ..." I think his circumstances influenced his judgement.

I left him, and went to gaze at several paintings of animals; here, the technique was always different: wild bulls, fighting; one could almost hear the charge, the snorting power. Monkeys playing, each one imbued with mischief. Finally, I came to a stop before a picture showing three people, two men and a woman, walking down a country road, returning from a funeral. They carried a small casket containing the bones of a relative. In outline they too were flat, but the attitude of the old man, supporting his wife, with his son beside him, gave a poignancy to the picture. I have a faint memory of being told that there is a time when relatives of a deceased relative place paper boats on a flowing river, each with a tealight glowing in it, and set them sailing away; shades of us lighting candles on All Saints' Night.

Daiwa Depato has hoisted a jolly Santa on its roof. Beautifully decorated white feather Christmas trees are illuminated in their display windows. But the Japanese work on Christmas Day! I wonder if I will? After my return from Tokyo I have agreed to teach several of Tara's classes. I doubt my expertise. I don't think my command of Japanese language is improving. Tonight, I will seriously press Keiko to start speaking to me in Japanese. Not for the first time I reckoned that this isn't fair to me. She is gaining experience, I am not. Before going upstairs I asked her.

"Keiko, please, please would you start speaking Japanese to me? I really need the practice. After all, it is what I came here for."

She looked at me, and sighed.

"Oh, Angela, it is so slow, trying to speak Japanese to you. It bores me to speak it slowly, because then we cannot talk."

"That's all very well, Keiko, but I need to learn. That is why I like to stay with host families. And I am studying so hard."

"You will never learn it in six months," she said, with perfect truth.

"But you could at least help me?"

"I am not a patient person."

"That much I do know," I told her, in Japanese.

Smiling, Keiko corrected my grammar.

I too smiled: "Arigato, Keiko-san."

I read my mail that night in bed. There was a long letter from an old schoolfriend, giving news of mutual friends, and talking about her dogs, and her plans for her garden in Norfolk. She ended her letter with a flurry of questions: did I now eat everything with chopsticks? Was I now fluent in Japanese? And, was it really true that they sat, and slept, on the floor?

I stood up to pull the tasselled light switch, and stubbed my toe against the dressing table. Cursing under my breath, so as not to offend Buddha, I slid carefully down under the coverlet, and shook the rice-stuffed pillow. Wind wailed through gaps in the windows, rattling them. "Yes, Pat! I still can't speak their language, but all the rest is true."

—∿∿—

At last it is Friday. Today, I am leaving Kanazawa and travelling to Tokyo. Sitting in the coach, I feel as excited as a child on her birthday. I am absolutely longing to be there, to be able to talk to an old friend in my own language. As the plane began its descent to Hanada airport, Tokyo, I've a wonderful view over Yokahama Bay, studded with fishing boats; each one enmeshed in a wide circle of nets, like a collection of spiders. The plane now circled over canals, passing ever lower across a marvellously delicate suspension bridge, linking what seemed to be filaments of wire across a river. As far as eye could make out, there were buildings; and yet, apparently, this city, home to millions of people, only encompassed the same amount of land as Milton Keynes!

I had left Kanazawa wearing my fur jacket, not realising how much warmer Tokyo, on the Pacific side of Honshu island, would be. Hunting for the monorail, lugging my case-on-wheels up and down stairs, along a myriad of passages where directions sometimes began in English but ended in Kanji script, I sweated. Half an hour later, leaning on an advertisement for 'Poka Swet' – the same ad that I had passed by several times before, I felt like Alice's white rabbit: 'I'm late, I'm late …'.

Guy, who is French, and punctillious, is going to be upset. I got into a taxi, driven by an inevitably grumpy driver, and asked for the Palace Hotel. Unusually, he knew it. Taxi drivers in Japan normally require their passengers to know the exact route to their destinations. Guy was waiting for me in the foyer, pacing. The first person in nearly three months who actually knew me! Someone who I could rattle away to in my own language!

"Oh, Guy! I can't tell you how wonderful this is !" I burst out. It was all I could do not to throw my arms round the husband of my old friend, and hug him. He said it was good to see me too, but we must hurry, because he had a car waiting to take us to a concert at NBC, and we were, nearly, late.

The National Broadcasting Orchestra of Japan is the premier orchestra; it has its own concert hall. We hurried through to the bar, and, over coffee and sandwiches, caught up on news of friends back in London. Guy's wife, Catherine, had sent him over with Bath Oliver biscuits and Lyons' tea bags for me. My command of adjectives had become depleted to one word: "Wonderful," I kept on saying, "oh, how wonderful."

All around us, people were leaving the bar.

"Perhaps we should take our seats?"

Guy checked his watch:

"No, no. It says on the programme that the concert begins at half past two. It is only ten past. We will finish our coffee."

We were the only couple in the bar.

"So, now we go."

The doors to the concert hall were closed. A steward mounted guard at the entrance. Faint strains of music could be heard drifting through.

"No. Too late." The man barred our entry.

"But no, there is time yet." Guy pointed at his programme. "You see? 2.30 it starts. And it is now," he indicated his watch, "2.20 precisely. We are not late."

The man still shook his head.

I could feel tension rising.

"Angela. You can speak Japanese. You tell him. It says here, on this programme …"

"Ssshhh," the steward said.

In a whisper, I wrestled with my 'puns' and 'funs': spoke of Igirisu-jins, and gaijins, and, ten minutes later, after the overture, he let us in. Guy was impressed at my skills. It didn't seem appropriate to mention that the steward was permitted to admit latecomers, post-overture.

The concert was marvellous; the orchestra played Ravel, Bartok, and Prokofiev, directed sensitively by a young Indian conductor; one of the finest concerts I have ever been to.

Back at the hotel, in deference to my English culture, Guy ordered afternoon tea, but this was not on the menu at five o'clock. We settled for a crepe and ice cream which arrived, displayed delightfully, but unrecognisable. We discovered the crepe, coyly disguised as a twig, accompanying the ice cream, fashioned as a flower. Miniscule, but delicious.

"Is it alright? I'm sorry, Angela, were we in France …"

"But we aren't. We are here in Japan, enjoying the differences."

He laughed. "So. You are happy to be here, in Japan? You are learning to speak Japanese, and you like your hosts?"

I had to pause, and think. Somehow, there hadn't been time to analyse whether I was happy; my thought processes had all been taken up by events, overcoming confusion, and trying to accomplish things.

"Yes, I suppose so," I said, "but it's hard to explain how different things can be over here. Many people have been incredibly kind to me, and the teachers are patient – more so than me, actually – but our wavelengths are different, if you know what I mean."

Guy said I was probably missing my family, and, of course, that is true, too. He had to leave for a meeting, but had arranged for a colleague to take me out to dinner that night.

Time to view my room. A bell-hop escorted me past stunning arrays of gladioli and bird-of-paradise flowers, displayed in marble urns, up in a lift, along a carpeted corridor.

"Your key, Madame. Here is your suite."

I don't believe this. Am I still in Japan? I walk in, treading on a soft, dove-grey carpet; I see silk-lined curtains pulled across one wall of the sitting room …

"And here is the bathroom, Madame."

I am still taking in the curtains: curtains mean windows, don't they?

"This is the mini-bar. Here, the fridge. Here the phone. Please ring if you require anything. Thank you, Madame."

He left, silently.

Me, I behaved like a child let loose in a sweet shop; running across to the big double bed, I bounced on it. I pummelled the pillows; not a rustle, not a grain of rice in them. Not wooden (to prevent geisha hair from disturbance), not macaroni filled. Feather pillows! There were armchairs and occasional tables with pretty lamps on them. They all worked. My clothes had been unpacked and placed in drawers, or hung in fitted wardrobes. There was a discreet tap at the door.

"Hai?"

"Flowers for you, Madame."

A maid entered, carrying a basket of carnations and roses from Guy and Catherine.

A little later, as I was running a steamy, bubble-scented bath, a basket of fruit arrived from Guy's firm. Waiting for the bath to fill, I investigated the mini-bar, poured myself a Scotch and ice, and opened a packet of cashew nuts. Delectable decadence!

'Because You're Worth It', I murmured, settling into the deep

Western bath, resting a few grapes on the edge.

I saved the best to the last; wrapped in the hotel's yukatta (bathrobe), Scotch in hand, I pulled back the curtains, and stepped onto a balcony. Before me was a floodlit moat, the waters glancing to and fro, and, swimming below, a pair of white swans glided, heading for the walls of the Emperor's old palace. All around, the lights of Tokyo glittered and winked like a Christmas tree hung with baubles, and nearby, suspended in the faint mist, an Eiffel tower glowed, pearly pink.

Perhaps I am dreaming. Perhaps it is the Scotch. Perhaps I have died and gone to Heaven.

I was watching an American channel on the giant TV when Guy's colleague, Debbie, rang to invite me to dinner at a nearby restaurant. We had an excellent dinner, and chatted until nearly midnight before I retired to bed, munching on the Belgian choccies placed on my pillow.

Breakfast in bed; croissants and good coffee, before meeting Guy and another colleague, John, in the foyer at eight. We left by car, to see the sacred mountain of Japan, Fuji-san.

Mount Fuji, normally so retiring that many have never seen her fully revealed, rising through veils of cloud. But on this glorious sunny late autumn day, we were incredibly fortunate. As we climbed a winding road through pine forests, skirting lakes that reflected the clear blue sky, snow plopped from sparkling branches, and Fuji-san herself grew evermore distinct, her outline surrounded by little puffy clouds, rather like an attendant chorus of Michelangelo's cherubs. This immense cone, surrounded by five lakes is, to one side, nearly a perfect triangle, the other side slightly curved; but the imperfection renders her all the more divine to Japanese poets, artists and philosophers.

The nearer we approached, the more Guy's eyes glistened:

"What a slope," he breathed, "just perfect. Marvellous ..."

Our driver smiled contentedly.

"...to ski down," Guy continued, leaning forward to absorb every contour.

"No, sir," announced the driver, "never … no skiing on Fuji-san!"

"But yes! See, it would be just perfect. Imagine! The ski-lift travels up there, or, maybe there, and a little chalet is placed …"

Our car took a bend sharply, and we three lost our balance. John frowned, and nudged Guy, as the driver, his back stiff with disapproval, corrected the slide, and carried on driving at a sedate pace.

Over lunch, John regaled us with stories about the lethal fugo fish, pointing out the kanji signs on the menu.

"It is considered a great delicacy here; very expensive. So, maybe, Angela, you will not be offered it by your hosts, but, if you are, try to refuse."

I reckoned if I could force myself to eat natsu (fermented beans tasting like chicken manure) I can eat anything.

"Ah, but this one kills," John warned.

Apparently, the fugo, a dreary-looking little brown fish, suffers from an unusually nervous constitution: when hooked, its adrenalin glands release poisonous toxins. Recently, John told us, one foreigner was left in a coma for weeks, only saved by the prompt presence of mind of a neighbouring doctor. A visiting film star was treated to fugo at a dinner, only to die in agony later that night.

"I'll certainly remember," I said, trying to commit the kanji to memory.

"Piscatorial Russian roulette," Guy observed, cautiously picking over his salad.

We abandoned the driver to commuter traffic and took the Bullet Train, the Shinkansen, back to Tokyo. It apparently travels at 150 mph, but it was so smooth, the speed did not register. Only when another Shinkansen passed us, going in the opposite direction, did it seem to pass like a bullet.

That evening, I again stood out on my balcony, watching the two well-choreographed swans still drifting balletically below (I wonder, are they real?) before joining Guy, John, and the chairman of his company, John W., for dinner at another restaurant.

And it was only then, sitting up at a vast steel counter, with cambric bibs tied round our necks, surrounded by the movers and shakers of Tokyo, that I began to realise just how little Western business executives know about the everyday lives led by ordinary Japanese people, even their own colleagues. I was amazed that the two Johns kept asking me so many elementary questions: Where did the families sleep? What did they eat? What was the role of women in the households? Curfew sticks. What on earth were they? What was talked about, in the home, with friends? What were their houses like inside? And, the monetary role of women: was it true that women held the purse-strings, and paid out not only the house-keeping expenses, but also for meals in restaurants, tickets for cinemas, and so on?

"But, you must know all this," I said. "After all, you, and your families, have lived here for nearly ten years. Surely you must have been into many Japanese homes?"

They hadn't.

Like all their European counterparts, mostly living in the goldfish bowl of Ropanji – an area of Tokyo – they had only shopped in supermarkets geared to Western tastes, and been entertained by Japanese businessmen in three-star restaurants, or sushi bars. Neither of the Johns had ever entered a Japanese home on more than a couple of occasions, and then only for big parties.

More and more food kept arriving in front of us, as did the beer and sake. Guy made one plaintive request for French wine, but was overruled. By the time we were served dessert, tongues had loosened. They told Guy about their attempts to communicate, their trials in trying to learn the language by studying at night, whenever they had an evening free, and, as the evening wore on and we were all drinking beer with sake chasers, the stories ranged from the bureaucracy here (a European business friend who had asked for an ex-directory number, had been given it, and then was denied knowledge of his new number by the exchange) to a favourite topic whenever two or more ex-pats in Japan gather together: lavatorial mishaps.

John W. began: Newly arrived in Japan, he had been invited to play golf with business associates at a highly prestigious club. The players arrived at some horrendously early hour, found all greens fully occupied, and retired to the lounge to drink copious cups of coffee. After an hour of pleasant conversation, John headed off to the immaculate Gents, where he noted there was no hook on which to hang his new trousers. He placed them, carefully, on the edge of a washbasin in the corner of the cubicle. This had U-shaped taps, reminiscent of a Teasmade kettle. The actual lavatory was a pristine trough set in a tiled floor. When he depressed the lever, he discovered, too late, that the washbasin was actually the lavatory cistern. Through the door, his partners were calling: "John-san! Now we can play! We await you on the first green ..."

And, shivering, feeling like an incontinent three-year-old, he was obliged to leave and join the others.

"The worst thing was," he explained, "that when I tried to explain my, er, dilemma, no one laughed! They ignored my soaking pants, murmuring their 'Aaa, so, so,so, ne. And we played on."

We laughed. A lot.

"It can be tricky," remarked the other John, downing his glass of sake, and signalling for another.

"I remember a party given by an Embassy official. Delightful, really. Much drink consumed by all, charming people, our host and his wife. I tootled off to their loo at some stage. Perfectly ordinary, sort of a loo – well, you know, heated seat and all that, but this one had a sort of dashboard of buttons on one side. Well, I thought about this for a bit, and then pressed the nearest, and watched as a metal tube began to rise up – damn thing had a sort of robot-like relentlessness – I was mesmerised, watching it, y'know, wondering what it would do next ..."

He took a sip of his replenished sake.

"And?" I asked.

"And, just as I was about to zip meself up, the damn thing goes like a wretched bidet, firing a socking great douche of water at my private parts."

I was starting to giggle: "So? What did you do?"

"Well, of course, I let down the lid, pronto. But, actually, that was not a clever thing to do."

"Why not?"

"Should have kept my hand on that blasted lid. Force of water spouted like bloody Versailles – sorry, Guy – it shot open the lid, went all over me, and flooded the floor. Water about half an inch deep, and, no drain. Must be plenty of water in Japan! And, it just kept on coming, until I found the right button to stop it. Sod's law, the last button. Very embarrassing. I mean, I could hear all this jolly chit-chat going on outside, trade delegates and whatnot, and all our Embassy chaps, and here was I, letting the side down, dowsing their nice loo…."

John W. is patently not the resourceful chairman of an international organisation for nothing. He began by trying to mop up the floor, using the remainder of the roll of paper, flushing at intervals. Unfortunately, Japanese loo paper is very thin. He made a foray into the bathroom, discovering more.

"Felt a bit furtive, actually – slipping to and fro with rolls of their bumph tucked under my armpits. Got through about six rolls, before I had to resort to bath towels. Didn't do my shirt cuffs much good, either. Rejoined the happy throng, and my wife said she thought we should leave. At once."

It had been a hilarious evening. I had laughed and laughed.

Next day I spent shopping in Ropanji with Debbie. Wonderful shops. I bought pressies for my children, and a black antique silk jacket for myself embroidered with pink silk flowers that had sleeves designed to accommodate a pekinese dog.

It was already getting dark when my plane took off and swept across Tokyo, over the pink Eiffel Tower in a sea of diamanté glitter, leaving behind the Palace Hotel and the Ropanji supermarkets; the businessmen eating and drinking in sushi bars, the two Johns returning to their wives and families, Guy drinking a glass of wine before catching his plane back to Catherine in London. A different world.

One hour later, my plane bumped down at Komatsu airport, and I caught the coach taking passengers to Kanazawa. The air was icy. All the coach passengers were either met by relatives and friends, or claimed taxis, whose drivers ignored my waving hand. Finally, there was only one unlucky cabbie left. He eyed me with distaste.

"Higashiyama?" I asked.

There was no other fare available. He jerked his head, and released the boot, simultaneously switching on the meter and his mini TV that was showing pictures of American football. Obviously determined to get this unpleasant business over with all possible speed, he weaved through traffic, taking small streets I didn't recognise. I crouched forward, peering out. Suddenly, we came to a familiar bridge, and I heaved a sigh of relief.

"Left, please."

He took no notice, continuing to drive past a string of pachinko bars. Perhaps he knew a more direct route? We arrived at another set of traffic lights that I remembered. Once more I told him to take a left, and once more, he took no notice. Could he be deaf? Oh great! The one and only deaf cab driver in the whole of Kanazawa, watching his blasted TV, and I had to be in his taxi, driving to God only knew where. Gradually, the buildings thinned out, and we started to climb. The meter price was also climbing, rapidly. I raised my voice.

"Higashiyama desuka?"

He muttered something that didn't sound complimentary. I leant forward, shouting.

"I want Higashiyama!"

We came to a screeching halt, and he turned round, red in the face with rage. I caught the words, 'yama', 'gaijin' and 'Amerika-jin' in the course of his diatribe. His patience was obviously exhausted, and he and I were on our own, halfway up the road to Utatsuyama.

I decided to get out. I paid him the exorbitant amount registered on his meter, and again humped my case from the boot. Still shouting, he did a U-turn, and headed back towards the lights of Kanazawa.

It took me more than an hour to find my way back to Higashiyama in the sleet, discovering to my fury that I had indeed been right about that first bridge. I told Keiko Takahashi I did not like the taxi drivers in Kanazawa, and she looked amused.

"Perhaps he was nervous," she said.

"Nervous? Look, I told him how to get here. At the bridge, I told him to turn left, but he wouldn't."

"What did you say to him?"

I repeated it, and she began to laugh.

"You didn't say 'left'. You told him 'green'! 'Hidari' you should have said, not 'midori', see? Poor man probably thought you were mad."

There seemed little point in going to the bother of lighting the kerosene stove; it always gave out more smell than heat for the first ten minutes. As I got ready for bed, I glanced over at my study books on the desk, seeing that one exercise book had got damp from the rain seeping through a crack in a paper shutter, and was lying on the tatami. That would never do. I picked it up, and noticed the title and maxim on its soggy cover: Corono Borders – All of Us Have Borders of Our Own – They Tend to Help Define Our Limitations. Light tugged off, I lay under the safety-pinned cover on the floor, and contemplated the limitation of my personal linguistic borders, as clearly defined, as well as the borderline of my self-control, this tending to be less clearly definable. Oh well, maybe, just maybe, both will improve before I leave Japan.

We ate a meagre breakfast of radish, toast, and tangerines. There was no soup, no fish, and no rice. Old Takahashi-san had left, presumably having eaten all Keiko's provisions. Is it traditional to have a paying guest in a room where the windows leak, I wonder? I remember Keiko telling me how once she had gone into my room and found snow all over the tatami. She had worried about that rush matting!

Winter is undoubtedly a'comin in. The rain slices at my cheeks, driven by a wind straight from the frozen tundra. All the streets stink of a mixture of oil, paraffin, and drains; the predominant smell comes from thousands of kerosene stoves, reminiscent of a rally of Italian Vespas. I don't know why the drains have started to smell, unless the extreme cold has fractured underground pipes … incidentally, each manhole cover is embossed with a different, often charming design of a flower, or a bird.

Pity about the stink.

I sit in the classroom wearing my old fur jacket, shivering. All because rules dictate that heaters don't get switched on until a date in December, no matter what the weather. I couldn't concentrate. I was too cold. After a while I told Shinchi-san – still my teacher – that I was going to cancel my lessons until the heaters came on. She apologised. She was sorry, but it was the rule. Lack of food was making me waspish. I said that, as far as I was concerned, the Rulers were going to lose money if the heat wasn't turned on, and added that I had spoken to other foreign students who felt the same. I know this will immediately filter through from the staff room, and may possibly influence the Powers That Be. I left for the Centre's library, one room that is always toasty warm – the room where the organisers and their office staff work.

Unfortunately, all the local schoolchildren who used to study downstairs have also discovered the warmth of the library. Youths have gravitated to it, first sprawling over benches outside the library, eating Mr Do-Nuts hamburgers and pot noodles, guffawing at the groups of schoolgirls gathered round a noticeboard outside the library door, all squealing with laughter. Recently, they had got bolder, invading the library itself, to giggle and chat.

This library is the one and only room where foreign students can study in peace. I glanced over at the senior organiser, diligently working at his desk. He did nothing to quell the noise. Half an hour went by, and more and more thirteen-year-olds joined their friends. Opposite me, a young Korean student put her hands over her ears, looking at me, raising her eyebrows in despair. Neither of us could study. I pushed my chair back and looked over at the children.

"You are making too much noise," I said, loudly. "Be quiet, at once."

Perhaps they were unaccustomed to rebuke. There was instant silence, followed by subdued tittering. I fixed my eyes on them, and waited as they picked up their books and tiptoed out.

Senior tutor later told me that I had been rude.

"Do you not think that they were behaving inconsiderately, and consequently, rudely, themselves?" I demanded.

She shook her head.

"We should never be rude to children, Angela-san."

I did get her to agree that modern children were insufficiently disciplined by their parents. Politeness, for which the Japanese are so renowned, applies, seemingly, only towards those to whom you have been introduced. Standing at the doors of Daiwa Depato, I had plenty of opportunity to observe a national trait; no Japanese would dream of holding open a swing door for the next incomer; what the Marx Brothers did with custard pies, the customers did to one another It struck me as remarkable that a person whose nose had just collided with swinging plate glass, promptly repeated the manoeuvre, never anticipated by the next, or the next, or even the next .

———

During my last meeting with Tara, I had agreed to take on two of her classes. Tonight was my first class, teaching the two daughters of a Dr Kishitani. He collected me from the Takahashis in his Land Rover, and we bowled out of Kanazawa, to the accompaniment of loud Japanese pop music, arriving at a large house set in gardens deep in the countryside. His wife was a pretty woman, a nurse in the local hospital. She led me over gleaming floorboards, past shelves filled with porcelain plates and vases, and into a study where her two daughters sat, side by side on the sofa. Yoshika is thirteen, and her sister, Yukika, eleven. I was seated opposite the girls, a coffee table in between us. Both the doctor and his wife pulled up stools, one at either end of the table, and settled down to listen, photocopies of the textbook in front of them. My heart sank. Surely, this was supposed to be an exercise in English conversation? The doctor rustled his sheet. "We begin, now, Cook-san? Page 54, girls."

Right. It was essential to radiate confidence from the start. I looked again at page 54, with a growing sense of horror.

"Now, Yoshika," I began. "That's such a pretty name, you have! I've never heard it before. But then, you have probably never heard mine, either. My name is Angela."

Silence. Not a glimmer of a smile, no sign that they understood.

"So. Let's see how much you remember from Tara-san's last lesson, shall we?" I began to read: 'Adverbs. These frequently, but by no means always, utilise the suffix 'ly'. Example: 'Sandy ran quickly. Mamie typed slowly.' Okay?"

My pupils nodded glumly.

"Good. Now, can you give me any exceptions?"

They couldn't.

"Look at the page," I suggested.

"Fastly," Yoshika muttered, desperately.

"No, Yoshika. That is not written on the page," interrupted Dr Kishitani, impatiently. "Did you not study this page?" His daughter reddened. She dropped her eyes. I decided to rely on the renowned Japanese ability to memorise by rote.

"I understand that there is a lot to remember, Dr Kishitani. Perhaps we should all read the examples given on these two pages, and look at the pictures."

Together we chanted our way through the lot, looking at the thumbnail sketches, and afterwards, true to form, Yoshika got them all right. Her mother relaxed.

"We continue?" asked the Doctor.

I read on: "'In common usage, blah blah blah, adverbs often come after the verb it qualifies. Example: 'Wayne played noisily'."

"Can you tell me which is the verb? No? Not to worry. Tell me, which is the adverb in that sentence?"

Yoshika's round face, framed with two ribboned bunches, was a picture of misery. Her lip trembled. Yukika, so far lost in a happy daydream, merely stared. Luckily, the telephone rang, and Dr Kishitani was called away. I closed the dreaded book. Tormenting small children for money, I won't do.

"Now then, girls," I said, sounding distinctly like Joyce Grenfell, "we are going to play a game. And we are going to score points! Wakarimasuka, Yukika?"

Yukika, arrested by the sound of her name, stopped playing with strands of her hair, and focused on me for the first time. "Ha?" she enquired. Yoshika filled her in, speaking in rapid Japanese, and she grinned, lazily. I wrote out a series of adverbs and verbs on scraps of paper, shuffled them, and made them guess which was which. After a few minutes of this, Yoshika began to understand. Yukika, ever prompted by her sister, murmured the correct responses, her brain cocooned in neutral. Kishitani-san popped in from time to time, smiling. She brought me a plate of prawn crackers, and I explained that the format of my lessons in future would always consist of revision, a new lesson, and finally a game. Yoshika smiled, quite enthusiastically.

On the drive back to Kanazawa, the two girls sat in the back, and I discovered that Yukika was the lively one, teasing her father, making him laugh; her blank expression had completely gone, and I saw a bright, intelligent, and cheeky little personality emerge. Next lesson, I vowed to myself, I am going to get that child to think for herself, if it's the last thing I do.

I had also agreed to teach the daughters of the Palfun Café because it was just across the road from the College, not realising that they would not be available for their lesson until the café closed. I also discovered that dear Tara had agreed a rock-bottom price for the lesson, which although it was scheduled to last one hour, invariably lasted nearly two.

I had haggled. "I am sorry, but, I am not prepared to teach for this price," I told the eldest daughter. "Especially not at this hour of night."

Her mother joined the discussion. "Tara did." She said.

"Well, I don't," I told them, firmly. "And, you know, some foreigners charge 10,000 yen per hour."

"Too much," observed eldest daughter, setting scarlet lips into a decisive line.

"I am only prepared to teach you three for 8000 yen an hour."

"No. We pay you 2500 yen. And that is 500 yen more than we pay Tara."

I hadn't been a street trader in London for nothing. We finally settled on 5000 yen – and a cup of free coffee thrown in.

Tonight was their second lesson. I walked into Palfun Café at 7 pm, finding it still crowded with customers. A long table had been cleared and placed in the centre of the room.

"Good evening, Angela sensei," I was greeted by elder daughter. "You see how the news of your good teaching has spread! More students are joining us tonight for our lesson."

In addition to her, her sister, and Kobo-san, who, as a local primary school teacher, had taken it upon herself to organise the format of our lessons, there were now three more women and two small boys, all seated expectantly round the table.

"And, here is your free cup of coffee," she continued, decisively, making it clear that although my charges had gone up, their personal contribution had not.

We all took it in turns to read a chapter from the textbook. This related to sushi bars.

"Sushi is delicious, no?" declared the schoolmistress assertively, pointing her prominent nostrils at me.

I returned a non-committal: "Mmm, chotto!"

She was instantly indignant: "But all Japanese people enjoy sushi! It is very good for the body condition, raw fish. So, why do you not like it?"

I spoke sweetly: "Tell me, Kobo-san, would you eat raw steak?"

Everyone looked horrified: "Ugh!"

"Well, there you are, then. Different countries have different habits."

"But, in our country, we eat much fish from the time that Buddha told us not to kill animals, Angela-sensei."

She spoke self-righteously, more in sorrow than in anger, like a nun defending the Friday fast.

"Pity he omitted to mention that large mammal, the whale," I remarked.

Stupid of me, really. It delayed proceedings while they looked up the word 'whale' in their dictionaries. Later, I explained that, although we didn't really go in for sushi bars, fish and chip shops were very popular.

"Fish and sheep? Fish and sheep? What is this, please?"

"Well, Jagaimo. Fried, like fingers, with fish, also fried. Sometimes eaten from newspapers."

Once translated, the small boys burst into uncontrollable giggles, and the cafe owner went back to scouring the counter, muttering to a friend: "Shimbun ni! They eat fish in newspaper!" in tones of disbelief.

I got back to the selected textbook, amazed at its lack of relevance in an English lesson: 'This is a picture of a Japanese temple'. On the opposite page were printed the correct questions. Obediently, I started with question No. 1: "What are the lady and the man in the picture doing?"

"They are clap hands and pray to Buddha," answered the school teacher, smugly.

I corrected her, gently: "They ARE clapping their hands and praying to Buddha."

"What tense you say?"

I had absolutely no idea. "The correct present tense," I told her, trying to recall parsing.

She gazed at me, brow furrowed, and then, suddenly changed tack:

"Do you believe in Jesus Christ?"

All thoughts of gerunds went out of my mind. A couple of businessmen at the bar, wearing identical grey suits, swivelled to gaze at us, curiously. Only their socks had a different pattern, I noticed.

"Er, yes, I do."

"What you believe about Him?"

Echos of the catechism came to my aid.

"I believe He is the Son of God."

Her large, flat face was solemn. "English persons pray much to Him?"

"Probably as much as Japanese people pray to Buddha."

She clapped her hands: "Aaaa, so hoka!"

Shades of the ex-geisha, Mother Takahashi.

Eldest daughter, mindful of precious time slipping away, suggested we return to the lesson. Our next class, I am informed, will relate to Sumo wrestling, described, of course, in English. I have already been in Café Palfun for well over an hour.

—⁓—

When I had walked to the College that morning, teams of women had been uprooting all the flower beds, replanting them with Korean cabbage plants. When seen together, grouped in mass display, they look wonderful, like full-blown cabbage roses, in pink, purple, cream, and green. All the male gardeners in Kanazawa were also out in force, carrying long bamboo ladders, and coils of hemp rope. Their job was to secure the branches of trees before the first heavy snowfall, especially in Kenrokuen, where the trees looked like maypoles, each branch tied into a wigwam of rope. Now, it is dark, and sleet is falling. More and more ominous thunderbolts grumble overhead. I wonder if it will actually snow in my room again, this year?

I am cold, hungry, and exhausted, but not scared to be walking in Kanazawa on my own.

The restaurants, bars, and pachinko amusement bars are always crowded with men of all ages, out after their evening meal at home. I spotted the Kitamuras' son-in-law, with a group of mates, entering one. Here, the entertainment is a little light gambling, as opposed to a little heavy drinking.

Married couples rarely go out together, and the wives do not seem to be upset by this. On some Sundays, a family may go out together, but frequently the husband leaves to play golf, or ski, or, go on company outings. However, everything changes, I have been told, once a husband is officially retired. Then, the man who has spent his entire working life within the confines of the company that may have even employed a marriage counsellor to find him his wife, is presented with the statutory watch, and his life is, to all intents and purposes, over. The resultant shock to both husband and wife is unimaginable. Her life, as well as his, is totally disrupted, and she is left with a man who has never had the time to develop a hobby, and has nothing in common with his own family. This is the most common time for a wife to divorce her husband, describing him as 'bad rubbish'. However, the Government is now coming to terms with this problem, and has been trying to promote schemes whereby a man nearing retirement age is allowed to work on flexi-time, gradually being weaned from his old position. I have not observed this for myself; the two host families I lived with had husbands who stayed home after supper, innocently watching panel games on TV.

I am longing to spot members of the notorious Yakusa (the Japanese Mafia), normally only visible at night. These are instantly recognisable by their tattoos, their smart silk suits, flashy ties, and Rolex watches. Look out for highly polished shoes, and a surrounding coterie of heavies, my informant had said. Their local office had been pointed out to me, inaccessible behind thick steel gates. In common with their Italian counterparts, they are associated with the drug trade, often running pachinko bars, brothels, protection rackets, and horse racing.

Very rarely is anything proved against them, and the police apparently are content to let sleeping Yakusa lie, not attempting to raid their headquarters unless a specific allegation is made. Such allegations seldom surface. One of the wonderful things about Japan, and certainly Kanazawa, is how safe a woman is, walking home in the dark. I saw no drunks, and never, ever, felt a threat from anyone. Once upon a time, shortly after the war, I remembered my home city, London, feeling like this …

Keiko had left my supper on the table: cold mushroom omelette, rubbery cuttlefish, and lettuce.

———

As the time drew nearer for Keiko to leave for Europe, it became clear that all those friends who had professed themselves willing to have me as their paying guest had got cold feet. Urgent phone calls revealed one who had developed bad back pains, another had a sudden influx of family descending on them, and a third announced herself incapable of cooking for a Westerner. I took my problem, as usual, to Miyazaki, dressed today in a lavender sweater with a design of cute kittens; as usual, she sighed:

"Oh, Angela-san … muzukashii desu." Well, I knew it was difficult.

"But, you will at least try?" I begged. "I don't have the money for a Riokan (a Japanese inn) and neither Keiko-san, nor I, want me to stay there on my own."

With only three days left, I called in again.

"Any luck?" I asked.

She shrugged her shoulders.

"Not after you rejected my last offer."

"WHAT? What last offer?"

"I telephoned you, to say that I had found you accommodation with a charming old man of sixty-five, who had a room available at the top of his house …"

"And?"

"You were out. Later, I spoke to old Takahashi-san, the mother of Keiko-san, and she told me 'Damme desu'. She said it was not suitable for you to go there."

A torrent of words flooded my brain.

"How dare she!" I burst out . "She had absolutely no right … I didn't know …"

Saito bustled into the office.

"Ah, Angela-san! How are you?"

"Furious," I replied.

She and Miyazaki had a rapid conversation.

"Aaa. I see," she said. "You must not distress the Takahashis, Angela-san. That is important."

Right.

"But, couldn't you explain to the old gentleman that I had not known of his kind offer?"

Miyazaki shook her head, doubtfully.

"I had to explain to him that you did not think his offer was correct," she explained.

Great. So now, vicariously, I had offended this kindly stranger, who had offered me the hospitality of his home. Saito spoke again.

"Do not worry, Angela-san. We will both try to find you another family. But remember, you should not mention this ... this unfortunate incident, to the Takahashis."

I promised.

Walking back, I reflected on the irony of my moral probity being decided by an ex-geisha.

On the last night, as Keiko was packing, Saito phoned.

"We have found you a family! You will be living with a large family; husband, wife, and their four children. But you will sleep downstairs in the house, with their grandparents. Now, it may be difficult," she added, "because the grandfather does not care for foreigners, especially because he worries that you may disrupt his grandson's studies."

I reflected that the next day was the anniversary of Pearl Harbour, and hoped it was not an inauspicious omen.

"Thank you very much, Saito-san," I told her. "I am very grateful."

Rules, rules, rules. It is nearly impossible not to infringe one or other of them, in this house. Tonight, my last night here, Keiko announced that she could not be bothered to cook, and would take me to a nearby café to eat noodles. I was standing in the porch, slipping my feet into shoes, when I slightly lost my balance, and stepped backwards. Keiko, at the door, looked on in disbelief:

"Did I just see you *stand* on the step, in your shoes?"

"Well, only one shoe, Keiko, I'm sorry, but I ..."

"Do you always stand on the step with your shoe on?"

"No, of course not. Look, I'm sorry. I just lost my balance."

She ignored the excuse.

"You may never, ever, put a shoe on that wooden step. I thought you knew the rule."

We set out to walk to the café in the pouring rain, Keiko slightly ahead, her umbrella held high.

"In my country," I told her, "the rules of a house are primarily designed to ensure the comfort and happiness of the occupants, and a welcome for their guests."

She did not answer, and we ate noodles in frigid silence. She left early the following morning.

I did not see her go.

CHAPTER FIVE

With the Kanekos

YASUKO KANEKO arrived precisely on the hour, driving an immense family car that had two rows of passenger seats. She looked tiny behind the steering wheel. Before I could step outside to greet her, she had run across the street, calling:

"Angela-san! I am so glad to meet you. You are very, very welcome."

My new hostess was wearing jeans and a mohair sweater. She had a pretty, fresh face, almost bare of make-up, her hair cut in a stylish bob with a feathery fringe. Her figure was decidedly enviable. With her, everything is done at speed; my case was whisked from me before I could lift it, and, within seconds of her arrival, she had wrenched the car, squealing, into a U-turn in the narrow street and we had left the old Pleasure Quarter and were bowling across Kanazawa, passing buses, and nipping in between cabs.

"Dai jobu desuka, Angela-san?"

"Hai. Taihen dai jobu," I gasped.

I did feel very much alright. I think I am going to like this young woman very much. If, that is, I survive the journey!

Her house was on the far side of town, in a select area of

Kanazawa, apparently renowned for its hospitals. Here, travelling up the sloping main street, men had, once upon a time, dragged stones with which to build Kanazawa Castle, each rock pulled by ropes made from plaited women's hair. We drove down a side street, lined with little shops, and vending machines for soft drinks and cigarettes. There were no pachinko bars here. Yasuko zoomed up a short, sloping drive, parked, and bounded out to collect my case. I looked out at an airy, light, modern house, surrounded by plants, and heaved a sigh of relief. We entered by two main sliding doors that led into the hallway. One doorway was for her parents-in-law, and one for her, her husband, and family. Because I was officially sleeping on the ground floor, in the parents' part, I was told always to enter through their front door.

We came in virtually side by side, slipped on our two pairs of fun-fur bunny rabbit slippers, and Yasuko took me to see my room, down a long polished wooden corridor. I was amazed at its size; and its colour. This was the first room I had seen since coming to Japan that had walls actually painted in colour, a rich shade of green. Two sides of the room had sliding windows giving onto an outer enclosed passage, and the back garden. In the distance I could see the slopes of Utatsuyama.

Inside the room stood a big television set, a wooden hat stand, and a pine rocking chair. Built-in shelves held some grotesque carved wooden gods ranged next to an exquisite Japanese doll, and, a vase of fresh flowers.

My eyes rested on a curious square formica-topped table, approximately the size of two picnic tables, standing on a quilt; from the table top, two more quilts fell to the ground, like a table cloth.

"Will you be happy here, do you think?" Yasuko asked.

I took in the size of the table contraption, reckoning it to be about three foot square. In stocking feet, I stand five foot three inches. Sleeping would have to be done in a strictly foetal position if I were not to echo Piglet's lament: 'Nobody knows, tiddly pom, How COLD my toes, tiddly pom ...'

[175]

I smiled, brightly. "Oh yes, it's a lovely room, thank you. Er, is that my bed?"

Yasuko pealed with laughter.

"You are joking, yes?"

"Um, no?"

"But surely, you must have seen a kodatsu before?"

She explained the many purposes, and advantages, of the kodatsu. It is, apparently, a uniquely Japanese phenomenon. Apart from their 'hottu carpet' that has heating wires running through it, or, of course, the kerosene heater, the kodatsu is most people's favourite means of keeping warm in winter. The quilt spread on the tatami is for sitting on, those on top of the table have an electric blanket sandwiched in between them, and once this has been plugged into a wall socket, one sits and sticks as much of oneself as possible under the kodatsu, pulling the upper quilts down tidily to the floor. The effect is similar to a tea cosy; legs soon get toasty warm. Oddly enough, even the bits of oneself left outside warm up quite quickly.

I discovered that the Japanese, those renowned inventors of so much high tech, absolutely love their kodatsu; children lie half under it, eating peanuts and watching TV, teenagers do their homework on it, often falling asleep on it, their heads cradled on their arms, and whole families and their guests group together companionably in the evenings, all with their legs tucked under the kodatsu, chatting and drinking beer, tea, or instant coffee.

"It is the heart of the family," explained Yasuko, flicking through her electronic dictionary, "like your English hearth. In the olden days, before the electric kodatsu was developed, there used to be a pit dug in the floor, with hot coals placed in it, and perhaps a kettle set to boil water for tea, and we would all sit around it, under the kodatsu, warming ourselves from the hot coals. This is the modern way."

She switched on a wall plug, its lead trailing across the tatami to the electric quilt.

"Try it, Angela-san!"

I sat on the floor quilt, and stretched my legs under the table.

Within a few moments, heat began to glow, and my legs felt warm, as if in front of a one-bar electric fire.

Privately, I thought that sitting upright on the floor, both legs stretched under a heated table was not the epitome of comfort for European limbs – but, perhaps they would become accustomed to the kodatsu. Perhaps I too would come to love it. And, at the very least, it didn't smell. Nor did I have to light it. Yasuko produced a thin mattress from behind the glass windows, and a bundle of quilts and blankets, and we made up my bed on the floor. This pillow appears to be stuffed with macaroni; it has a miniscule frilled cover showing rabbits on one side only, secured at the back by knotted tapes.

We left the ground floor, and went upstairs to her part of the house. Here was a dining room, obviously used as a family room, with shelves full of trophies and framed photographs, and children's artwork pinned onto cupboards. We sat at the long refectory table with matching chairs, and had a cup of coffee, looking out at a balcony where lines of washing flapped over crates of beer bottles. I felt at home; this could have been anywhere – Ireland, or England. Even the coffee came from a familiar jar marked Maxwell House!

Today is Saturday, so all Yasuko's children returned for lunch. First to arrive was Ryo, a serious fourteen-year old. He is the one studying for his High School Entrance, the one whose studies I must be careful not to disrupt. Ryo is struggling primarily with his written English. His grandparents are worried that hearing English spoken would confuse the boy, and disrupt his concentration. He made his bow to me with averted eyes and disappeared into his room; from there, strains of Bartok seeped into the room. Ryo is a classical music buff. Masaya clattered up the stairs, telling his mother that he was starving. His mother looked at him fondly.

"My son is always hungry. But just look at him!"

Certainly her oldest son, at seventeen, did not fit the Western concept of a typical Japanese. Masaya is a good-looking, bony six-footer. He sprawled at the table, looking longingly at the food Yasuko was preparing in the long kitchen leading from this room.

[177]

Finally, the door burst open and the twins entered, chattering noisily. They stopped short in the doorway, and lowered their eyes. Yasuko introduced them:

"Angela-san, these are my daughters. They are named for 'Love' and 'Gentleness'. This is Ai, and this is Yu."

They were identical.

"Konnichi wa," they said in unison, looking like a mirror image.

We ate a delicious lunch; home-made soup, salad, and fruit, after which Yasuko took me shopping in the neighbourhood. In these shops, most of the customers seem to know each other, pausing to chat before a tempting fish counter, where the fish is strung like a daisy chain, marigolds protruding from their open mouths, and crayfish are arranged on fresh ice.

Yasuko, swinging her basket, appeared to know every child in the shops. She crouched down beside one little girl, who was chattering at her, excitedly, rummaging in her pink plastic satchel. A group of other children joined her, squatting on the floor, watched indulgently by their mothers. The child finally extracted a crayon drawing, and thrust it into Yasuko's hands:

"Asanagawa, desu!"

And so it was; the river, running between green banks, with trees full of pink blossom, and a fisherman reeling in a huge fish – the latter larger than either the fisherman, or the tree!

Shop assistants joined us to admire: "Hai. Kore wa Asanagawa, desu. Subarishii, Naoko-chan!"

Yasuko told her she must bring it to the Christmas party, and to remember to write her age at the bottom. Naoko was five years old.

"And this is my friend, Mrs Angela! She will also be coming to our Christmas party, to see all your paintings."

"Konnichi wa, Mrs Er…" said everybody, politely.

Walking home, Yasuko explained that she helps to teach art to a group of local children, and they would be holding their Christmas party in a few days' time.

"But, I thought you didn't celebrate Christmas?"

"We don't," Yasuko agreed, "but we do have a Christmas party."

I unpack my textbooks from my briefcase, switch the kodatsu to medium heat, rest my elbows on it, and settle down, grimly, to try and master the next chapter of Japanese grammar.

'The particle 'wa' indicates the topic. This is frequently the same as the subject, though not inevitably. Maybe the object is actually the topic. And, on occasions when the topic is obvious, it is customarily omitted.'

Ah.

I press on, hoping that light will suddenly dawn: 'It is a mistake to identify the word 'hai' as always corresponding to the Western 'yes', or, indeed, 'iie' as always meaning 'no'. One should regard the former as corresponding to 'that is correct', and the latter to, 'that is incorrect'.

Example: 'O'kashii ga arimasenka?' (So, you have no cakes?) Reply: 'Hai arimasen'. (That is wrong, we have some). As opposed to: 'Yes, they aren't' which is how I would have read it. I wonder if some Japanese grammarian had been responsible for the old music hall refrain, 'Yes, We Have No Bananas'?

My mind, and toes, are becoming overheated. I switch the electric blanket setting to low and rub my aching back.

'Care must be taken in pronunciation. For example, the negative 'iie' must not be confused with the word for good, 'ii'. The word 'ie' means 'home' whereas 'i' means 'stomach'. Now, let us take the particle 'mo' ...'

Let's not. I move over to the rocking chair, and close my eyes.

Yasuko called me for supper. Her husband, Jin-Ichiri, is a delightful man, with a keenly intelligent young face that belies his shock of grey hair. He offers me a beer as we sit down to supper, and pours one for his wife. Yasuko and the twins were busy bringing food to the table. Jin-Ichiri, Masaya, and Ryo sat, awaiting its arrival. As ever, even in this sophisticated family, the female role remains clearly defined; no male may ever be denied a second helping, no matter what stage mother, daughter, or sister may be at their own meal: "More rice, mother" or, "More soup, wife" and "Hai, hai, sumimasen" she apologises, rising from her place to replenish their plates. It is noticeable also that clearing up and washing up is also regarded as exclusively women's work. The boys retire to study, or play, men sit and smoke. That is the just the way things are. I reckon that Womens' Lib will have a long and stony path to travel in order to gain an equal footing here.

I attempted to help, but both husband and wife insisted I was their guest, and should sit and rest myself. Yasuko finally fluttered to the table, and lifted her beer glass: "Kampai!" she and Jin-Ichiri toasted me.

"Tonight, we have a treat for you, Angela-san. A special Japanese fish."

"What is it called?" I asked.

"This is fugo," she announced. "Very special."

There were slices on my plate. I looked at it: innocuous, pinkish-white, thin slices, bordered with lettuce leaves. Good manners have their limits. I thought of my children. I thought of my medical insurance cover.

"I'm sorry, Yasuko-san. But fugo I do not eat."

The eyes of the family switched to me. "Why not?"

"As I said, I'm very sorry, and I'm sure it is delicious, but, if you don't mind, I'd really rather not try it."

Yasuko looked puzzled: "But why?"

"Because you are not licenced, and, anyhow, people can die of eating fugo," I blurted.

Jin-Ichiri laughed. "So, she has heard," he said.

Yasuko reassured me. "Angela-san, I buy from a licensed premises. You are perfectly safe to eat fugo here."

Dubiously, I took a forkful. It had absolutely no taste whatsoever.

"Delicious," I said. "Come on, are the rest of you going to have some too, or are you all determined to kill off this gaijin?"

We all laughed. Jin-Ichiri poured me a glass of sake, and the twins, once the joke had been explained to them, were reduced to helpless giggles. After supper, kneeling on the tatami of the room which doubled as the master bedroom, the family taught me a Japanese card game. We laughed a lot, and I enjoyed the evening. That night, pummelling my macaroni-filled pillow, I couldn't drop off to sleep, subconsciously afraid that I might not wake up. Also, my bones ached. Perhaps I have lost weight recently, because hips, shoulders and elbows seem to grind against the floor. The long hours roll by as I toss and turn on the thin under-quilt. Oh, for my beloved Serena to curl up behind my knees and warm them! Humphrey hot-water bottle, has long since lost his warmth. That infernal pillow, whether placed under my skull, or at the base of my neck, affords no comfort at all. I finally discarded it, banging my head against the TV set in the process.

Before I go to bed tomorrow night, I vow, I am going to creep out into that outer passage and collect all the cushions stacked there and put them on the floor, directly under the quilt. If I am careful to replace them each morning, no one will be offended, and perhaps I will get a good night's sleep.

—⁓—

I can just make out the time on the dial of my alarm clock: 6.15 am on a grey, chilly dawn. Someone is shuffling across the tatami in the room next door, panting. Maybe this is the disapproving grandfather? I lie very still. More stertorious breathing, and then a key clatters in a lock. Hinges squeak, and silence falls once more. Suddenly, I hear one sharp, musical 'Ting!' an intensely pure sound coming from some tiny metal gong. The note reverberated through the room, and hung, golden, on the air. Now I could hear whispering, until a door was relocked, and the heavy breather left.

I am very, very stiff. And cold. My clock now shows 6.30 am.

Down the corridor, the grandparents are receiving visitors. I hear them being greeted, and shown into the nearby livingroom. Mixed smells of kerosene and Nescafé drift into my room. There is a cooing of womenfolk: "So, so, so…" and the sound of men talking. One man laughs like a jolly Santa Claus: "Ho-ho-ho! Ho, ho-ho!" I wonder, is that my host?

The kodatsu has quite a few basic faults, in my book. Currently, the fact that it is not designed to dress under, on a freezing early morning. The room does contain hot air vents from a boiler, but these have not been timed to come on until later.

A tap on my door: "Angela-san, breakfast!"

We are all treated to a breakfast special. The early morning visitors had come with a present for Jin-Ichiri's family; homemade New Year cakes. These looked like little round blanched marshmallows, or bread rolls in need of partial baking. Yasuko placed them on the rack of her toaster for two minutes before giving them out. Their colour hadn't changed.

"Aaa, o'mocha!" Yu said, or, maybe it was Ai?

The twins were delicately pulling the balls of dough apart with nimble fingers, and every appearance of delight.

"Oishii desu, ne, Angela-san?"

"You should be careful," Yasuko warned me, "sometimes, when old people eat these at New Year, they choke …"

O'mocha is a gooey rice dough, steamed for many hours, before being pounded flat, and finally shaped into balls, dusted with rice flour. They have absolutely no taste whatsoever, but can be pulled into long, glutinous strands, like bubble gum, but minus the flavour.

"Another for you, Angela-san?"

"No, no, really, I couldn't possibly manage more than one," I insisted, unclamping my back teeth with an effort. I remembered last night's particle, and tried it out. "Mo chotto!" And they understood. This was an occasion when 'mo' meant a composite of the words 'sufficient, also, and already' (as in Jewish households: 'Enough already', I presume).

Later that day, Yasuko asked me if I would like to visit a local temple.

"Surely," she suggested, "you have studied enough for one day?"

She told me that the temple was a place to achieve peace of mind, and that seemed like a very good idea.

We approached this temple across a verdant lawn of thick green moss, surrounded by glades of pine trees. Once inside, it was dark. Gradually, I was able to see shrines. Gilt figures squatted in ornate splendour, each surrounded by flickering lights, brass bells, heaps of oranges, bottles of sake and tiny bowls filled with rice. Great ornamental mobiles hung over each, tinkling, as we passed by. There was a smell of joss sticks. Yasuko led me on through more rooms, all containing another statue of a god, until we came to one guarded by two gigantic wooden creatures, one allegedly male, the other female. They were painted red, and stood approximately 12 foot high, each wearing an expression of hideous menace. They had apparently been carved 400 years ago.

I stood, staring up at these gods of thunderbolts. The custodian of the temple materialised, silently, beside me, and I jumped as she touched me on the arm. A squat, dumpy little old lady flashed me a smile, and vanished again into the darkness.

"Angela-san. She wishes to welcome you. She will make us some special tea." Yasuko explained.

I blessed Naoko Kitamura. I was prepared for the sticky pink sweet, made my obeisance to the tea bowl and my hostess, drank the bitter ingredients in three appreciative slurps – having made sure to turn the bowl twice – making sure that the prettiest pattern faced away from me, before finally rotating the bowl to show due appreciation of its design and workmanship. And I did remember to upend it, so as to gaze at the indecipherable maker's name on the base.

The old lady flashed me a gold-toothed smile. Now, she wanted to know about me. Was I married? What did my husband do? Had I met the Queen? Had I children? So, was my husband rich? Was I rich? I told her that, having spent a weekend in Tokyo, I certainly wasn't, and she clutched the sides of her kimono and rocked with laughter at this little quip.

"How old was I?"

"I prefer to forget," I told her.

She and Yasuko burst out laughing. I envisaged another bowl of tea about to be served

"Iie. Mo kekko desu. Arigato." I said, firmly.

Perhaps more of that grammar had sunk in than I realised. As we left, I was presented with a small circlet of blue beads. At its base, a larger bead had a hole in its centre, and a tassel hanging from it. "When you look through this, you can see Buddha," the old lady assured me. Back in my room, I have tried. Without success.

―――――

My room gives onto a magnificent view, once I have pushed the panels aside. Grandfather specialises in bonsai, all in their own special ceramic bowls. Many of these he has staggered on slatted shelves; tiny clusters of maples, now turning carmine and purple, miniature beech woods, twisted azaleas, and a stand of six-inch pine trees. Beyond rooftops the lamps of Higashiyama gleam, and, rising above these, dotted among trees, an occasional light shines from the mountain of Utatsuyama – the large houses of the Yakusa, bought from their ill-gotten gains.

I heard a story of one such Yakusa, living in splendour in one of these houses. He and his wife had invited some wealthy acquaintances to take tea, and admire the view from the mountain. The evening was warm, and the windows to the garden were pulled back. As they sat there, gazing out, the ladies in the party drinking the best green tea, their fingers glittering with diamonds, the men quaffing the finest Scotch whisky, there came suddenly a burst of glorious bird song. They were amazed, because, as previously said, birds in Japan rarely have a melodious song, usually squeaking or chirping. A few moments later, another bird began to sing, its song even more beautiful, trilling in from the garden.

"Those birds? Such wonderful singing! What sort of birds can they be?" they asked their host. The Yakusa was delighted.

"Ha! You enjoy my garden birds? I tell you the secret of my wild birds. I have the Dial-a-Bird system installed! What bird you like to hear now? I can give you the nightingale, or maybe you prefer the little lobin led-blest?"

Yakusa love flashy jewellery, both for themselves, and for their female relatives and girlfriends. Their difficulty was that the giving of presents, apart from omigyage (souvenirs), or maybe as a gift at New Year, rarely happens in Japan. Once married, a woman seldom receives any jewellery; if she does, it is regarded as compensation for some marital misdemeanour. So, how were they to display their expensive trinkets? Large jewellery shops solved the problem, obviously seeking repeat business: they started to throw glittering parties, at which their customers could seek to outshine each other. Such gatherings were a huge success, and, of course, proved very profitable.

Today, I took my Christmas cards to the local Yubinkyoku to buy second-class stamps. The official behind the counter promptly opened the envelope and laboriously counted each word, and the spaces in between: 'Look forward to seeing you in the New Year. Lots of love, Angela.' Pencil poised, he replaced each card in its envelope and clucked reprovingly.

"Too much words. First class stamps for all."

Japanese officials are nothing if not accurate. Bureaucracy, bureaucracy! I then went to the City Hall to obtain my alien's registration form, and filled in my home postcode: London SW fifteen, six LL. The young man perused the form carefully, enquiring: "What is this SW?" He frowned, as if I was sending an encoded message to MI5.

"It stands for South West," I explained.

"Not good enough. You write South West." he insisted.

I finally had to complete the address phonetically: London South West, 15 6 EL EL. He was, however, perfectly happy to accept three snaps of myself taken at a local shop wherein I resembled the spouse of the God of Thunder. Perhaps, there are none so blind as them that cannot see ... Next stop, the local branch of Customs & Excise to try to get them to revoke three months' duration of stay in Japan. My teachers had assured me that this could not be done. I would have to fly to Korea, or Hong Kong, stay a couple of days, and then fly back with a new three-month tourist visa. This I could not afford to do; my funds were getting dangerously low, even though I had cut down on food, and even bus fares.

I had left the Kanekos that morning in bright sunshine, but had

had the foresight to carry a raincape and plastic wellies. But now, I had to take a bus. I got off it in a remote industrial estate, and had walked a few paces when the rain began; not just an initial drizzle, a sort of 'grand soft day thank God' rain; this was an instant torrential deluge, soaking me before I could even extract my rain cape. I wedged squelching tights into the wellies, huddled damply under the cape, and swore.

And got lost.

One hour later I was still trudging through the rain, with no idea of where I was. I rang the bell outside a warehouse. The manager, summoned by his receptionist, stared at me with a mixture of horror and pity, Western bag-ladies being a rarity in Kanazawa. Together, they consulted a phone directory, shaking their heads. The manager, still shaking his head, turned to me. But, did he say 'kimasu'? Or was it 'ikimasu'? Bowing, I turned to leave. They stopped me. I recognised two words: 'obásan', and 'jidosha'. The receptionist fetched a sheet of polythene, and motioned me to a plastic chair. A few moments later, that kind man placed the polythene sheet on the passenger seat of his car, and drove the foreign 'Grandmother' all the way to Customs & Excise.

The Principal Immigration Officer was a large man, seated behind an imposing desk. He wore big horn-rimmed glasses that magnified his eyes, giving the impression of a frog. Beside him sat a very small man, wearing rimless glasses. In the corner, behind a word processor, a secretary was busily clicking away. I approached the Great One, bowing humbly.

"Please, do you speak English?"

"Sure," he growled.

I explained that I was trying hard to learn Japanese, how much I was enjoying his wonderful country, and my regrettable lack of cash. He looked unconvinced.

"Why you come to me? Why you want more time here in Japan?" he demanded.

I had rehearsed my reply.

"Because," I said, earnestly, "I need to be able to help your countrymen to enjoy England when they come as visitors. I am a Shakespeare Guide," I told him, "and that is why I need to learn more of your language, in order to explain our culture to them."

I stood, dripping on his nice clean floor, looking at him imploringly.

The two men consulted, passing my passport and registration document between them. The small man spoke. He had a shrill, reedy voice:

"So, you go to Korea, and then you come back?"

"Unfortunately, I do not have sufficient money to do that," I explained, "and, I really do want to improve my Japanese, and then help the good, interested Japanese tourists who come to Shakespeare's country."

More unintelligible conversation ensued. Resolution! Frog Prince slid open a drawer, and produced a rubber stamp. He announced that, just for this once, I might extend my visit for a further three months.

"But" he said, sternly, tapping his nose with a stubby forefinger, "you tell no one. This, for you, is special!"

I was suffused with gratitude:

"Oh! Oh! Arigato! I mean, domo arigato gozaimasu!"

Passport and papers in hand, bowing, I made for the door, but was recalled.

"Passport again, please!"

Faltering, I again handed over the precious documents.

"One day little, for deep year, is all," he reassured, banging down the stamp once more.

Deep year? What on earth? Light dawned. This was a leap year! I beamed at him, remarking conversationally:

"Did you know of our tradition? In England, during leap year, ladies can propose marriage to a man they want to marry."

The typist emitted a little yelp, and then continued pressing keys, rapidly. An expression of horrified disbelief flowed over the face of Frog Prince. His adam's apple twitched. We stared at each other in mutual alarm. I mean, surely he couldn't possible imagine … Little Reedy Voice broke the silence, wagging his finger.

"You GO! And remember, you are an Alien. And, if you do not leave Japan on this date, our police will fingerprint you, and maybe even put you in …"

I didn't wait. The door closed behind me. Clutching the papers, I went hastily down the stairs and out into the street. The rain had stopped, and a pallid sun glinted on puddles. 'S'wonderful … S'marvellous … That you should care for …'

Well, no. Perhaps not. It had been a long and gruelling day.

Back at last on the main street in Kanazawa I made my way to the bus stop for Takara-machi. Usually I would walk back from here to save the bus fare, but, not today. I put my new leather briefcase down on a low wall outside a bank, and discarded my raincape; it was too much trouble to discard the wellies, and, my back was aching. Once back at the Kanekos, I vowed, I would turn on the kodatsu, pour myself a beer, and do absolutely nothing. After all, I now had three extra months to study, thanks to the two I mentally christened Frog and Tadpole. Enough of a breather. Only a few hundred yards to the bus stop.

When I picked up my briefcase, chunks of wall came away with it; what I had thought to be a solid pink and grey stippled wall revealed itself to be a mass of molten pink plaster goo that stuck to my hands and the black leather briefcase, like gritty strawberry mousse. I tried to get it off with a tissue, without success; the more I tried, the more it spread. With the mess now clinging to my handbag and my sleeves I swabbed and cursed. My bus passed on its way.

A passer-by stopped to watch.

"I help," he said.

He fetched a small tin of water from a nearby garage, and began to scrub vigorously, at the briefcase. As he worked, inadvertently touching the wall, bits of the soggy pink stuff got stuck on his trousers adhering like chewing gum. The door of the bank slid open, and the bank manager tripped neatly down its steps, wearing a pinstripe suit, gold rim specs, and a benign expression. He stood beside us, watching.

"Hora!" I said, indicating my briefcase and hands. I also indicated my unknown helper, busily scrubbing. The bank manager waited a few moments more, not addressing a word to either of us, before retiring back into the bank. We continued scraping. Minutes passed. More buses passed. He reappeared, and, with a flourish, presented me with a small gift, and another for the man, still rubbing away furiously at my briefcase. Each present, wrapped in see-through cling-wrap, contained a plastic lemon squeezer, and a very small pair of scissors also made from pink plastic … to match the wall?

The fruits of his benevolence received, both the manager, and my good Samaritan, bowed.

"Well. Arigato," I said, between gritted teeth. I mimed the placing of a notice.

"Good idea, huh?"

The manager treated me to a gold-toothed smile, and went back to his sanctuary.

I thanked the passer-by effusively, pointing to his trousers, with many a 'gomen nasai', but he didn't seem fazed, leaving with a cheery wave and lots of 'dai jobu's', as in: 'No problem!'

———

I am hugely enjoying my stay with the Kanekos. The two weeks are going all too fast. This is such a relaxed, happy family, so concerned to make my stay with them memorable. My only regret is that I cannot speak enough Japanese to really communicate with Jin-Ichiri; his spoken English is on a par with my rudimentary Japanese. He is a charming, intelligent man, with a puckish sense of humour. Over supper tonight, we were struggling to understand his view on current happenings, the importance of Russia to Japan, and the misconceptions of politicians throughout the Western, and American world, each of us appealing to Yasuko to translate.

"It is so ridiculous, our school system," he said. "It dates back over centuries; to when our Emperor decreed we should learn how to read and write in English; for commerce, you understand, but that the purity of our language should not be defiled by our having to speak it! And, nor should we be ..." he paused, reaching for his dictionary, "seduced? Eh? Into foreign cultures. And," he continued, "to this day, schoolchildren, like myself, learn English for six years, but, we have never heard it, and were never taught to speak it. And now, it is too late for me."

"No it isn't," Yasuko said, casually tapping at her empty glass. "I study English every day. You, husband, are just too lazy!"

Jin-Ichiri grinned at me. "You hear that, Angela-san? You hear about our gentle Japanese wives. Not true. Me, I am like American husband: chicken-pecked!"

We all laughed, except for Masaya, their seventeen year-old. On paper he can translate Jane Austen, but is utterly incapable, or maybe unwilling, to understand a word of English. Jin-Ichiri poured us three glasses of beer, and, before I went off to bed, Yasuko put on a selection of CDs from their collection. We sang along to music from 'Oklahoma', through to 'Mary Poppins', 'The Sound of Music', 'Cats', and 'Phantom'. I tiptoed out to the corridor and collected cushions to put under the ground coverlet. It does make the bed warmer, and means Humphrey retains his heat for longer. I do not understand why Japanese people always fold up their bedding, even if the room is not going to be put to different use during the day?

Today, at the International Lounge (motto: 'Let us stretch hands across a cup of tea') I met a very distressed Naoko Kitamura, who told me that Hoshiri had been taken to hospital, suffering, as far as I could gather, from trouble with his stomach. For one week he has been unable to eat. Such a sweet and gentle man.

Passing a flower shop, I decided to buy him a little cheer-up present, that I would take to Naoko the next day. Japanese flower shops are an absolute delight, full of bonsai, lilies, and displays of orchids. But, because Hoshiri enjoyed his garden, I looked at the selection of plants, finally settling on a pretty little pink and white camellia. I told the shopkeeper I would pay for it, and collect the following day.

"Please tell me, what should I write on the card?" I asked Taniguchi.

"What are you giving him?"

I explained it was a pot plant. My teacher looked horrified.

"But, Angela-san! He is in hospital?"

"Well, yes?"

"Never a pot plant. Not for a sick person in hospital."

"Hospital rules?"

"No, no, Of course not. You see, pot plants, they are rooted ..."

"Naturally, Taniguchi-san."

"So, of course, they stay in their pot. The message you send is that you hope he stays there, where he is."

It was my turn to be horrified.

"What? Oh my God! How awful ... thank you for telling me. I didn't know. I just saw this pretty little camellia plant, and I thought he'd like it, and ..."

"A CAMELLIA!"

Taniguchi spoke as Lady Bracknell, pronouncing on that infamous handbag.

"Do you not know of the bad habit of the camellia, Angela-san? The flower heads drop off. Now, do you see what I mean?"

"Yes," I admitted, humbly.

The episode served to prove, yet again, something every foreigner here would do well to remember: if in doubt, ask – in fact, even when not in doubt, ask, because the symbolic pitfalls for the unwary are innumerable.

Guided by my teacher, I bought a card bedizened with a red, purple and silver cord – for good luck. It showed a sprig of cherry blossom, and a fan, all of which I was assured had encouraging meaning, and were patient-friendly. The staff at the International Lounge told me that Hoshiri was too weak to raise his head from the pillow. I was devoutly glad not to have sent the camellia.

Joji Uno has telephoned to invite me back to Mattoh to have supper with Mieko and Fumiko. In view of the weather forecast, he suggested that I spend the night with them.

I did indeed awake to a grey and white world; brilliant snow on the ground, and a swirling dust of snow particles driven in all directions from a dirty grey sky. Snow over here is never crisp and powdery, and in Kanazawa they have developed a special method of de-icing roads and pavements: at every few yards of pavement, round metal discs send out low jets of water, and because the temperature rarely drops below freezing, the water from these jets is fractionally warmer than the snow, so melting it into slush rather than ice. Apparently, in the northern island of Hokkaido, where temperatures drop to -29 and icicles form at the end of exposed noses, a system of heated pipes runs under pavements and streets and does the same job.

I took the bus from the Centre to the railway station, sitting behind a small boy and his mother. The child was leaning against her shoulder, reading his book, sucking his lips in concentration, following the lines of print, starting bottom right of the page with his finger, moving up the lines of print, and then down again to the bottom. Something about the pictures rang a bell with me, and when he turned the next page, and I saw a pirate with a hooked arm being followed by a crocodile with an alarm clock in its tummy, I recognised it at once.

"Waaaah!" the little boy said, snuggling closer to his mother. She smiled down at him.

"Ee, dai jobu, dai jobu. Hora! Tinka Beru kimasu!" And there, sure enough, was Tinkerbell floating in from the top right-hand corner of the left page. Of course, the story was printed not only from bottom to top, but also back to front, with the first page at the end, and the last being first, from our point of view. I am indeed at the other side of the world.

Christmas decorations were out all over Kanazawa station; huge silver and white wreaths that appeared to be made out of cotton wool, and arrangements of lace and foliage. The pots of live chrysanths now had flowers like white snowballs. The musical accompaniment played before each train leaves has not changed, however; arpeggios of harp music heralds the guard's whistle, a sort of 'Seraphs Awake', or a version of the signature tune once used as the theme for 'Mrs Dale's Diary'.

The Unos gave me a wonderful welcome. Fumiko had learned a new piano piece and was instructed to play it for me, as a possible prelude to her being invited to play a solo at her school concert, Joji told me with his customary enthusiasm. Mieko had cooked a celebratory tsuiaki in my honour, and I was shown their winter kodatsu, now established in their kitchen.

"In my house, you are always welcome," Joji said, as he, Fumiko and I sat together after the meal, our feet tucked under the kodatsu, while Mieko brought us all a constant supply of roast sweet potatoes, coffee, biscuits, and nuts. She slipped upstairs to switch on the electric blanket in my bed, and light the stove in my old room.

I realised that, since staying with the Kanekos, my language skills must have improved, because much of our conversation was in Japanese, and even Mieko seemed able to understand me. She actually told me that I had improved, and I felt a small glow of pride. Who knows? Maybe, just maybe, I will master reasonable Japanese by the time I leave, and then all the cudgelling of brain, despondency and exhaustion will have been worth it. Joji was in fine form, extolling the delights of his o'mocha – those New Year cakes I had eaten at breakfast at the Kanekos. Had I ever tasted them? He asked.

I crossed my fingers. "Er, no, Joji-san."

"Then, Angela, you must come to us in the New Year, and I will make you some of my special ones. They are the best. I will show you how they should be made, the old, traditional way. I make them in my garage, with Fumiko." He reached for his electronic dictionary.

"Yes! I have my mallet, and my tree trunk, and I hit the rice many, many times – like this!" Joji raised both arms dramatically over his head, like an axeman felling a tree. "And Fumiko, she shapes the rice in the tree trunk, eh, Fumiko?"

"Hai," Fumiko remarked, laconically.

"But, Angela, you must be very careful, eating them, because, every year, about twenty old men die, when the o'mocha gets stuck in their throats."

"What about old women?" I asked.

"No, no. It is the old men who die," he assured me, seriously.

I remembered Yasuko being more unisex in her caution. I went to bed in a toasty warm room. Oh, the joy of sleeping in a Western-style bed! I had not experienced such bliss since leaving Tokyo. I slid open the window a crack, praying that Mieko would not check on it, and with a last glance at the crinolined blonde doll in her glass case, fell fast asleep.

The next morning, Joji took me to watch Fumiko's fencing class. Young Fumiko, looking apprehensive, was already togged up, wearing a powder blue tracksuit, pads, gloves, helmet, and guard. Only one other girl was in the class, and no other parents were present. When it was Fumiko's turn to be attached to a wire that registered each touch electronically, Joji leaned forward, tensely. The two small adversaries faced each other and bowed. Fumiko was set against a boy of about fourteen.

"HAI!" snapped the instructor. With wired swords clenched in gloved fists, the two feinted and darted to and fro, trainers squeaking on the boards.

"Attack!" growled Joji. "Attack, Fumiko, attack NOW!"

She lost the joust, and her father sat back, disconsolate.

"She has not the brave heart! My daughter, and she has not the brave heart." He muttered.

Later, we went into Mattoh museum. Joji was a wonderful guide, explaining how the exquisite swords on display were crafted; a process involving the extraction of river mud to give strength to the inner core of the sword, and that, somehow, this gives the outer surface suppleness and flexibility. Once the blade has been perfected, more mud is taken from the river, and the craftsman then creates a pattern of incredible delicacy; sometimes a tracery of spray, or bubbles from a river, or, occasionally, the mud is applied in a soft irregular shadow that, when eventually put to fire, is transformed into the curves of a mountain range.

The artist sees no dichotomy between scenes of such natural beauty, and the killing purpose of the weapon.

We saw rooms devoted to agricultural tools, and medieval – as I thought – practices. Practically everything was made from wood, iron, or, of course, rice straw. Life-size models showed a procession of men wearing rain capes made from overlapping woven matted rice straw. The man at the head of the procession carried a huge hide drum, shoulder high, beaten by a small boy, others carried flaming torches. For control of pests, Joji explained.

"The insects are frightened by the noise of the drum. They fly up, and are burned by the torches. I remember being there. It was I who used to beat the drum."

"You? When, Joji?"

"Oh, after the war. When I was a boy."

And this, I reflected, is a country now using robot-control helicopters to spray their crops!

I was privileged to be driven back to the Kanekos in Joji's new car, complete with all the erstwhile 'optional extras'.

"Waah, Joji-san! Have you become a Yakusa?" I teased him.

He laughed, slightly nervously. "You should never say such things in Japan, Angela. Ever."

We stopped off at a garage for petrol, and almost before he had switched off the engine, a team of young people rushed forward, emptying the ashtray, polishing windscreen, windows and lamps, and hosing down the wheels. One leggy youth, wearing a baseball cap inscribed 'Joyful Sky Harmony' actually removed the rubber mats from under our feet and shook them. No wonder no father or husband has to waste his weekend cleaning the family car.

I am wondering how on earth to repay the Kanekos for their kindness and hospitality. I have bought them sweets, but shy away from the symbolism of flowers. It occurred to me that they might like to sample a Western dinner?

"It would be very interesting," Yasuko agreed. "But I don't know how my sons would … I mean, the boys are rather … well …"

"Conservative? Mo chotto?"

She smiled. "Perhaps, a little. But, thank you. Let us try."

We went shopping together. I bought my tried and tested chicken pieces, together with vegetables, potatoes, butter and milk, with bananas that I planned to flambé in butter and brown sugar for pudding. Yasuko also seemed to be buying a lot of food. Unpacking our purchases took up most of the kitchen work surfaces.

I peeled the onions and carrots laboriously, without a peeler, watched curiously by the twins. Then I coated the chicken with flour and garlic salt, fried it, and set all the ingredients to simmer, slowly, on one of the two gas rings. Meanwhile, Yasuko was deep-frying her prawns in batter, presumably in case of resistance from the menfolk. We squeezed past each other in her long, narrow kitchen, as I mashed the potatos with a fork, adding the butter and milk, whilst simultaneously stirring the sauce for the chicken stew.

The moment had arrived. Our two meals were ready. Holding a pink and gold platter, Yasuko had arranged her prawns prettily, interspersing them with segments of sliced tomato and lemon. My stew, by invidious comparison, looked like nursery nosh. Everything was placed on the table at the same time, barring the banana dessert which I insisted on preparing after the main course, to serve with cream. The meal was a great success. Even Masaya and Ryo came back for second helpings of stew, pronouncing it 'oishii'. Jin-Ichiri declared it to be like a Western Christmas Day!

"If I ate like this every day, I should become fat – then, no more skiing," he declared.

Ai and Yu are rewarding me by teaching me the Hiragana alphabet. We three knelt together on the square of hot carpet, and they doled out a set of animal cards, like the Kitamuras had for their granddaughter. The twins took it in turns to ask me what sound the individual symbol on each pictorial card stood for in Hiragana. In both alphabets, Hiragana, and Katakana, a consonant is always linked to a vowel to make a sound, so the cards each had a squiggle that represented a consonant combined with a 'a, i, eh, o, u': ie. 'ka, ki, ke, ko, ku'. Or, 'sa, si, se, so, su', etc.

Three- and four-year-olds master this. I gazed at the squiggle.

"Sa?" I hazarded.

Two heads shook in mock sadness.

"Chigaimasu, Angela-san"

"Mu?"

"Chigaimasu!"

"Ti?"

They clapped their hands, delightedly.

Gradually, over the evening, I improved, reaching the standard of a dim three-year-old by about ten o'clock.

"Futari tomo ii sensei ne," I told them. And they had been, very good and patient teachers. We went into the living room and watched Yasuko, Jin-Ichiri, and their sons playing mahjong; an intensely complicated game.

<hr>

Apart from all the decorations in the shops, nobody seemed interested in celebrating Christmas. Daiwa Depato is running a tape with a Japanese version of 'I saw Mummy kissing Santa Claus'. The Japanese for Mummy is 'Ha-Ha', rendering the jingle comical to Western ears. I wonder, will my three children have a Christmas tree, like we used to have?

Who will be decorating it with our special rude china cherubs, one of which insists, no matter how it is hung, on twisting so that its bum faces the onlooker? Will my son be hanging his special three-legged giraffes under the Christmas fairy? I am absolutely NOT going to sink into homesickness, but I do wonder how Keiko Takahashi intends to celebrate the 25th of December. Probably we will have some sort of mini celebration, because, after all, as courier, she has spent quite a few Christmasses in Europe. I imagine we will be raising our glasses and toasting family and friends at some stage. Come to think of it, I shall be closer to the actual biblical scene, in essence, sitting on straw mats, in a wooden house, surrounded by snowdrifts. I doubt Joseph rustled up noodles for Mary, but then, nor would either of them have been surrounded by flocks of red-breasted robins fluttering haphazardly around the ox and the ass. This morning, a Christmas card arrived from my daughter. Yasuko was watching me.

"You know, Angela-san," she remarked, casually, "I have been thinking that, this year, we will have a special little Christmas here, before you return to the Takahashis."

The twins, once they understood, were ecstatic at the idea, jumping up and down like puppies.

"We will have a special party meal, and some presents. And," she added, getting quite carried away, "we will light candles on the Christmas table!" She flapped her hands at the excited twins: "Enough. Enough now. Off you go, or you'll be late for school."

Like me, Yasuko Kaneko loves to shop. We went together into the heated, scented world of Daiwa Depato; up the thronged escalators, visiting floor after floor, trying on gloves, fingering materials, calling each other to come and admire a pair of earrings, or marvel at the prices of imported china and glassware. She decided to buy Ai and Yiu socks for Christmas and went to find them, while I lost myself happily in the hair decorations department, where counter after counter showed every sort of conceivable bow, comb, and slide: the sole adornment most Japanese women allow themselves in an otherwise incredibly boring wardrobe that features mostly beige, brown tweed, or navy serge; here were glass-fronted counters of embroidered, sequinned, beaded, or jewelled decorations – tiny feathered birds in crimson and turquoise, elaborate diamond drops quivering on little springs, artificial flowers clustered on velvet bands, hand-painted ribbons – the choice was endless. I finally decided on a batik bow slide for one twin, and a comb decorated with tiny bunches of grapes for the other. But that was before I came across a drawer full of delectable lacquer pins and combs, from which I was dragged away by Yasuko.

I broke away to buy a slide decorated with tremulous blue glass flowers for my daughter. An extra late Christmas present!

Yasuko despairs of me: "To go shopping, it is NOT necessary to buy!"

"Well, just you wait until you come to London," I told her.

She was very nearly late back to cook lunch for her family, but, oh, we had had fun. I think a good motto for a foreigner in Japan would be to always expect the unexpected. I had promised to return books to Shakyo Centre library that afternoon, and was surprised when Yasuko insisted on driving me.

"But of course, we go together. This is the plan," she insisted.

Plan? What plan? Whatever route she was taking to the Centre, it was not one I knew. She was driving her husband's large car, seeming to peer through the steering wheel, and finally zooming into a parking space with sublime disregard for kerb, or white lines.

"Quick! We are late!"

I followed her across a side street, and up concrete steps.

"Yasuko-san. Excuse me, please, but, wait … where are we going?"

For an instant, she turned to look at me, smiling; a neat, slim figure in sloppy-joe jersey and jeans, and then opened a door.

"Kaneko-san! Kaneko-san!"

She was immediately surrounded by about forty or fifty small children, and a few young women, in a room festooned with Christmas decorations. I was introduced:

"Kochira wa Igirisu-jin, Mrs Angela!"

This was the children's Christmas party. Everywhere, children were busy, shifting refectory tables, hanging up decorations, cutting fruit, and hanging up their artwork. All were participating, not leaving the work to the adults. I was asked to help make the hottu keki.

"Yes, of course. But, I'm afraid I don't quite know how to, er, do a hottu keki?"

"Naoko-chan will show you," a teacher told me.

Looking round, I recognised the little five-year-old Naoko as the child who had shown Yasuko her picture of the Asinagawa river. Solemnly, we bowed to each other.

"Konnichi wa Cook-san."

"Konnichi wa Naoko-chan."

From then on, I was her personal responsibility. She led the way to a single electric ring, its wires, as ever, trailing across the floor from its socket, with a heap of flour and water paste waiting to be cooked, beside a frying pan.

"Now" she said, releasing my hand. "Now, see, I cook hottu keki."

She poured a drop of oil into the pan and placed it on the ring. I looked round, nervously, for some adult supervision, but everyone was still occupied; children slicing oranges and lemons to make fruit drinks, others mixing the flour and water into the raw keki, others still tugging at tables. Naoko scooped up a few blobs of the mix and tipped it into the now sizzling pan, hovering over it with intense concentration. They bubbled and spread, rather like a fried egg. Naoko's wooden spatula, grasped in her small pudgy hand, lingered over the hot fat. I couldn't bear it. Such a little one shouldn't be allowed …

"I will cook these, Naoko-chan," I said, decidedly.

Politely, without argument, she relinquished her spatula to this foreigner. I attempted to turn the mixture. It refused to budge, the fat hissing and spitting. Naoko sighed, shaking her head. Patently, I was a terrible responsibility. Not only was I a simpleton who couldn't speak Japanese, but I couldn't even cook hottu keki. After a few minutes, I tried again.

"Iie, mo chotto, Mrs Angela. Mo chotto!" she insisted.

And, of course, she was right. I had under-cooked them. I gave up, and left the cooking to her. She produced a pile of perfectly browned flour and water dough pancakes which were taken away to be doused with a very small amount of diluted strawberry jam. When the teachers called everyone to sit at the tables for this Christmas feast, Naoko kept me under her wing, sitting beside me, and chatting away – quite inexplicably – as everyone tucked into their hottu keki and fruit juice, and jugs of tea, all of which had been made by the children, maximum age nine. She was a perfect hostess, introducing me to her three-year-old sister, and then producing a scrapbook of her paintings, taking me through each one, jabbing her finger at all focal points of interest:

"River, this. My mountain. My house. Look, rice field here. My sister. This is our cherry blossom, see, Mrs Angela? Beautiful, isn't it? My father and mother …"

She watched me keenly as I ate my hottu keki with chopsticks, and I felt that at any minute she might produce a bib and mop me.

After tea, the teachers showed examples of all the childrens' paintings, bringing each up to the stage to explain them, and all children and adults applauded each one in turn. I was amazed at their talent. All their paintings were vivid, fresh, and encapsulated aspects of their chosen subject. Later, the children cleared away all the paper plates and cups, and cleaned the room. It had been a lovely party, and I was sorry to leave little Naoko. I thanked her for showing me how to cook, and helping me to enjoy the party.

"Do itashimashite," (not at all), she said, kindly, as she left with her mother and sister.

It was growing dark when we returned to the house. I had been silent in the car, comparing the joy and happiness displayed at that party with others I had either hosted, or been to, back at home, where everything had been done for the guests. But those indulged European children had reacted so differently. Nothing much was expected of them. They in turn expected to be takers, never partakers, and, of course, responded accordingly. They are called upon to contribute nothing, barring a modicum of insincere: 'Thank you very much' as they collect their expensive party bags at the door; what low expectations we place upon our young children. I shall not forget this Japanese children's Christmas party.

―――

We met Jin-Ichiri's father, still pottering about in his garden. He straightened up and smiled at me.

"Angela-san is very interested in gardening. She admires your bonsai," Yasuko told him.

Slowly, painfully, the old man walked from plant to plant, telling Yasuko how he had grown each one, pausing while she translated. Apparently, he would have liked to talk to me, but suffers from a degenerative disease that affects his speech.

―――

The Kanekos' house is now a house of secrets. There are rustlings, and giggles, and scampering up and down the stairs. There are places I may not go, and I must cough and wait for permission before entering their kitchen. I also have placed my room out of bounds. It is the 22nd December.

I have only two more days here.

I am in the process of creating something I once saw being made at a Flower Club meeting in Ireland; the invited expert had explained that all one needed to create an unusual, sophisticated Christmas wreath that would epitomise the very spirit of the Season was a wire coat hanger, plenty of polythene bags, silver and gold spray, and of course, lots of time. And scissors. Right. Watched with polite surprise by Ai and Yiu, I collected aproximately twenty assorted polythene bags from their mother's kitchen, and retired to my room, armed with scissors. Kodatsu switched on, the coat hanger resting on its table top, I started slicing the bags into narrow, four-inch strips, like old-fashioned curling papers. Half an hour later, the tatami was littered with uneven, dog-eared bits of bag. My feet and knees were roasting, my back stiff, and my bottom numb. Not for the first time I marvelled at the affection the Japanese hold for this heating method. Either their physiology is differently shaped, or my joints are well past their sell-by date. A tap on my door:

"Don't come in!"

"Shokuji o suru, Angela-san," calls a twin. Suppertime. Already?

"Coming…." I looked at the Christmas circle. Half an hour's busy tying had only filled a few inches, but had used up practically all the bags.

Jin-Ichiri poured me a large glass of beer.

"Ashita wa Kurismasu, ne?"

We had all agreed that tomorrow was going to be our special Christmas.

December 23rd. Yasuko had obtained a generous supply of polythene bags from her in-laws, and I finished the Kurismasu circle shortly after lunch. There remained just enough time to buy gold and silver spray, an Andrew Lloyd Webber CD for Yasuko, Elvis for Masaya, and Daniel Barenboim for Ryo. Plus a bottle of Baileys for Jin-Ichiri. All easily accomplished in Kanazawa, except, of course, the spray, which I finally located behind a counter displaying crackers. I sprayed the circle in the back garden, after dark, in a brisk gale. Hopefully, dawn tomorrow will not reveal rows of bonsai, all glistening silver and gold.

The following morning, I suspend all the lightest presents from the wreath with strands of ribbon. I go up to the kitchen, keen to hang up my Christmas wreath, but the children bar my path. All of them.

"Not now, no, Angela-san!"

Back in my room, I pack my clothes back into my suitcase. Tomorrow I return to the Takahashi house. On Christmas Eve. This time, it was Ryo who came to call me.

"Angela-san! Kurisimasa oshokuji ga suru! Ima!"

In the kitchen, the dining area was in darkness, dimly lit by candles. Ballet music played. I produced my Christmas wreath from behind my back and Jin-Ichiri nailed it over the arch into the kitchen, while everyone else was supposed to keep their eyes shut. He stood back, admiring his handiwork. Actually, once suspended, it did look very pretty.

"Okay! You may all look now!"

Parting the dense strands of gold and silver took a gratifying length of time, as I had hidden all the light presents deep within the polythene furbelows, and tied them in with strands of silver ribbon. However, at last, each twin had found their hair ornaments, and tried them on, preening in front of a mirror. The boys also discovered their presents. Yasuko promised to play her CD immediately after supper, and Jin-Ichiri said that if he didn't eat soon – very soon, he would start on the Baileys before the Christmas feast. But, shimmering in the candlelight of a gilt rondell, was the highlight of the Christmas decoration: angels, on horses, revolved, each carrying its own candle; music jingled an accompaniment. The room had been decorated with papier-mâché Christmas trees, embroidered angels and Santas, stuck all over the walls. A fabulous evening! I was given a Japanese diary for the following year, (months written up in Hiragana only), a pictorial calendar, and small tokens that I would never had found for myself. Jin-Ichiri and Yasuko presented me with a hand-made cloth jewel case for earrings that snapped open when pressed. The dinner was superb. We all toasted each other, and anything else we could think of:

"Kampai! Kampai!"

And then it was the turn of the twins to produce the Christmas cake they had made; a three-layered Victoria sponge, interlaced with strawberries, buttercream, and jam. It was iced with a snowy scene: here was Santa Claus, heading out on his reindeer-drawn sleigh, up over a mountain, towards a Christmas tree.

"You never made this?"

Yasuko and the twins nodded, beaming.

"But, how? I mean, you don't have … I mean, like, without an oven?"

"We don't need an oven," Yasuko said.

Their sponge cake was so light, it would have taken off if blown on. It tasted absolutely delicious. I can only assume that they had steamed it over one of the gas rings. Fabulous!

Such a special, lovely evening. Such a happy time.

Tomorrow, I will go back to a different world. The geisha house in Higashiyama, in the old Pleasure Quarter of Kanazawa. And Keiko Takahashi.

CHAPTER SIX

In the Bleak Midwinter

KEIKO TAKAHASHI greeted me with her usual inscrutable small smile. She kindly invited Yasuko, Ai, and Yu in for a cup of peppermint tea. They stepped reverentially into the vast dark house and sat at the dining table, the twins awed and silent. The two women discovered they had been to the same school. After tea, Keiko showed them round her home. Yasuko was very impressed with everything; the long stone-floored corridor on one side of the inner garden, the two ancient wooden stairways resembling polished ladders, and the dark passages bisecting all the six, eight, and ten tatami rooms.

"Ee, taihen omoshiroi, ne?" she kept exclaiming to her daughters, gasping at such a wealth of vacant space. They left shortly after midday, with kisses and handshakes for me, and profound bows to Keiko, Yasuko barely achieving a three-point turn in the narrow alley, rising in her seat like a jockey. Then, the big car drove off through the slush, with one last cheerful toot. Keiko turned off the main lights and cleared away our tea bowls.

"Well, she seemed a nice woman," she observed, "and her children were good."

"They are a lovely family," I said.

She washed up, and I dried.

"Oh, not in that cupboard, Angela," she snapped. "You have a very bad memory. Will I have to show you everything again?"

"Will you also remember to talk Japanese to me?" I countered. "I did explain to you that I need the practice. After all, this is why foreign students try to stay with host families."

She sighed. "But ... you do not understand it, Angela."

I imagined the Kaneko family, now eating lunch, laughing, teasing each other. I remembered their patience, as they encouraged me, dictionary always to hand, looking up words, with even Jin-Ichiri essaying a few words in English as I floundered through far too complicated sentences, trying to exchange ideas. I took a deep breath.

"Look, Keiko. Today is Christmas Eve. Suppose I talk English to you until after Christmas, and then you make an effort to speak some Japanese to me – slowly – so that I too, can improve?"

I bent down to pick up my suitcase.

"I'll just take this upstairs, and then, because it is Christmas Eve, why don't I take you out somewhere, and buy you a glass of sake?"

Keiko stared at me.

"O'sake? Now? You want to drink it now? At one o'clock?"

"A Christmas drink," I suggested.

"I do not celebrate Christmas," Keiko said.

I lugged my suitcase, handbag, canvas grip and satchel out of the living room, through an outer room, changed slippers, and started up the first staircase; through the gloom, along the upper corridor towards the second set of stairs. Where the Hell was that wretched bit of string that turned on the light? Carefully, I put down my school satchel, and started fumbling along the lathes. My toe found the bottom step of the next staircase, and I lost a slipper. Stepping backwards, two schoolbooks tumbled through the treads. Instantly, a light came on, and Keiko emerged through a bamboo wall. How she had got there, I will never know.

"Whatever are you doing, Angela?"

"Sorry ... I couldn't find the light."

"That too, you have forgotten? Please, turn it off when you arrive at your room."

The wall slid shut.

I arrived. I found the light string in my room. The room was freezing, but at least the kerosene stove still had my box of matches on top of it.

"Please, dear God!" I prayed, "let me not have forgotten how to light it. Let there be light, eh?"

And, third match lucky: wick flickered, flame travelled in a hesitant circle and flared, emitting a strong smell of paraffin, and at last, an all-round blue flame! Heat! My left palm stings, but, the tatami remains unscathed.

Tonight, I shall walk to midnight Mass. I think I remember where the church is.

―――

In the distance, thunder is rumbling.

Christmas Eve. Now – well give or take some nine hours – red-eyed florists would be hard at work. In homes, spare rooms would be ready for relatives, best sheets turned down. fathers despatched to buy more lights for the Christmas tree, and my son, in company with most of the male Irish population, would be preparing to do all his Christmas present shopping in the space of a couple of hours, before meeting up with friends in a local pub. Wives are making stuffing. Defrosting turkeys. Wrapping awkward objects, and hiding them under their beds.

Keiko tapped on my door.

"Hai?"

"May I come in? I have bought us some beer."

Kneeling on either side of the stove, we toasted each other.

"Kampai!"

"Kampai!"

She told me about her European trip.

"It was dreadful. All they wanted to go to were the brothels of Europe. Not the Tower of London. Not the Sistine Chapel. And, they didn't like foreign food. Every evening, they wanted me to take them to dirty night places. I said, I am a woman, I do not go there. I find you a porter, he will take you. These Japanese men who have never left Japan, probably never left their own small towns – foreign culture is wasted on them. So, I warn them about AIDS, and I go to my bed. I do not like being a courier to such people."

"Can't you change your job?" I suggested, shifting onto my other haunch. She shrugged.

"Like, to what?"

"Well, maybe what you once told me you wanted to do. Like, selling foreign teas from here, and trinkets from other countries; Venetian glass, beer steins, English china?"

Keiko snorted.

"Angela! Think! You have met my mother. This is still her house. My brothers' house. Our family home, where our family tablets are. A change would not be allowed."

I persisted.

"But, such a tea shop would be very respectable. And it would make money. Perhaps you could persuade your brothers …"

"My dear brothers come to see my mother, maybe once a year, for a few hours. My sisters-in-law tell me how lucky I am to live in this wonderful house."

She got up briskly, collecting our glasses and the beer cans.

"But, I just might ask them. Anyway, Angela, now I am going out. I will leave you a salad, and cuttlefish, and tangerines, in the kitchen."

"I too shall be going out," I told her. "I am going to go to Midnight Mass in Kanazawa. Please don't lock me out."

I heard her start down the stairs, calling out: "Merry Christmas! Be careful. It is now snowing, very much."

And, it certainly was. Flurries of snowflakes skittered against the windows. Wet snow oozed through the gaps. Was this to be another year when it actually snowed inside my room, I wondered?

Midnight Mass was lovely; the great church lit by candles, the three priests con-celebrating in their ornate vestments, the familiar scent of incense pervading over the congregation; it didn't matter that I could only join in the words 'Noël, Noël', it was calming. It felt right.

On the steps, afterwards, I met an American friend of Saito's who told me there would be a party for gaijins on Christmas night, given by an Indian couple who ran a restaurant in Kanazawa.

"You pay for your dinner, and bring a small present to exchange. Could be great."

She would not be there, as she was teaching that night. Perhaps I had been stupid to refuse to teach on Christmas Day. But, it was too late now.

Keiko's doctor friend turned up again at breakfast. Once more, he produced his origami set while she concocted a gruel from fish stock and onions. This time he snipped even more miniscule objects out of green, pink and yellow paper, placing them on the back of his hand, gesturing me to blow. Midges! When I blew at them, they rose in a cloud, hovering on my breath. He collected them in a small phial and presented it to me.

"Angela-san. For Christmas!"

Keiko smiled at him, indulgently.

Back upstairs in my room, ignoring the time, I poured myself a stiff Japanese whisky, in an effort to keep myself awake, and decided it was time to start opening the Christmas presents sent from home. By the time the kettle on the stove had started hopping, the tatami was covered with giftwrap, the whisky level had gone down, I had finished the packet of Bath Oliver biscuits, and was feeling much happier. I decided to go the gaijin party.

Was there ever a night in Kanazawa when it was not blowing a gale, pouring with rain, or blasting sleet and snow? The glowing meter of an empty taxi was irresistible, and, what was more, perhaps infected with seasonal good cheer, the driver actually stopped for a gaijin!

Inside the Indian restaurant, it was warm, and smelt of curry. A large lady wearing a red and gold sari ran up to me and hugged me to her bosom.

"Welcome! Merry Christmas! The ticket is 500 yen."

The room was crowded with foreigners, none of whom I recognised. We stood around, politely, making conversation of the 'How long have you been here?' variety. I found myself talking to a young Finnish wife, married to a Japanese. She was of the school of thought that believed restraining her children might damage their egos. Her daughter was four, her son two-and-a-half. Both their egos were in tip-top condition. I observed a group of Indian children watching, wide-eyed, as the toddler tried to reach a glass of orange juice by swarming up the tablecloth. His sister, meanwhile, was sitting on the floor, kicking ankles, and pulling faces at the other children. One Indian boy stuck out his tongue at her, waggling fingers in his ears, until noticed by his father. Lightly cuffed on the cheek, he subsided silently. Meanwhile, the Finnish baby had been hauled from the tablecloth by an Indian granny, and returned to his mother, where he threw a major tantrum, rocked in her arms.

After a delicious lamb curry, and a novelty produced just for us – mince pies! – games were announced. People were pushed and persuaded into teams for a jolly game that resembled Oranges and Lemons, followed by Blind Man's Buff. Perhaps this love of childish games is universal throughout the Far East, eliminating the necessity of conversation between strangers.

I had experienced this twice before in Japan at parties given by, and for, adults, where middle-aged businessmen are at ease playing these games. American and Aussie students have no problem in joining in, enthusiastically, sometimes leading the general merriment among adults, playing musical chairs, or a sort of tip and tag.

I find it difficult. Perhaps the British are too inhibited.

But now, most people here seemed happy. The noise volume had increased, and a young, busty Philippino woman in a scarlet harem trouser suit and high-heeled diamanté sandals began to dance with the children, uttering loud whoops. A conga line of guests started up. Beside me, a young Biafran student I had met before the meal raised his eyes, murmuring, "I think I now go back to my room."

He had previously told me that he found the Japanese very racist.

I walked back to the Old Quarter, awaiting a phone call from my children, and found Keiko sitting by her coffee table, drinking sake. She waved the bottle at me, expansively.

"You want some?"

Whisky at lunchtime, beer with the curry; I thought it best not to round off Christmas feeling sick.

"I won't, thanks. But, tell you what; I'd love a cup of your peppermint tea."

Keiko shook her head.

"No. I do not want peppermint tea."

We sat in silence, awaiting my phone call.

From the other side of the world, my three children, and my god-daughter, talked to me: they opened my presents. I could actually hear the sound of the paper unwrapping! They described the Christmas tree, and yes, the cherubs were on, and the three-legged giraffe. They held my dog to the receiver, and although she refused to bark, I could hear her snuffling. And they ended the call by opening a bottle of champagne and toasting us all – a big 'pop'! We spoke for about forty-five minutes, during which Keiko Takahashi sat right beside me, listening avidly.

"What a lot of people wanted to speak to you," she remarked.

"Yes. It was lovely. Absolutely lovely."

"It must have cost them a fortune."

Sake does not appear to have a softening effect on her. However, when an old friend phoned half an hour later, she called up the stairs to say I could take it on the upstairs phone. I had not known there was one. It took a bit of time to locate, costing him a fair bit of money.

———⁓⁓⁓———

Gusts of wind are now whining through the gaps in my windows, bringing with them the occasional whisper of a flute, and a sudden bombardment on the skin drums. Sometime later in the night I woke up suddenly, instantly conscious that something had moved within the room. Everything was pitch black. The drums were silent, but the wind had increased in fury, striking the glass with an iron fist, making it rattle like an old-fashioned glasshouse on the verge of collapse. And yet, something HAD moved. I know it. This house … it doesn't want me here. It is as alien to me as I am to it. I am right! There is something here. I can hear it rustle across the tatami, approaching my bed, through the open sliding doors. I am lying rigid under the quilt, waiting. Very slowly, so as not to make a sound, I reached for my torch, and then switched on the beam, leaping, frog-like, towards the sound.

"HAA!" I shouted.

Yet again, another fierce gust of wind hit the house, causing the two sheets of the *Asahi Shimbun* to rise on a current of air, and drift, rustling, through the open doors, into my bedroom. I watched the newspaper subside on the tatami, seeing a jagged blade of window pane stuck through it.

What on earth is wrong with me? I was sick with fear, like never before.

Actually, that is not true. The memory came flooding back.

Once, when I was a child, living in London during the war, a V2 rocket had fallen in the next street, and the force of the explosion blew the white curtains in the nursery off their pole, causing them to fall on top of my face. I remembered screaming, and then my parents rushing into the room, pulling them off me. I had forgotten that incident.

Until now. Here.

I secured the newspaper on my desk and went back to bed.

There was no sign of Keiko when I went downstairs. And no sign of breakfast. I went downstairs several times, but she had not surfaced. Finally, I left for my lesson with Taniguchi. She was disappointed with my progress.

"I think you must be tired, Angela-san. You have already covered much of this work. I am sorry that you do not concentrate."

I could not. If I tipped my head back, I felt dizzy. However, the Centre was about to close for ten whole days over the New Year holiday.

"Perhaps you should rest from study during the holiday? Travel, and enjoy Japan?" she suggested.

I knew that the New Year holiday period was the one time in the year when all Japanese people went on holiday. And, of course, all prices went up.

I smiled at her worried face.

"Later, perhaps, Taniguchi-san. I would truly love to visit Kyoto. But, for now, I will try to learn Hiragana properly, and perhaps Katakana. Next term, you will be surprised how much I will have learnt, eh?"

I retired to the foreign students' library, having decided the rain was too strong to venture out to Daiwa to buy a sandwich. Miyazaki startled me, placing a light hand on my shoulder.

"Ah, Angela-san! Takahashi-san telephoned me, to say that you had left her house without taking breakfast?"

Her face swam before me.

"That's right," I said.

"She say, why you not make your own?"

I told her that it did not feel right there, to do that. Twice before, I added, I had left the house at 10.30 without breakfast, or seeing my hostess.

Miyazaki clicked her tongue. She left, saying nothing, and I carried on studying, attempting to grasp the finer points of Rao-san being shown round a factory by his ever-kindly boss, Howaiti-san, with virtually no success. This is ridiculous. Why can't I concentrate? Miyazaki reappeared at my elbow, wearing a dripping mac.

"Come with me, Angela-san. Together, we have a picnic."

In the tiny staff closet, barely large enough to accommodate one small table and two chairs, she had laid out our picnic: a loaf of bread, chilli beans, a tangerine, and a carton of yoghurt.

"Please, you sit down, and enjoy," she instructed.

Using a bent bamboo twig, she ladled out the beans onto paper plates. We shared the loaf, and the tangerine. The yoghurt was for me. Kamada, Senior Tutor, edged her way through the door and looked at us with raised eyebrows. Miyazaki launched into a flood of explanation.

"Aaa, so, so, so."

Kamada accepted a segment of tangerine, and gave us both a cup of scalding black Japanese tea from her thermos. I left them, feeling astonishingly much better.

Back at the house nothing was said, but the following morning Keiko was up early, giving me an unprecedented breakfast: coffee, juice, ham and an egg, and two slices of real toast. Supper too was a treat, with the ubiquitous cuttlefish taking a back place for once. We ate a delicious risotto, followed by an assortment of fruit as well as the tangerines.

"I cannot eat any more fruit," I protested. "That was a lovely meal."

Keiko was dissecting each section of a tangerine, almond-shaped nails picking out each strand of pith, her small black eyes inscrutable as ever.

"Then, you must take a tangerine upstairs with you, Angela. I cannot have you feeling hungry, can I?"

I do not want to stay here for another eight weeks.

I arranged with Saito to meet for lunch at a café in Kanazawa, to see if perhaps she could arrange yet another place for me. She had been so good, inviting me to her home, before Christmas, always interested in my progress.

She arrived on her bicycle, late, her hair standing on end.

"So sorry ... telephone calls ... my son needed collecting ... then people came to my office with problems ... sorry, Angela-san."

She plonked herself down at the table, a pencil still sticking up behind her ear. Such an endearing human dynamo; one who was exceedingly efficient at dealing with organisational problems as well as assisting Miyazaki who was now in charge of handling problems that might arise in connection with those few foreigners still in Kanazawa. And here was I, yet again about to inflict another problem on her, long after the course, and basically her remit for the year, was over.

Over a hambagu (minus bun) and some pasta, well drowned in soy sauce, I explained that I felt unrelaxed living in my present surroundings, and that, famous although the house might be, it was also much colder than I had anticipated. Also, since my hostess spoke such very good English, I was getting inadequate experience at speaking Japanese. Perhaps, soon, if Keiko Takahashi was to leave on another trip, it might be possible for me to leave? No way did I want to be the cause of any friction between my hostess and the Centre, and I was anxious to be tactful, but please, Saito-san, later in January, I really, really, would like to move elsewhere.

She heard me out, keen eyes vastly magnified behind pebble glasses.

"I am so happy to hear that you enjoy living in such a historic house," she remarked, loudly.

I blinked. Perhaps her English wasn't as good as I had thought?

"Yes indeed. And, I am happy to have seen you before our holiday."

She pulled back her chair and turned to smile at Keiko Takahashi's good friend, a teacher from the Centre, and Miyazaki, newly seated at a table behind us. We left shortly afterwards, having chatted about her experiences in America. I watched as Saito tightened the hood on her anorak and pedalled furiously downhill in the teeth of a brisk breeze out of Siberia, hoping that our meeting would not have embarrassed her with her colleagues. Probably not. Probably I was just becoming paranoid. Self-important. The time had come to think of other things: like the necessity of withdrawing some money to pay my rent and to live, during the holiday.

Today was 27th December. Only one more banking day before the annual holiday. However, thanks to the ever-efficient Saito, who had not only lodged my money in one of her unused accounts, given me the code number for the cash machine, but had also written out a request for me to hand to a staff member if I couldn't operate it, this should be easy.

Every customer entering the bank is greeted by a taped voice uttering a welcome. On another wall, for our convenience, a large flat TV screen was showing a sports programme to ease the tedium of anyone facing a few moments of delay. To my amazement, the screen was showing a soccer match between Ireland and Scotland, and, as it panned across the watching crowds I could have sworn I saw one of my daughters and her boyfriend! I sat on the pink plush bench with clean ashtrays conveniently placed at intervals and watched, forgetting my surroundings, occasionally letting out a squeal: "GO FOR IT, IRELAND!" Other customers eschewed my bench.

After half an hour the scene changed to show sumo wrestling, and I came back to reality and lurked by the cash dispenser watching other customers collect their money. Only a quarter of an hour left before the bank closed. I decided to show the request to a pretty young teller: "Sumimasen?"

She left the counter and came to help me. "Cardo de gozaimasu?"

I handed her the card and the machine gollupped it up. On screen, a cartoon character appeared, wearing a broad grin.

"Ansho bango o kudasai?"

Furtively, I gave her Saito's number and she punched it in. The machine made curious clunking noises, and lights flashed. More cartoon characters now appeared, but this time they did not look happy; more in sorrow than in anger, they wagged their fingers reproachfully, high pitched robot voices squeaking disapproval. Then came horrid digestive noises and the machine spat out the card.

"Ee to," breathed the young assistant, a slight pucker furrowing her cloudless brow.

"Mo ichido?"

And she did. Try again. And again. In desperation we tried all the other machines with exactly the same result. A Superior Being was approached, and came out wearing a patronising smile. The girl had obtained a little silver tray; from it she handed him the card, and, shaking his head at our inefficiency he inserted it. With the same result. I was told to telephone Saito. Her voice was disbelieving: "If you cannot operate the machine, Angela-san, ask for help … I told you this."

I gritted my teeth. "I have. No one can work it with the number you gave me."

"So. You forget the number?"

"NO!"

"And, do you need money?"

God, give me strength!

The Superior Being touched me on the shoulder. All the staff, including the security guard, had lit up and were staring at me, restlessly.

"You must go now. We are closed. So sorry."

"Saito-san. I am in the bank. I have been here for a long time. Of course I need money."

She told me to come back and see her. She would wait for me. In her lovely warm office I stood, my umbrella, blown inside out lying beside my feet.

"I think perhaps I made a mistake," she said, slowly. "I think perhaps I gave you my son's birth date number, and it should have been the number for my mother's date … or even … I am sorry."

She lent me money to pay my rent and carry me through the weekend, cut me a generous slice of homemade cake, and promised to withdraw my money on Monday, the final day before all banks closed. Since all my pupils had now gone on holiday, and I had no more paid lessons for the next fortnight, I was deeply, if damply, relieved.

I just wish my head did not ache, or my bones. Sometimes, everything spins sickeningly before my eyes, and I cannot unstiffen my neck because my head is too heavy for it. Nothing that a good, sound night's sleep wouldn't cure. Maybe it is the rice-filled pillow giving me earache during the night? More probably I am feeling the effects of sleeping on the floor in a raging draught.

I make myself tea and take two aspirin, settling down to read some of the English books from the college library. I am reading a fascinating book on myths of Japan, compiled by Lafcadio Hearne. So many of these legends are about the spirits of dead children. This one really intrigues me; apparently, somewhere on Honshu island lies a beach, only accessible from the sea. This beach is covered with fine pebbles and sand, and when the tide recedes, the bay is filled with tiny heaps of pebbles, shells and sand, stacked like sandcastles.

If, inadvertently, a human knocks one down he must immediately rebuild it, for these are sandcastles made by dead children, and a broken castle makes a ghost child weep. Each day, as the tide sweeps away from the beach, little bare footprints of small children can be seen, running across the sand. This story haunts me.

So much of Japanese culture relates to the spirit world, and nature; from the Deities of Noh Theatre, to their reverence of Fuji-san, the sacred mountain; their celebration of cherry blossom; even the apology made by farmers to the lowliest insect, before applying pesticide to the crops.

On New Year's Eve, all the temples throughout Japan will sound their gongs 108 times, beginning shortly before midnight, and people try to visit as many temples as possible to pray for their dead relatives. The number of boings was decreed, of course, by an ancient Emperor, who had worked out that there are precisely 108 Evils and Ills that afflict the human race, and each stroke of the gong is supposed to dispel one. Keiko intends to visit temples on behalf of her mother, who is now too old to visit them herself. She suggested that we might go together. I do hope she does, because I feel it might be considered intrusive for a foreigner to go alone.

Old Takahashi-san has come to stay for the New Year. I found her kneeling at the table, a fine brush poised over a pile of cards, expertly swooping intricate curves and coils of calligraphy. She looked up and gave me one of her twinkling smiles:

"O'Shogatsu," (for NewYear) she explained. Beside her stood another old lady, showing her garlands: traditional New Year garlands, made from loops of rope with maize, the outer shucks pulled back like petals, with pine for prosperity/good luck/long life, and ribbons; all intricately hand-made, and all different. Each was subjected to close scrutiny by the two Takahashis, and finally, after much discussion and laughter, they chose and paid for a half dozen. This same old lady had been coming to the house, selling her garlands, since Keiko was a child.

Perhaps Keiko had phoned her brothers. The following day a very nice nephew arrived, and the day after that her brother came to visit.

I watched the transformation of Takahashi-san. Her face glowed with pleasure; wearing a beautiful silk kimono, her hair elaborately coiffed, she knelt straight-backed on the tatami, her son on one side, her other brother's son on the other, coaxing stories from the two men, her eyes as brilliant as the large emerald ring she wore on the third finger of her right hand – a gift from Keiko's father, many years ago. But, after supper, she would have to return again to the nursing home in order to retain her right of a bed there.

During supper, I again witnessed the curious habit of Japanese people to laugh at disaster. They were discussing an accident that had happened to an old family friend. He was a keen handyman, always making improvements to his home, further down the street. One day, possibly due to an electrical fault, his entire house had burned down. The episode amused the Takahashis hugely; old Takahashi-san cackled with laughter, Keiko was smiling broadly, and the two men roared.

I remembered being told that to become involved in another's misfortune, or even to observe it, is considered unlucky. Even someone else's grief is in some way tainting, and caring about it simply invites personal ill. Road accidents on TV? Each family reacted the same way:

"Oh yes. It was in Kanazawa. Many killed. Bad drivers." And then they laugh. If someone breaks a leg skiing, they are helpless with mirth.

Keiko's role that evening was to cook, and keep all plates filled. We ate copiously, of delicious food. Not a cuttlefish in sight! After her mother left, Keiko and her brother sat talking late into the night. It is easy to see why she is so jealous of her brothers; both of them have done well for themselves, own their own businesses, have homes and children, rarely bother with their mother, and yet are plainly adored by her. But, whoever said life was fair?

Friends of Keiko are giving their end-of-year party, and have kindly included me. The husband, Asami, drove us to his modern, grey, pebble-dashed house in a new estate on the far side of Kanazawa. The interior was similar to other houses I had been to;

universal G-plan utility furniture, totally lacking in character. We were led to the inevitable long low table in the centre of the room, knelt on zabutons, and were entertained by our host showing us all his collection of wine bottle labels, collected by himself and his wife on a recent holiday in Europe, steamed from bottles they had drunk there, and now painstakingly stuck in an album. I got the impression that he had chosen the wine according to how the label had caught his eye; some featured jolly lads and lasses frolicking in lederhosen, plus a motley number of matadors and bulls, a few sultry senoritas embracing red roses, or young French demoiselles pensively gathering grapes in their aprons. More and more guests arrived, all bring gifts of food or sake, and the wine labels circulated again to admiring coos. Now, wine corks are being pulled from many label-less bottles, and the wife and her sister presented her guests with red lacquer bowls and chopsticks, beseeching us to eat. First on the menu came sliced tongue and raw broccoli. Then we were helped to bamboo spears and some sort of pod. Next arrived more bowls containing a thick yellow custard with chestnuts and shrimps, delicious, but taxing my chopstick proficiency to the hilt. Now the hottu platu was lit, and our host poured a little oil on its surface, followed by hot gruel, into which he tossed packet after packet of pastie-shaped pasta. Meanwhile, the wine was circulating constantly; we are drinking rough red wine, sparkling white wine, an acid rosé, a glass of sake to break the monotony, followed by a fruity Sauternes, a dry white, and a rich ruby red. A wine taster would have run out of expletives. I am running through a few in my head, ranging through: 'Insolent', 'Quirky', 'Masochistic,' 'Lively', 'Pure Cowslip', to the 'Downright Lethal'. Under the rules governing Japanese hospitality, it is imperative that no guest's glass should ever be empty. My glass was refilled whenever it reached halfway level – previous colour immaterial. Honour dictated that no guest, perhaps more especially a foreign guest, should refuse. I took tiny sips, very, very slowly. Asami's charming daughter sat beside me; speaking in halting English she explained she was studying at a ballet school. I asked her whether she lived to dance?

Did she dream of becoming a prima ballerina?

"Yes", she said, hesitantly, "but there is a small cloud ..."

"Small cloud?"

It transpired that for the past three years she had shared a small room, containing bunk beds, with two other girls, one of whom was making her unhappy.

"Three years? Why do you not ask to change rooms?"

The twenty-two-year-old was shocked at the notion of doing something so unthinkable. To do so would be to question the wisdom of her superiors in making the room placements, and this would be grossly uncivil.

A huge boiled bream appeared on the table as Asami was questioning me about London. He was asking me what I knew about Mr Sherlock Holmes. Having been asked this already by my unknown rescuer in Osaka, I put a bit of imagination into my description of Baker Street, hoping he would never get to visit it and be disappointed.

"Aaa!" he breathed, translating my description to the other guests. "I have always been a big fan of your Mr Holmes."

I was rewarded by an extra large New Year rice cake which I ate carefully, mindful of those unfortunate old men who choked to death, guzzling them, each year.

Everyone watched me. "Oishii desuka?" they chorused expectantly.

"Interesting," I mumbled, feeling like a seal at feeding time.

Keiko, having learned the expression from me the previous day, leaned across the table, smiling sweetly:

"Is it an acquired taste, Angela-san?"

I agreed, and she translated, to much laughter.

My host took the opportunity to refill my half-empty glass to the brim with another wine; a new taste sensation, blending creosote and cheap Madeira. My feet have given up the ghost. They're now numb. Asami's daughter helps me to a generous helping of pork casserole, layered between leaves of Chinese lettuce. However, I do think the meal must be drawing to a close, because the women of the household are producing the inevitable bowls of sticky rice, served tonight with chopped herbs and a delicious, but incredibly hot pickle. Choking on it, I downed half a glass of wine, promptly replenished with a sparkling white. Covertly, I glanced at my watch: 10.30 pm. We had been kneeling, and eating, for over four hours! Well, Edwardians did it. Perhaps 'Pekineses at the Ritz Did It'... but not on their knees.

By now, all the men were flushed and expansive, and their womenfolk had reached a stage of uncontrollable giggles. Every male remark reduced them to further paroxysms, and our hostess was leaning against her best friend, screeching with laughter, tears running down both their faces. Another daughter produces a tureen of pumpkin soup, followed by her speciality, slices of cod roe, tinted in New Year colours, pink and white. Keiko ate calmly on, her eyes flirting with her neighbour as they took turns in toasting each other, the female laughter level went off the Richter scale. How such a skinny woman can consume so much food is beyond me, and her alcohol tolerance would put an Irish navvy to shame. When Keiko's gift of tangerines was presented, I heaved an inner sigh of relief; surely, after these, we would be given green tea, and I could stagger up, and maybe have a cigarette?

No. There was chocolate cake to follow, made by Mrs Asami, served with dollops of cream – and tiny raw fish that tasted of horse sweat. Our hostess was certainly a prodigious cook, but her merriment was now deafening. I could cheerfully have muzzled her. The topic that was convulsing all the women – except Keiko – related to which of the men present would lose their hair first.

I was starting to feel sick.

Getting up, my thigh bone cracked like a pistol shot, but luckily, no one noticed. Even Keiko Takahashi was laughing now, holding out her empty glass for more sake, as I took my bag and crept out of the room. Slippers off, door slid open, shoes on, front door shut behind me. I stood on the porch, got out the pack of Salem, extracted my lighter, lit up, and inhaled, luxuriously. Bliss!

Unfortunately, this was the moment when the Asamis' guard dog, luckily on a leash, emerged from his kennel and discovered this curious-smelling foreign female smoking on his porch. After one disbelieving look, he emitted a ferocious snarl, and the most menacing bark I have ever heard. With it, he alerted every other guard dog in the neighbourhood, and, like tic-tac, the cacophony spread from street to street, huskies straining at their chains, hurling themselves stiff-legged, into the air, all barking hysterically. Lights came on, and heads peered out. Hastily, I pinched out the fag, chucked it in the direction of the kennel and beat a retreat. My absence had not been noticed, thank Heaven. The last bottle of sake was drained some time about 2 am. We drank green tea and Asami-san actually drove Keiko and I back home.

A garda breath test would have probably qualified for *The Guinness Book of Records.*

Assorted vinous fumes seeping from every pore, combined with the stink of kerosene, were not conducive to my learning Hiragana. I kept tip-toeing down to the kitchen to replenish my kettle, and drank copious cups of Earl Grey. Looking at the little row of New Year cards given me by my students, I remembered promising myself, and them, that by the end of the holiday I would have mastered the whole of Hiragana, and some of Katakana. Would it disturb some celestial plan if I were suddenly enabled to Write in Alphabet, or Speak in Tongues? Just one tongue would do. I adjured the Almighty: Give me fluency in Japanese, and I will – well, for today at least – GIVE UP DRINK.

My kettle needed more water again.

Down in the kitchen, old Mrs Takahashi was quietly at work in her kitchen. Unseen, I watched her moving slowly from cupboard to work surface. Somehow, she imbued every action with a sort of ritual significance; the shadow on the wall as she raised her hands to grasp a bowl reminded me of the Dürer etching of hands raised in prayer.

This is the most dignified, graceful old lady I have ever seen. With large cooking chopsticks she began to separate out the tiny fish for her o'miso gruel, her lips moving as she counted them: "ipiki, nihiki, sanbiki …"

She stooped to select the right-sized saucepan, stroking its burnished surface.

I had never before seen her smile like this.

The whole work surface was crowded with cooking utensils, ceramic bowls, sauces, fish, and baby mushrooms, and, old Takahashi-san was having a lovely time. She even began to sing, very softly. It was quite five minutes before she spotted me beyond the doorway. I apologised for startling her, and offered to help:

"O'tetsudai shimashoka?"

She refused, of course, as I had known she would, and gestured for me to sit at table. Mrs Takahashi, senior, was once more Mistress of her house, entertaining a guest. She laid the table reverentially, bringing out more bowls, and then rejecting them as not being perfect for the occasion, like a child giving a dolls' tea party. Come what may, on this, the last day of the fading year, I resolved to eat every mouthful of whatever it was she was preparing – raw fish, raw egg, raw onion, raw jellyfish – just this once even if she served me natsu (a revolting fermented bean curd) I would eat it.

Keiko broke the spell. She arrived in the kitchen, sliding open a wall panel and emerging from some undiscovered passageway at the far end. She stood, hands on hips, taking in the scene; kitchen in total disarray, me seated at the dining table laid with the best china, and mother pottering to and fro in the kitchen. Whatever it was that Keiko Takahashi said to her mother, it did not sound filial. Old Mrs Takahashi subsided meekly into her place, complaining in a querulous chunter, whilst Keiko in her turquoise tracksuit whisked from kitchen to table, clattering crockery. She looked like an angry dragonfly, and sounded like a virago. Old Takahashi also kept up her stream of complaint, and, for an instant, tucking her napkin under her chin, the old lady caught my eye, and, very delicately, she stuck out the tip of her tongue in the direction of her daughter. I raised an eyebrow, and lowered an eyelid.

We are going to visit the temples at midnight, but first, Keiko and I must eat noodles. This is traditional. It brings good luck.

The narrow streets were full of people. Under umbrellas they jostled, chatting and laughing, greeting friends. Small girls proceeded more or less sedately with their elders, but little boys ran ahead, or chased each other around the family group as Keiko and I joined her neighbours on the cobbled street. I watched her bow and greet neighbours, wishing them a Happy New Year on behalf of her mother and herself, before groups of people began to separate, each heading for a different shrine. Keiko also turned away, leading me away from the throng. We began to climb a footpath that I thought led up to Utatsuyama. I followed the pinprick of her torch as we climbed steps cut into the mountain. All at once, the temple gongs began to sound; not all at the same time, but first one solitary great boom, answered a few seconds later by another, clanging, further away; then others joined in. Alone, we continued to climb, up sodden steps. Thickets of bamboo sighed and shook wet branches on either side of us as Keiko paused, her head on one side.

"This is curious. By now, we should hear my mother's special temple on the mountain," she said.

The only sound was the wind, and the echo of gongs, far below. We walked on.

Suddenly, she raised her torch, its beam illuminating an abandoned shrine. Ivy sprawled across shutters that rattled in the wind. Deserted stone gods were revealed, staring down at us impertinent mortals that dared to disturb them.

"Let's go," I pleaded.

Keiko didn't hear me. She stood, staring at the overgrown building, lost in reverie.

"Every year, when I was a child, this is where we used to come, my mother and I."

Rain pattered on our umbrellas. I stood back on a twig. It cracked. All round us, pine trees sighed, and branches groaned and squeaked. Keiko began to walk round the building shining her torch at its walls. More and more flat yellow sandstone faces came to life behind their covering of creeper; malevolent faces, grimacing at us with protruding mad eyes, with fangs – and, as the creeper thrashed about them, and the torch light flashed from one god to another, they seemed to come to life.

"Please, Keiko," I whispered, "I think we ought to go …"

A shutter banged violently above our heads.

"Keiko!" I said urgently, touching her arm, "We should go now. C'mon, Keiko, we're leaving …"

She allowed me to lead her away, back down the mountain path, towards the gongs of Higashiyama.

Back in the town, the streets were loud, thrumming with the sound of the ever-present gongs; charcoal braziers burned on stanchions at the foot of temple steps, stall holders were doing a roaring trade selling prayer slips, or large hollow paper fish, like windsocks on an airstrip, and, over all, the smell of roasted nuts. We joined the crowds on the temple steps, waiting to enter.

Once in, the routine did not seem reverential; people surged in, chucked money into a box in front of the altar rail, then clapped their hands and bowed briefly, before leaving, chatting jovially to friends as they went out. I lingered, watching. The altar itself had screens to the side of it; shadows flickered behind them, and I heard the notes of a flute, followed by a slow, muffled drum beat. On the steps leading to the altar I saw a woman kneeling in the unmistakeable stance of a supplicant. Approached by a priestess dressed in scarlet, she accepted a branch, bowing her head to the floor. To my eyes, she seemed grief-stricken.

"I will see you outside," Keiko said, throwing some money into the box. "I am joining friends on the steps."

I nodded, silently. From behind the screens appeared a preternaturally tall figure wearing magnificent robes, and a hat resembling a bishop's mitre. His shadow loomed huge against the screens, gliding in time as the music swelled, and he advanced, towards the crumpled figure on the floor before him. In his hand he carried a cane with long white paper streamers flowing from one end, and, when he shook these over the head of the woman the streamers rustled – a rattlesnake sound. The flute squealed like a creature in pain. And then stilled. Silently, the priest glided away, disappearing once more behind the screen. Nothing moved beyond the altar rail; the woman remained as before. Suddenly, more young priestesses approached her, offering oranges and a glass of sake, and slowly, inch by inch, the woman uncurled, knelt upright, and accepted the gifts. I do not understand. Was it a ritual cleansing? Was she in deep trouble? Grieving for someone? I left the temple.

Outside, in the drizzle, it was was like a night scene in a Breughel painting; gilded faces grinning, illuminated by the light of the braziers, people chatting, children scampering, old people passing slowly through the crowds, and people, more and more people of all ages; all circulating, in an ever-shifting pattern of faces and hands, all gesticulating, waving at neighbours, eating, locked in conversation while their sons and daughters moved closer together, eyes seeking each other.

We went to one more shrine that night. This too was very different. Within its doors only a few couples gathered. I saw an elderly man and his wife, and two couples, both young. Here in the dim light was the altar rail, and the box for money, but, surrounding it, on the walls, were dolls; not statues, not shadows, but real dolls, and teddy bears, and children's dresses, and lines of white, pink and blue babygros, hanging limply. I glanced across to the far side of the shrine, and saw one of the young women sobbing. I felt intrusive, and looked away.

On the wall beside me were rows of granite figures, ranging in height from approximately one foot to three foot. All wore scarlet knitted skull-caps and matching shawls. I had already seen such statues before, up in Utatsuyama, in the cemetery. I knew they represented the spirits of dead children. On another wall, deep in shadow, hung hundreds of babies' bibs, some soiled, some clean.

Keiko Takahashi tossed her money into the box, clapped her hands sharply, bowed for an instant, and instructed me to leave.

"This was a special favourite shrine of my mother's," she told me. "Here, tonight, she wanted me to come, because, when I was a tiny baby, I was delicate, and sometimes ill. So, my aunt and my mother brought me here, and left a dress I wore. And, then I grew well again."

"Why was that woman crying?" I asked.

"Well, I suppose her baby died," Keiko said, abruptly. "This is our shrine for children. Some who live, some who die. Understand?"

"But, tonight, why do …"

"Why? Why what? Why do you always have to ask 'why'?" She sounded thoroughly exasperated.

"Sorry."

I had obviously offended her. I hadn't meant to, when she had been so kind, taking me with her on such a special night. But, I still wondered whether parents and grandparents went to that shrine to intercede for their children, or to give thanks to the gods for saving them. Or both. I remembered a legend I had read about a wicked woman who stole babies from poor peasant women to feed her monster king. But, when she too lost her child, and was weeping in anguish, a spirit came to her, promising that her own child would be cared for, according to how she cared for all children in the world. Thus, she became the custodian, the Goddess for children, as in The Water Babies: a 'Mrs Be-Done-By-As-You-Did'.

The streets were still full of people. The rain still poured down. The gongs still sounded. Keiko said that she had visited enough shrines. It took a long time to return, because of the many friends and neighbours who stopped her to wish her mother, and her, a Happy New Year:

"Oshogatsu omedito gozaimasu!" … "Oshogatsu omedito gozaimasu!"

Another 2 am. Now, another New Year. I wonder what it will bring for me?

"Today," Keiko announced, the following morning, "we will eat a true Japanese breakfast, because this is the first day of the New Year."

Her mother said nothing, shovelling lumps of rice into her mouth, washing them down with sake. Sake at 9.30 in the morning? She smiled, but did not greet me with her usual 'Ohaio gozaimasu', merely passing her empty glass to Keiko for a refill. Perhaps her daughter's drink capacity is inherited? Keiko, setting before me a bowl of black fermented beans (tasting of silage), four walnuts, and four thin slices of sliced radish covered in tiny green fish eggs, explained that her mother was carrying on the old tradition of not speaking until the first meal of the New Year had been taken. The little fish eggs were a virulent spinach green, and slimy. I gagged on the first mouthful, and then noticed Takahashi-san's eyes fixed longingly on my plate. We swapped dishes whilst Keiko was in the kitchen serving my portion of o'miso and rice. She seemed surprised at my empty plate.

"Have you had enough, Angela?"

"Hai, arigato. Oishii desu kara," I told her, smugly. Beside me, her mother's jaws moved slightly, with a flicker of amusement, but her lips continued to move in silent prayer.

My kerosene stove had run out of fuel, and a horrid stink hung over all. I carried the canister down to the porch, and had just started to fit the plastic tubing from the main drum when Keiko materialised through the door, demanding what on earth was I doing.

I thought it obvious.

"You need to fill it AGAIN?" she barked.

"Yes, I do," I said, shortly. "My room is cold, I am cold, and the heater has run out."

Back in my room, for some unknown reason, it occurred to me to write down the food I had been given by Keiko for breakfast and supper as I remembered it over the past few days and weeks. I don't know why. I also reflected maliciously on the breakfast menu I would set before her if ever she came to England: porridge, traditional Scottish style, to start with, followed by steak tartare, and a very ripe Brie …

The Takahashis ate before me that night, Keiko leaving my supper on a tray: the remnants of breakfast gruel, now containing a raw egg, a sliver of meat and pimento, and a spoonful of rice that had sat long in the steamer. Very, very long. My tummy is setting up an opposition to the drums tonight – boom, boom, rumble, rumble.

Tomorrow, I resolved to try to find a shop still open during the holiday, and buy myself something nourishing, like fruit cake, or a lump of cheddar cheese.

The old lady in the tiny corner shop recognised me. She shuffled out from behind a curtain, wearing her usual apparel; woollen kimono, navy apron and gumboots, as I walked round the shelves hunting for something to eat.

"Nani osagashi desuka? Nani ni shimasuka?"

Her gold teeth glittering, she followed me, trying vainly to ascertain what I wanted. There was absolutely nothing substantial to eat. Finally, I bought a few bananas, a replacement jar of Nescafé, two packs of cigarettes, and a bottle of Japanese whisky to warm the cockles over the New Year. She insisted on giving me a pack of tissues and a lighter: "For service, Obaa-san!"

In the evening, after a supper of three slivers of meat fried on a hot plate, accompanied by chopped onion stalks, I retired again to my room. Mashed banana in whisky and milk powder is an acquired taste, but, maybe it will grow on me.

Friday, January 3rd, in the Year of the Monkey, is a day I shall always remember. It dawned bitterly cold, as usual, the heavens blanketed in thick grey cloud, shedding flurries of snow, creating a scene identical to those little glass globes children shake to create a snowstorm. I feel exhausted. If someone said 'Boo' to me, I might burst into tears. At breakfast, Keiko was at her most monosyllabic, reading her mail. She looked up only once, giving a pained sigh when a brimming jug dripped onto the tablecloth. She fetched a damp cloth and gave it to me, pointing to the drops with long, well-manicured nails. Inwardly, I counted to ten, and calmed myself by imagining which form of counting was applicable to a drip: was it the long thin form, derived from the shape of the jug, as in bottles and roses, or the flat thin form, as the drip melted into the tablecloth? Keiko turned a page of the Asahi Times with an impatient rustle as I got going with her Dinky-car Bissel, chasing a few errant toast crumbs across the cloth. We washed up in silence.

I brought some tights and blouses down to the mosaic

sink/washbasin in the room of the three lavatories, being careful only to step on the duckboards, since any more sins commited that morning would undoubtedly cause confrontation. I washed them in the cold water, wrung them out carefully, and went to hang them on the line that stretched along an outer corridor beyond the living room. Keiko was kneeling at the table, writing, as I pushed open the partition, using an elbow.

"Not THAT one, Angela!"

I gave an exasperated grunt and pushed another identical panel, luckily, getting it right; there, before me, stretched the line.

"Now, shut that door!"

I gave it an inadequate shove with my foot, thereby causing two panels to gape slightly.

Now, Keiko was on her feet, shouting.

"I said, SHUT THAT DOOR. NOW, SHUT IT!" she yelled.

I turned to look at her, my arms still full of wet washing. I had promised myself once, that I would never allow myself to be bullied again. My throat closed, I couldn't swallow. I couldn't speak. I could only hear my heart pounding, and feel my body go stiff, my neck, my face, flaming. Rage! I must get out, or I would hit her. I pushed past her, gasping, leaving all panels open.

In my room, I paced up and down with clenched fists, muttering: "Calm down, Angela. Right? Just, calm down. Look, it doesn't matter. Breathe deeply, OK? There, you're grand. It's alright ..."

But it wasn't.

Not so long ago, I had left an uncaring husband. Twenty-seven years of sad marriage. I had left my beautiful home. Gone to a strange country, away from direct contact with my children. Perhaps I was more vulnerable than I had presumed? But, in any event, I actually couldn't tolerate this abuse. And, I would not.

I was still me.

I knew that I had reached the end of my endurance, whether through inadequate sleep, lack of nourishment, or loneliness. Perhaps I was being irrational, impulsive? Whatever. That was irrelevant. What was clear to me at that moment was that I could no longer stay here, with my hostess, in the old geisha house. I was not prepared to wait until Saito returned from her holiday. I was going to leave this place today, right?

Decision made.

I am in control of my destiny.

Perhaps there would still be someone who spoke English in the Centre; maybe one of the teachers, reading in the library, who could give me the name of a cheap bed and breakfast for a few days, just until the holiday ended?

I strode out into the blizzard, sloshing through empty streets, using my umbrella as a shield. From under it, I hardly ever saw another pair of feet, but did occasionally bash into a lamp post. Sometimes dizziness swept over me, and I lent against a wall.

At the Centre, iron chains were stretched, padlocked, across the car park. I climbed slowly up the long flight of steps to the main building. The water cascade was switched off, the only sound, snow, plopping from overhanging branches. I walked through the silent gardens, up the steps to the entrance doors: no fluorescent lights, no telephones ringing, no clacking of word processors, and, of course, no people. I leaned against the glass doors, staring out at the dancing snowflakes, and thought.

Options:

Option One. Go to the nearest phone booth, and look up hotels, or cheap ryokan (shared rooms, Japanese-style, plus breakfast).

Option Two. Return to Higashiyama for ten more days, then try to push Saito into implementing her promise to find me alternative accommodation. No. That was not an option.

The wind was increasing its intensity. A slate blew off the roof of the Centre and embedded itself in the snow. I walked back down the steps, remembering a phone booth in the street below. It was impeccably clean. It had directories in swing racks. It had a clean ashtray on a shelf. It had a workable biro suspended from a string.

And all directories were written in a mixture of Kanji, Hiragana, and Katakana.

[232]

I checked in my pocket, and found the Unos' phone number. Mieko's small voice answered, sounding ridiculously far off.

"Mieko-san? Oshogatsu omedito gozaimasu! Angela desu."

"Uno Mieko desu."

Yes, I knew it was her. I tried again.

"Oto-san wa doko desuka?"

She sounded drowsy. Probably enjoying her rare favourite occupation, smoking and drowsing under the kodatsu.

"So when, I mean … Oto-san ga, erm, kimasuka?"

I could actually hear her puffing out smoke from a cigarette.

"Oto-san to Fumiko suki shimasu! Sayonara, Angela-san."

If this blizzard persisted, people could soon toboggan down the main street. Presumably the local government office had also closed down and shut off the anti-freeze jets. I left the phone booth to a loud, stagey roll of thunder, lightning flickering through the snowflakes.

'I don't care. I am not going back. Bugger Buddha, the thunder, and Japanese phone directories.'

My steps were leading me up the road to Takara-machi. Perhaps the Kanekos would be in and could phone a ryokan for me? The Kanekos' car was in the driveway. Upstairs, I saw their fringed lamp shining in the dim afternoon daylight. Yasuko herself came running downstairs and pulled open the door.

"Angela-san! What a surprise! But, you are to come for coffee next week, no?"

I had forgotten.

"I am so sorry to bother you," I said. "It is just that I cannot read your telephone directories, and …"

She looked at me.

"You do not look well. Something is wrong. Come in and tell me the problem … Come, I take your coat. You put on these slippers, remember? These are your slippers."

Upstairs, sitting at their dining table while she made coffee, everything looked so normal, so warm and reassuring; the same sort of family muddle and memorabilia that all of us have: knitting wool

[233]

on the table; a golf trophy of Jin Ichiri's; the framed photograph of Ai and Yiu wearing ballet tutus; funny fridge magnets, and coloured pictures drawn by Yasuko's small art students stuck on a cupboard door.

A world away from that great, gloomy house in Higashiyama. I explained, carefully, that I was not very happy staying with Keiko Takahashi.

"Oh, but, why?"

This was a difficult one. It had always been impressed on us foreign students that absolutely all Japanese people, especially the good people of Kanazawa, were universally kind, polite, and welcoming, and that, even if we had difficulties, it ill-behoved us to point them out.

I said that I found the house very cold, and Yasuko nodded, sympathetically, stirring her coffee.

"And, Takahashi-san... Does she help you with your Japanese?"

I explained that Keiko was very busy, caring for her elderly mother.

"Aaa, I see. And had you a happy Christmas?"

To my horror, I felt my lips go shaky, and the back of my eyes get hot; if I wasn't very careful, I would succumb to a bad attack of self-pity. If she would just book me in somewhere, I could leave her in peace ...

"Thank you, yes, Yasuko. It was, well, very quiet, but I spoke to my children on the phone, and that was ..." I sniffed, biting back tears.

Yasuko said: "I think you must tell me why you are so unhappy, Angela-san?"

Her kindness completely undermined my resolution to be guarded.

"Oh, Yasuko! I am so miserable. I am an alien there. Everything I do is wrong, and I can't ... please, could you find me a ryokan, just until term starts again, and I can talk to Saito-san?"

"Tell me," she insisted. "Tell me what has happened."

And, I did. Everything. The broken window panes in my room,

the cold, the stove, the food, and Keiko; finishing up with her yelling at me for mistaking the panel doorway.

"And so, I am very sorry, but I had no one else to ask. I

"No! No, I am so glad that you came here. When I hear how things have been for you, I feel ashamed to be Japanese."

She was crying. Me too. It was such a relief to let the tears come. We were both standing there, tears running down our cheeks, when Jin-Ichiri came in.

"Oh, husband …"

And those were the only words I understood over the next five minutes, as she launched into explanations, her words flowing out from her like a river in full flood, while Jin-Ichiri stood there, listening, nodding his head from time to time. I had never seen him look so serious.

I felt curiously remote from the situation. Never before had I been in a position where there was absolutely nothing I could do. All thoughts of being in charge of my own destiny counted for nothing now. At last, Yasuko fell silent, looking at her husband. That Oracle, that normally whimsical, humorous man, was looking downright severe. He fished in his pocket, handed her his car keys, and turned, reassuringly, to me.

"I too am so sorry, Angela-san. But now, you no worry. You put all your luggage in my car, and we welcome you back in my home. When Uno-san come back, we telephone him."

Yasuko parked the car opposite the Takahashis, and I ran in, intending to tell Keiko that I was leaving, but, to my horror, she had gone out, leaving only her mother in the house, watching TV.

Upstairs, I whisked round my room, gathering up my possessions in a frenzy, higgledy-piggledy, stuffing them into my suitcase and my canvas grip, my satchel, and assorted polythene bags, lugging them down to the porch.

Now, the old lady was stirring something in the kitchen:

"Dai jobu desuka?"

The last thing I wanted to do was upset her; she had always been gentle and charming to me, in fact, sometimes we had seemed almost in league.

"Hai, hai. Dai jobu desu." I called back, reassuringly, from the porch.

Fortunately, at this moment, Keiko returned. She stood staring at her crowded porch.

"Cleaning out your room, Angela?" she enquired, her lip curling.

I said: "I will speak to you in a moment, Keiko-san."

One by one, under her astonished gaze, I placed my belongings onto the street, closed the door behind me, and came back into the porch.

"I am glad to have the opportunity to tell you that I am leaving your house," I said.

She gasped. "But … but why?"

"You ask me why? When you shout at me, like a market woman?"

Old Takahashi-san had come to the porch, peering nervously round the panel door.

Keiko stamped her foot.

"I do not shout at you!" she shouted.

"Keiko Takahashi," I told her, formally, "here, in your house, I have been cold, lonely, and hungry. You have refused to help me speak Japanese, whereas you have learned much English from me, which was not fair."

"Keiko?" queried her mother.

"But you cannot go! Where will you go?" she demanded, furiously.

I turned to leave. "I am going to stay with friends. Kind friends, who know how to welcome foreign guests. If ever again you are given the chance to entertain a foreigner in your home, I suggest you learn how to control your temper."

For a brief moment, we locked eyes, before she whirled about and turned on her heel, nearly knocking her mother over, to disappear back into the house.

Old Takahashi-san still stood there, utterly bewildered. For her,

I gave a deep deferential bow, and quit the old geisha house in the Pleasure Quarter. For all time.

Yasuko had loaded up the car, and we drove off in silence.

Had I been foolish? I wondered. Unfair to Keiko? After all, she had taken me to the temple ceremonies at New Year, and included me in the Asamis' party invitation. But then, perhaps she had not wanted to be alone. And she had gained kudos by her expertise in English, and saved herself the necessity of cooking me a supper when we went to the party. I had not intended landing myself on the Kanekos. I felt confused, and disorientated.

It wasn't until we arrived back at her house that I discovered I was shaking all over.

Jin-Ichiri carried my bags in – through the designated front door. Someone had put a vase of carnations on the kodatsu in my room.

"Coffee, or beer, Angela-san?" enquired Jin-Ichiri. He looked at me with a small grin, and decided. "I think beer would be best."

"Maybe for me too?" Yasuko said, smiling up at him.

To be back with my Japanese friends again was an unbelievable relief.

With Good Friends

THAT NIGHT I SLEPT as if someone had slipped a Micky Finn in my beer. No one disturbed me, and I woke at the disgracefully late hour of 10 o'clock, macaroni pillow and Humphrey lying beside me on the floor.

In the afternoon, Yasuko took me to an amazing art exhibition. The entire show was devoted to the works of a single artist, a nonogenarian, who had died only recently. A poster in the entrance showed his photograph: a life-size depiction of a genial old man with crinkly humorous eyes, white hair, and a full beard – a sort of Ernest Hemingway figure, but more benevolent looking. Each room followed his development as a painter; his work during the thirties, painting scrupulously accurate portraits, always depicting their characters. I stood for a while in front of his early portrait of his mother, trying to imagine their lives. Another room was devoted to a later period in his life, when he had turned to stylised, detailed watercolours of insects, butterflies, and frogs (my personal phobia). Then came primitive paintings in primary colours, and, finally, a room devoted to scrolls and screens, in his exquisite black-on-white calligraphy. These collected the largest crowds, and the most awe-struck reaction from them. I, on the other hand, returned to the first room, to an oil painting that had fascinated me. It showed a fast-flowing river, painted in furious oils. Beneath the water lay the body of a woman, her long hair streeling out; one dimentional? Perhaps; but she was so obviously limp, so pathetic, so very dead. I stared at it for a long time. Later, Yasuko, reading from her brochure, told me that the artist's daughter had drowned herself. The last painting was one that had advertised the exhibition: a huge ginger and white cat, supposedly asleep, but with a glint of green eyes, and tail taut.

The artist was Moriichi Kumagai, who had died, aged ninety-seven. A stunning exhibition.

Another evening, Yasuko announced that we were all going to her parents' house for a party. She and I walked there, making our way through narrow streets that connected with no seeming purpose; garages linked shrines or temples, ancient timbered houses were squeezed into spaces beside factories, the usual coils of overhead wires draped from telegraph poles on either side of the street, occasionally crossing it, looping across buildings, and sagging between spaces where two high buildings were hyphened by a single-storey corrugated iron-roofed dwelling, the wires hanging like suspension bridges, swaying in the wind. Small girls, well wrapped up in coloured anoraks, played skipping games outside their houses, chanting in unison, businessmen walked purposefully in identical navy raincoats against a background hum of rush-hour traffic coming from somewhere else. Here, the only traffic was the occasional bicycle. A miasma of spicy cooking hung on the night air. No youths lounged on street corners, not so much as a cigarette butt lay on the street.

Her old home was full of people, family, and friends. A toddler waddled to and fro, launching himself from one adult knee to another, as children chased each other round the room, laughing. The kitchen was at one end of the living room, full of busy, chattering women, all chopping vegetables, stirring large saucepans. Yasuko's mother greeted me warmly, sleeves rolled up, elbow-deep in flour. As Yasuko wriggled into a floral pinnie, like all the other women, I was acutely aware that I was the only woman present without a job to do. I looked at the crowded kitchen, however, and doubted whether there was a square inch of space left.

"My mother says, please to go and sit down and rest yourself," Yasuko said.

Her brother was deputed to lead me to a chair and pour me a beer.

Jin-Ichiri arrived, bringing Masaya and Ryo. And then came a very, very old man, his head like a skull, with wisps of white hair. He limped into the room, his hands almost transparent on his two sticks. He was followed by a girl who could have been a prototype for the St Trinian's cartoon schoolgirl: protruberant teeth, straight fringe, pigtails, and rimless glasses. She wore a white shirt, school tie, navy gymslip, and felt hat. This was Mariko, a niece of Yasuko's.

"Now, Angela-san," her Father said, beaming paternally, "you will see if, this time, the calculator of my brother Jin-Ichiri, and the beads of my Father, can win against my daughter."

This was to be their entr'acte before the feast, a variant on wine labels or holiday snaps.

Jin-Ichiri and Masaya produced pocket calculators. The old man sat in his armchair, his head nodding involuntarily; he brought out a small, well-worn set of abacus beads. Mariko sat upright on the sofa, face impassive. From behind her magnifying spectacles, her eyes blinked rapidly. Jin-Ichiri called the first few figures, alternating with his brother-in-law, as both men tapped their calculators: "Seven thousand, three hundred and ninety-five, plus twenty-seven, plus ninety-eight, divided by thirty four, multiplied by seventy-nine, plus one million, three thousand and fifty six, minus eighteen, divided by …" They were reeling out figures at random, at ever increasing speed, rather like auctioneers getting into their stride. Beside me, Masaya, scowling in concentration, prodded the buttons on his calculator, and, from the depths of the armchair, came the sharp click of ivory beads.

"Equals?" queried Jin-Ichiri, sharply

Without missing a beat, his niece reeled out the answer. Jin-Ichiri's calculator and the abacus came second, in a dead heat, followed by Ryo. All gave the same answer. Masaya's, however, was different.

"That is because you made a mistake. You MULTIPLIED by thirty-four, and DIVIDED by seventy-nine," remarked the prodigy, composedly, taking a sip from her can of Coca Cola, smoothing her gymslip over her knees. They tried again, several times, but Mariko always gave the correct answer quicker than the calculators.

"But that's incredible!" I said. "I mean, taihen odorakimasu! Seriously, in England, on television, you could make a great deal of money, demonstrating that gift."

She giggled. "Many persons can do," she said, lowering her eyes.

"How old are you?" I asked, having learned that this was a perfectly permissible question to ask in Japan. She was just seventeen.

The old man was shifting uneasily in his chair. He was uncomfortable. Helped by the other men, he made his way to the traditional Japanese end of the room, up a polished step onto the tatami, and settled his creaky bones into a lotus position with a sigh of relief. He lit his pipe, and the men all knelt or squatted round him on the tatami, chatting companionably, occasionally stubbing out a cigarette in the big glass ashtray beside them, having lit a fresh one from the previous stub. Ryo and Mariko produced comics from their school satchels, swapping them, and laughing, while Masaya was talking to another group, ignoring the toddler who was making strenuous efforts to climb up his legs.

Yet another mighty feast! This was held in another long room, where, as before, three coffee tables had been joined together. Yasuko suggested that I sit sideways, beside her: "So you can relax." This time, I was prepared for the ensuing orgy of eating, and took tiny first helpings. The pretty daughter-in-law, frequently with a child on one hip, tirelessly served dish after dish, only joining us at table several hours later, but showing no resentment, merely sitting down on the zabuton beside her husband, accepting a glass of beer, and scoffing a bowl of boiled rice. Her small daughter carried on careering round the room, singing quietly to herself, self-absorbed in some imaginary game. Once, her arms touched the pyramid of tangerines built in front of the shrine to Buddha, and the whole neat pile collapsed, rolling amongst the bottles of o'sake and goblets of rice placed before the statue. No one rebuked her, and she and Yasuko carefully built it up again. A little later, she fell asleep in Yasuko's lap.

As we left, Yasuko's mother gave me a gift she had made herself: a small fabric-covered box, three-sided, shaped rather like a plump iris pod; when squeezed at both ends, it opened like a duck's bill, ready to receive earrings. I have it still. Nearly all the Japanese women I met spent leisure time creating artistic handiwork; Naoko Kitamura, whose exquisitely dressed geisha dolls won prizes at exhibitions, Keiko Takahashi, kneeling on the floor beside her Singer sewing machine, making herself a fully lined, tailored jacket and skirt from an advanced Vogue pattern; another student of mine, Sakano-san, who painted each evening, although vastly pregnant, and of course, Yasuko, who knitted, sewed, made gift cards, collages, and flower arrangements in between cooking two delicious meals for her family each day. Mieko Uno was the exception, but then, she worked each day, and, by the time she had washed up the evening meal, begged and bribed Fumiko to do her homework, and got her to bed, it was time to steep the family's washing and start on the ironing.

On his return from skiing, Joji Uno returned the Kanekos' phone call. The conversation between him and Yasuko went on a long time, but I realised it was coming to a close when Yasuko, rather like a small bird on a branch preparing for flight, started to make the usual series of fluttery little bows and bobs – the customary ritual before actually saying goodbye:

"Hai, hai, Uno-san … hai, arigato… hai, so desu … domo – so, so, so, hai, wakarimasu … domo arigato gozaimasu, Uno-san…"

She passed the receiver to me.

"Angela-san!" boomed Joji's voice. "I am very unhappy to you. Kaneko-san has told me of your bad experience. Tomorrow, you come to my home to stay, and we talk. Okay?"

"Thank you very much, Joji-san," I said.

I heard the familiar: "No problem!" And he rang off.

The following morning we again loaded my baggage into Jin-Ichiri's car, and set off for Mattoh, Jin-Ichiri driving, with Yasuko beside him, clutching a large tin of biscuits for the Unos, and a box of chocolates for Fumiko. It felt like my dowry! He had no map, and I was getting increasingly doubtful about my ability to find the way. Under his breath, Jin-Ichiri began to grumble, and I grew tense.

Dear God, I was an awful nuisance to these lovely people!

Suddenly, on a straight stretch of road, a car that had been huffing and puffing on our tail, accelerated, shot ahead, and squeezed into the narrow space between our car and a lorry, causing Jin-Ichiri to brake sharply.

"Disgraceful! That was downright dangerous driving," I said, indignantly.

No one said anything. Not by so much as a flicker did Jin-Ichiri express emotion.

"Well, didn't you think it terrible driving?"

He shrugged. "Ee, wakai no hito" he remarked, resignedly.

I don't understand why the fact of the driver being young mitigated his offence, imagining a Western reaction: the blaring of horns, shouted insults, gestures and shaken fists, plus, of course the righteous chorus of disapproval from all other occupants of the car. Here, it is considered unmanly to express irritation over such incidents. Adults are supposed to have self-control. I remembered discussing this with Bertram Pocock, agreeing that the two emotions seemingly absent throughout Japan, in public at least, were cynicism and aggression. Certainly, self-discipline is highly prized here as seen in the prelude to two of their favourite sports – sumo, and kendo (Japanese archery). However, this comment was made before I had encountered Keiko Takahashi.

The Kanekos having decided it would be good for my Japanese if I gave directions in Japanese, we finally found the Unos' house more by dint of Jin Ichiri's judgement than my guidance. He had been wonderfully patient as I called: "Oops, er, migni, kudasai oh, sorry, er, gomen nasai, I meant hai, ima hidori … er, yukkuri, yukkuri, and, ima …" testing male self-control to the limit.

Mieko, wearing her well-remembered navy tracksuit, welcomed her guests on her knees. Yasuko, who is probably the same age, elegant in a caramel sweater and Levis, responded with a deep bow. Two such different women, both now dear friends of mine. Joji and Jin-Ichiri, wary-eyed but genial, ducked heads as I introduced them. The two men rapidly discovered a shared interest in skiing that led to much showing of Joji's medals and photographs after Fumiko had played her piano piece. Yasuko regretted that her own two daughters were not as skilled at music as Fumiko, the cookies were appreciated and recognised as coming from one of the best shops in Kanazawa, and, gradually, Mieko relaxed. The two women began to discuss children, ballet classes, and homework. Finally, they left, having greatly praised everything about my old room, and Joji set about making his special spaghetti for me, as before.

"So now. You tell me about this Takahashi-san," he invited.

When I had finished explaining, he was snorting like an enraged dragon.

"Hidoi hitoda," he growled. "From now, you will stay in my house until you return to England. You are a part of my family." He turned to Mieko: "Wife! Angela-san has grown too thin."

Mieko, eagerly pushing the cookie tin nearer to me, agreed. Joji had more surprises in store for me. Tomorrow evening, he and Fumiko will show me how to make his special New Year rice cakes, and, the family are going to take me to Kyoto where we will stay overnight in a hotel specially reserved for civil servants.

"We will repair your wounded heart!" he declared.

I am so grateful, and so thrilled at the thought of seeing the most famous ancient city in Japan. Mieko and Fumiko are also enormously excited at the prospect of going to Kyoto.

⁓

The following day, after a wonderful night's rest, I telephoned the Centre, to find out when they were officially due to open.

"The office open today," the telephonist told me.

"Ah, I see. And, tell me, Miyazaki-san – when does she return?"

"Also today. Who speaks, please?"

"My name is Angela Cook …"

A gasp. "Aaaa, COOK-San! You wait, please!"

Miyazaki came on the line. She wasted no time on preliminaries. "Where are you?"

I told her that I was in Mattoh, staying with the Unos.

"I need to talk to you," she said, coldly.

We arranged to meet at the Centre at midday.

All the classrooms were still officially shut, but the lower part of the building where the offices are, was at full complement: porters, car-park attendants, council officials wearing the statutory navy suits and white shirts or blouses were all back in business. I walked up the three flights of stairs to the library, and had no sooner pushed open the door than one of the young assistants came forward, ducking her head nervously, not meeting my eye. A secretary, Hiroko Kono, who I had often talked to, also avoided my glance, and even the Administrator, seated at his desk at the back of the room, talking on the phone, gave me only the faintest glimmer of a smile.

"You come with me now, please, to see Miyazaki-san," said the assistant.

Miyazaki got up to greet me. Today, she wore a fluffy charcoal-grey angora jumper, and a pinched expression. Beside her, thank goodness, was Saito, looking serious, but otherwise her usual, slightly dishevelled self.

"You please to sit there," said Miyazaki, motioning me to sit on the far side of the table. "We have heard from Takahashi-san …"

"And," I told the two women, "I do not want you to blame yourselves. I know that you were both on a well-earned holiday when my problems – some of which you, Saito-san, already knew about – became impossible to tolerate."

Saito translated for me, and I let her finish.

"However," I continued, "I now find myself in a difficult position, since I know that Miyazaki-san is a friend of Takahashi-san's, and I do not wish to distress her by speaking frankly."

Again, the translation, leaving Miyazaki slightly flushed.

"No, no" she protested, shaking her head, "I know her very little.

[245]

Just to speak to on the phone to fix your stay, Angela-san."

"Then that's all right. I can feel free to explain to you both that I consider Keiko Takahashi to be an unsuitable hostess for foreign visitors. She refuses to speak Japanese, preferring to receive free English tuition. She was frequently bad-tempered, and she fed me very badly. Sometimes, not at all, as you may remember, Miyazaki-san?"

I got the distinct impression that this interview was not going the way it had been intended. Miyazaki, however, rallied:

"I know that Takahashi-san apologised for this," she said, reproachfully. " And she told us that it was you who had been most rude, and she worried where you went."

From my handbag, I produced my diary.

"Perhaps you would both like to know exactly what I was given to eat by her over the last few days of my stay?" I read from my notes: "Octopus and black spaghetti with lettuce. Ham omelette, lettuce and a tangerine. Fish gruel, a slice of bread, and cuttlefish ..."

"And rice, of course," prompted Saito.

"No, not with rice," I said.

She looked horrified. "No rice?"

"Correct. No rice on those days."

Saito burst into rapid explanations to her colleague. The absence of rice in my daily diet was apparently a telling point. A massive black mark against the housewifery of my hostess. Miyazaki looked shaken.

"And, as to my being rude," I continued, "I cannot believe that it is part of the Japanese culture to shout at their guests. In my culture, such behaviour is described as being like a fishwife ..."

Saito's brow furrowed: "Sorry?"

"Fishwife? Like a market woman."

"Ah, thank you," Saito said, noting the expression.

I told them about Keiko's delightful old mother secretly sticking her tongue out in response to being shouted at by her daughter, and the two women looked at each other, amazed. I explained that the snow actually came into my bedroom, but that my hostess had resented my refilling the stove in my room.

"So, as I am sure you will both appreciate, the situation had become impossible, unfortunately whilst you were unable to help me. However, I was fortunate. Two kindly host families in Kanazawa understood and sympathised with my problems, and helped me. Both the Kanekos, and the Unos, have proved themselves to be very good friends."

In true Japanese fashion, the two women consulted together, speaking in low voices.

Finally, Saito said: "Miyazaki-san says she is sorry, but she does not think she will be able to find you another host family, because you are teaching, and accommodation can only be found for students who do not have other jobs."

I looked at her quizzically. We both knew full well that virtually all foreign students subsidised their stay by teaching.

"That is perfectly alright," I said, "because Uno-san has generously offered to let me stay with his family until I return. And, at a specially reduced rate for me."

Saito's eyes twinkled at me from behind her horn-rim glasses. I handed over Takahashi's key.

Miyazaki took it, saying, "Takahashi-san says that she owe you back rent for days you paid for after you left?"

"Please tell her she can keep it," I told her, graciously.

"We are sorry you were not happy."

"We will say no more about it," I said, getting up to leave.

There was still one finale to the episode. A few days later, Miyazaki stopped me in a corridor. She looked embarrassed:

"Er, Cook-san ... Takahashi-san has returned your extra rent money, and asked that I give it to you," she said.

"Fair enough, thank you."

"But, she has kept some back, to pay for her having to change all her locks when you go," Miyazaki said, her face now hot pink. In my mind's eye, I envisaged the cement-floored porch, with its boxes of tangerines and daikon, the empty bottles, the sit-up-and-beg old bike; the line of old shoes on the step; my memory retraced the endless expanse of cold, gloomy rooms. The idea that I might even conceive of breaking in tickled me. I made a strenuous effort not to

[247]

laugh, choking it back, but a small snuffle escaped me, and, before I could help it, I was laughing out loud.

"Oh, Miyazaki-san! Did she really imagine that I would … ?"

Miyazaki stared at me in bewilderment.

"Look, I'm sorry, my dear woman, but I just find it one of the funniest things. I reckon it shows that woman as she really is, and I absolutely assure you that I do not mind at all!"

But Joji Uno minded. He was livid, striding up and down the kitchen, muttering "Baka na!" and, "kurutteru yo!" and apologising to me, apparently on behalf of the entire Japanese nation. Perhaps my integrity has been grossly impugned, but I can still only see the funny side. Saito also buttonholed me to mention, quietly, that, if ever it was snowing, or I was teaching a late night class, I would be welcome to stay with her and her son in Kanazawa.

"Just between the two of us, eh?"

Watanabe-san, the Administrator, called me over to his desk, wondering if, perhaps, I would like some more students? I said I would be most grateful.

"My friends look for a teacher who speaks real Queen's English. They are a group of sewage-purifying executives who go in America in March, to inspect American drains."

"I would like this, very much," I told him.

"Then I fix for you. And, they pay well."

He grinned at me, and, could that possibly have been a conspiratorial wink? His phone rang again for the umpteenth time: "Hai, Watanabe desu."

I left the library on a cloud; with this job, I could continue all my lessons, and still stay solvent. Bless you, Mr Watanabe!

I had forgotten the degree of energy that Joji can generate. Tonight, I was leaning over my desk, eyes shut, chanting yet another irregular past verb that could also be conjugated differently if combined with an adverb, when I heard his car scorch down the track. Koro was barking. I heard him imitate his bark, and then the front door slid open and slammed shut. Joji Uno, I reckoned, had a project.

"Angela-san? ANGELA-SAN? Tadaima"

Well, half of Mattoh now knew he had returned.

"Itte rasshai, Joji-san," I returned.

"Fumiko? FOOMIKO!"

His daughter crashed past me on the stairs. Mieko peered from the kitchen, dishcloth in hand. Joji ignored her.

"Tonight, Angela-san, as I told you, I mend your poor bruised heart, okay? Tonight, you help me and Fumiko make our New Year cakes. Right? Yesterday, I soak the rice. Now, today, we steam it."

The special steamer was produced, ceremoniously, from the kitchen. It was a square wooden box exactly resembling a 'super' – that special box in a beehive. This was filled with the pre-soaked rice, covered, and set on top of a saucepan filled to the brim with boiling water.

We all ate supper, keeping an eye on the gas ring, and an hour or so later, the kitchen was full of steam, and the rice had become sludge.

"Ha!" cried the Master Chef, stirring it experimentally with a bamboo stick: "Is ready now."

We trooped after him into the garage, Mieko staggering under the weight of the rice box. In the middle of the garage, Joji placed a big, upright log, hollowed out in its centre. He stood beside it, as Fumiko handed him a long-handled wooden mallet, and knelt beside the log.

"Pour, wife," Joji instructed.

Mieko obediently tipped a steady stream of glutinous rice into the log basin, until the box was empty. Then she and I stood back as Joji raised his mallet high above his head, and brought it down onto the soggy mixture. It came away slowly, with a soggy squelch, as Fumiko sprinkled flour rapidly onto the goo, before her Father struck it again. They developed a rhythm, reflected weirdly as giant shadows on the garage wall; Joji, gum-booted, legs straddled wide, both his hands clasping the mallet high above his head; Fumiko, always crouched intently by the log, hands darting from the flour, attempting to knead the mixture before her Father struck again:

'Whoosh, bang-plop, pat pat. Whoosh, bang-plop, pat pat …'

After ten minutes of this, Joji was sweating. He wiped his forehead on his sleeve:

"You like to try now, Angela-san?"

"Ee, ki o tsukete Angela-san," Mieko worried, "abunai desu kara!"

I did not see how it could be dangerous, but I allowed her to help me into a pair of gumboots, and duly took up stance beside the log. The mallet was surprisingly heavy. Luckily, Fumiko dodged as I brought it down heavily on one side of the hollowed-out bowl.

"Sorry, Fumiko," I gasped.

Fumiko shrugged, grinning. She did, however, move slightly further away. My second stroke I played more cautiously, only raising the mallet a foot or two, managing to hit the doughy mass, rather ineffectually. There seems to be an art in hitting it so that the rice doesn't come away, stuck to the wooden head. Fumiko had to claw much of it away before being able to mould it into shape with the flour. I swung several times, teeth gritted, muscles tense, and did improve slightly, but never achieved the mighty swing of Joji, or a steady rhythm for Fumiko. Then, both Mieko and Fumiko had their turns – rather like a family stirring the Christmas pudding – Mieko light but dextrous, Fumiko dealing the mix a series of mighty wallops, until it was adjudged ready to be brought back into the kitchen and rolled out on a board, sprinkled with more flour, and pinched out into blobs on our plates. Bowls of soy sauce and grated radish were produced, and I was invited to try the first one, dipped in the sauce. I took a very small blob, and chewed. And chewed, praying that my expensive bridgework would not be dislodged. At last, I managed to swallow the lump, watched, proudly, by the family.

"Oishii desuka?"

I nodded, temporarily speechless. Honour-bound, I also managed another before pleading that, delicious as they were, my stomach was now full to overflowing.

"Very traditional," Joji said, contentedly, reaching out for another. "All my neighbours come to try my o'mocha."

From what I can understand, this nation is obsessed with food;

[250]

schoolchildren on buses or trains remark on what they ate for supper the previous evening, boys talking noisily about their favourite dishes; matrons sitting closely side by side (not actually looking at each other, direct eye contact being deemed impolite) exchange recipes, or plan the family meal, day after day, with shared nods and clucks of approval. And I had observed that if someone either left their food, or omitted to comment on its excellence, the wife is either cut to the quick, or assumes the worst, knowing that they must be sickening for something.

All conversations seem to be kept firmly on the trivial.

But, there are so many things I long to know. Like, what is the current national percentage of arranged marriages? In an election, what encourages a voter to vote for a particular candidate: family tradition? Conviction? Loyalty to a known candidate? And their allegiance to religion puzzles me: why is it that many people will present their children at the Shinto temple for the ceremonies at ages three, five, and seven, having married in a Christian church, and yet be given the last rites at a Buddhist shrine? I don't suppose I shall ever find out, and it would, I am convinced, be improper for me to ask. I have been told by several people that the essence of Japanese good manners is to suppress any display of overt spoken emotion, the exception to this rule being the display of valour by Samurai warriors, and the grief expressed in Noh Theatre.

In real life, most Japanese people excel at stiff-upper-lip behaviour. Joji Uno once told me that: "Our smile hides all our feelings. It is only foreigners who believe it means friendship."

And yet, and yet … to this day, mutual suicides of couples denied permission to marry are not uncommon, and, on occasions when family pride is at stake, or a person feels he has been grossly and deliberately insulted, revenge is legitimate, regarded as the only honourable course, in fact. But, even then, there is no public show of temper, nothing so vulgar. The issue is not even discussed between friends, and there is certainly none of the "And then he actually had the nerve to …" "So, I told him …" "Would you believe what she did?" In Japan one merely smiles, and bows. And broods, privately, on revenge. Their media system on reporting crimes such as homicide is also different. I saw on TV a report of a murder in Osaka, and the police were seeking a specific person. But, there was none of the 'police are looking to interview X in connection with the crime' reportage. The man was named as a murderer before he was even located. I also recall an incident recorded in the memoirs of Lafcadio Hearne, where he described the scene when a man who had killed the father of a family was brought, shackled, to stand before the small son of that family, and how the man begged the child that he should suffer death to atone for his crime.

It is hard for a foreigner to grasp the differences in thinking and reasoning between us and the resident Japanese. I have also heard that expatriate Japanese people returning to their homeland find it hard to be reaccepted. However, there is incontrovertible belief amongst all Japanese that there is absolutely no difference whatsoever between the European and the Japanese mentality, and nothing is more calculated to infuriate them than to suggest otherwise.

"Of course not there is no difference between us," my teacher insisted, hotly. "We all think alike."

How then could I say that therein lay one prime difference?

———

I never really liked the sea, much. Friends used to marvel at the view from our house in Cork, and, not wanting to seem rude, I used to agree, although I did not understand why anyone could admire such a treacherous, cold, usually grey-green tossing mass. I was also scared of the air – flying through it in a capsule seemed unnatural, and possibly doomed. But, I love the earth; its seasons, its growing grass, its fields of wheat and barley, the hedgerows, and the hills on the horizon. I took pleasure in the rich brown earth of ploughed fields; the safety of it, with my feet on the earth.

I had just left the front door when the earth tremor shook. Koro let out a ululating howl, wrenching at his chain, and the good earth shuddered under me. I fell to the ground. And then, it was over. A few rotten pomegranates tumbled down. The house creaked, and then was still. Everything returned to normal. I got up and looked around. Just a few seconds had destroyed my belief that nothing unnatural could happen if my two feet were rooted on the ground. Washing still flapped like flags from neighbouring balconies. A car drove past on the distant main road. And I carried on walking to Mattoh station, as intended, my itinerary planned; first a two-hour lesson, then a visit to a floral exhibition in Kanazawa, and finally, my first class with the sewage-purifying executives. I asked my teacher about the tremor. She shrugged.

"They come often, at this time of year. You get used to them."

I felt foolish. "Oh, right," I said.

Ever since the Ikebana demonstration, I had been studying the book the tutor had given me, and really wanted to see varied Japanese flower arrangement techniques, en masse. This exhibition was amazing: all made, of course with the bare modicum of flowers, using twigs, moss, stones and bare branches to create an effect. One large arrangement was contrived by intertwining birch twigs to resemble a gigantic bird's nest, lined with fluff. Protruding from the design a sharpened twig looked like the beak of a bird, while floating from the nest was a stream of camellia buds unmistakeably characterising the semi-quavers of bird song. The picture this created was poetic and entrancing; I had never seen such perfect interpretation of a theme. So much beauty had a calming effect on me. The reverence of the nation for all things of nature I have already noted; however, it is not replicated on nearby beaches. I took Koro for a walk – on his lead – to the seashore the other day, and found it to be like a local dump, littered with rusty bits of metal, old batteries, shoes, broken bottles and beer cans, crates of rotten oranges, and smelly vegetables. Amongst the seaweed and shells, polythene bags full of possible nasties swayed to and fro in the tide. Koro, of course, loved it. His idea of beachcombing is not the same as mine.

<hr/>

The executives from the sewage purifying plant were a large group, gathered in the conference room awaiting my arrival. Their chairman was a man in his late fifties, his colleagues mostly late thirties and forties. There were two women among them.

For the first hour we read together from a textbook – the best yet. I read a sentence, then the group repeated it after me, and subsequently they recited individually. This was the accustomed method, and they were content. During a fifteen-minute coffee break they began discussing their favourite TV programmes:

"I think programmes about hospitals are very good programmes," declared Higashino. "My wife thinks them very fine."

His choice was greeted with universal agreement.

Various other Western soaps were suggested, until Miss Kawata spoke of an old video she had recently seen.

"Demo – The Fripper wa ii no purogramma, ne, sensei?" she suggested.

'The Fripper'? "I don't think I …"

"Ipiki sakana yo," put in Ikebata, helpfully. "Ipiki is number one, for animals, 'sakana' is the word for fish …"

Light dawned. "Flipper!"

"Hai, hai, fripper," they agreed, enthusiastically.

This seemed like a good exercise. I put down my paper cup. "La, la, la, la," I chanted.

"Altogether, now: la, la, la, la…"

Obediently all my students joined in: "la, la, la, la…"

"Now, everybody say 'Flipper'!"

"FRRipper," they chorused.

Well, I can't talk. I still cannot distinguish the difference between 'Byoin' and 'Byoeen', which could make a significant difference, since one refers to a hospital, and the other a hairdressing salon. Other ancient videos were quoted, and absolutely everybody had at some time watched 'The Little House On The Prairie'.

"We all like these people very, very much," explained Mr Kobo. "Do you watch them as well?" I said they had been very popular.

The second hour I decided to spend doing role-play. No more of this standard repetition.

First, I explained that, in America, when entering a room, it was a case of 'ladies first', and we practiced this, returning from the coffee machine. The male members found this an extraordinary custom, as the two women scurried through the doors, eyes averted, giggling.

"And this is polite, in America, and England?" Oki-san asked, incredulously. I explained that it was a tradition, like that of men walking on the outside of a woman on the pavement, and Oki was dumbfounded.

"But then, senior members would get their trousers splashed," he exclaimed.

"Exactly. But the men are supposed to protect the women from getting splashed!"

We practiced getting lost in New York, asking the way from busy strangers, booking a table at a restaurant, and ordering from a menu. Mr Higashino, who had appeared a reserved, supercilious individual, became quite animated, saying he only wanted to discover American nightclubs with small lights, and loud music. Everyone laughed.

"You would!" said his boss, "But this is a business trip."

The boss is a far more conservative character, wanting to order green tea, raw fish, and absolutely no cheese, at a sandwich bar. I told him it might not be immediately available in all localities, but, the prime essential was to decide what to order, and give the order loudly, and clearly. The women found this very hard, tending to whisper. As a final exercise I stood at the far end of the room, pretending to be the sandwich-bar attendant, and made them shout their order:

"'Scuse, please... I like shrimp and salad ..."

"Can't hear you, lady," I bawled. "Come again?"

"'Scuse please ... I like shrimp and ..."

"You'll have to speak up, lady – I'm busy."

Miss Kobo was now pink with embarrassment. She cast an anguished look at her boss.

"I like a ..."

"Huh?"

"SHRIMP" she yelled, desperately.

"Well done, Kobo-san."

Miss Kobo lived near the Unos, and drove me back. She told me her hobby was Japanese dancing, and that she had been performing it since she was five. This season, she was due to appear in a theatre in Kanazawa, dancing the solo role. She told me she had enjoyed the lesson, and now knew how to order a sandwich in America.

"Ah, but suppose you wanted a ham sandwich?" I enquired, getting out of the car.

"HAM, please!" she shouted.

Mieko, opening the front door, jumped backwards, and Koro shot from his kennel, barking.

It had been a mutually interesting evening. I like this group very much, and am determined that they will not be travelling throughout America unable to fend for themselves, whenever an interpreter is not present – although English speakers worldwide are better at decyphering meaning than the Japanese.

Last week, Kamada told me that snow was going to be brought down by the army, in specially refrigerated trucks, from the northern island of Hokkaido, and then the army would construct colossal fantasies out of the snow. She was unsure when exactly, but thought the ice sculptures would be on display in a building beside my bank. A few days later, I asked the young girl in the bank, in my best rehearsed Japanese:

"Can you tell me, please, where is the snow exhibition, and, when does it close?"

She looked confused. This was not a banking question. Her fellow colleagues became, suddenly, very busy. Over her head, through a window, I could actually see the top of a giant snow edifice towering.

"Now look," I pointed. "Just look. Yukki, ne? Yukki means snow, ne? Doko no made arimasuka?"

She glanced nervously out of the window, and then her carmine lips parted:

"Gomen nasai. Aa, Snow Festival arimasu. Ashita, to omoimasu."

It was a Snow Festival. Not, as I had said, an Exhibition of Snow. However, it would not close until tomorrow, so I would go and see it at lunchtime. I duly arrived next day to discover the army packing the snow back into the trucks, closing the trucks, so as to return to

Hokkaido. That sort of closure. I fumed. I mean, if someone asks where the damn exhibition is, and then, when does it close, surely it is obvious that they want to see it BEFORE it has closed? Or, they do not want to see it AFTER it has closed? Perhaps it has to do with there being no future tense in Japanese. But, surely …? That day I had learned a new phrase: 'Zannen ga tsugi wa warui' which, broadly interpreted, apparently means 'unfortunately, circumstances are unfavourable'. This may be used if unable to attend something – or even not wanting to – but, in any event, it was a pity that the former interpretation applied to me today. I would have loved to see the Festival of Snow – sorry, the Snow Festival. This weekend is also all going to be about snow. For days, Joji has talked of little else but skiing; looking at weather forecasts, estimating the likely depth of snow, the crispness of it, and the prospective weather conditions.

Supper tonight was especially tense because, tomorrow, Sunday, is the long-awaited day when Joji's dreams of fame for his daughter comes true; the great day of Fumiko's Junior Ski Contest. Joji had been rehearsing her moves, shifting the salt and pepper, slaloming sideways between tea bowls, re-arranging cutlery to indicate parts of the piste where Fumiko should lean further out, or bend her knees, or something;

"Wakarimasuka, Fumiko?"

Fumiko, chomping on fish with her mouth open, nodded sleepily. Mieko knelt on her kitchen stool, her eyes half closed, blowing smoke over her half-eaten supper, while her husband recalled every bend on the slope, weaving and swaying, rice bowl in hand.

"Is that not right, wife?" he demanded.

I watched Mieko jerk back to the present. I could almost hear her eyelids click open.

"Yes, indeed, husband."

Now, Joji was gearing up for his daughter's grand finish down the slope, winning all before her, down through the final two chopsticks set side by side. We all retired early.

They left at 4.45. I heard sleet hitting the windows, and snuggled deeper under the quilts, hearing Mieko shuffle upstairs, tidy Fumiko's room, and shuffle down again. Later, she left for work. Perhaps on overtime, working on a weekend? A Sunday morning. No church bells here, of course. Mieko had left me two packets of her factory's sandwiches on the kitchen table, and I took them upstairs to eat as I studied, remembering Kamada telling me that I should try to think the language: make my brain Japanese to comprehend its beauty, its symbolism. This morning, my brain remains obduately Anglo-Saxon. Perhaps this is why the staff have apparently nick-named me 'Mrs Why-jin'! Today I am wrestling with the construction of one paragraph, before having to write my own exercise that follows the rules explained in it. Translated roughly into English, it goes: Speaker One: "Station towards going road, do you not know it?" Speaker Two: "No, very well I don't know it." Speaker One again: " Issho ni Nihon ni, ikimashoka." I'm guessing here, but it seems to mean, "Yes, together to Japan shall we go?" Probably not! My brain is becoming overheated. I decided to abandon this exercise, and settled down with a mug of Nescafé to learn the connotations of a simple little word like 'near'. 'CHIKAI'. When used before a verb, becomes 'CHIKAKU', right? Its negative form is 'CHIKAKUNAI' plus a DESU popped in in polite speech. Past tense, it becomes 'CHIKAKATTA'. Exploring the potential positive tense, we discover it under the guise of 'CHIKAKATTARA', whilst the negative potential tense requires the use of 'CHIKAKUNAKATTARA' And, that is before one has conjugated the flaming verb, let alone remembered where to put it in a sentence.

It is, after all, the Sabbath day. I am going to go downstairs and give myself a treat, listening to the tape sent to me by my god-daughter. Tape recorder switched on, I waited to hear her familiar voice.

"Dumty-dumpty dumty-dum, dumty-diddledy-dum!"

And there they all were, transported into the Unos' kitchen; Ruth and David on the farm, Brian organising some new deal, Jennifer shopping with Lilian, Clarrie bemoaning some recent misdemeanour of Edward's, and, of course, Eddie Grundy's well-remembered voice, discussing how to make a quick buck with his Dad, Joe! A whole omnibus-worth of 'The Archers'.

It made me feel chikakattara.

The front door slammed, and I heard running footsteps upstairs. It was only 1.30 pm.

"Okaeri nasai" I called.

"Tadaima," came the response, as Joji entered the kitchen.

His head hung down. He slouched onto a kitchen chair.

"Fumiko didn't win?" I guessed.

"Dame desu."

"Well, I'm sorry, Joji-san, but …"

Jojo began to mutter, his fists clenched, banging the table.

"I'll make coffee?" I suggested.

His voice rumbled on, crooning with disbelief.

Fumiko came down and switched on the television, lying under the kodatsu, whilst her Father's voice keened in sorrowful lament. The kettle on the stove began to hop and emit steam.

"Of course, she was only a woman. She did not have a man's heart. She did not bleed like a man. She bleed like a woman. No use. He, her father, had shown her how to win – how to ski, like he himself had learned to ski – but, she had not been brave. When it mattered, she had not been brave." I poured his mug of coffee.

"Well, sometimes, perhaps it is character-forming, not to win. Like, not always, perhaps, Joji-san?"

Joji Uno raised his head to look across at his daughter. His only child. His beloved daughter. Not a son. Fumiko, stretched under the kodatsu, reached out for a packet of crisps.

"No," he said. "I do not think so. My daughter's name could – should – have been in the newspaper. A Winner."

He cheered up the following day when we all went off to Hatsuon mountain, he and Fumiko to ski, Mieko and I supposedly to watch.

It was Mieko who threw the first snowball at me. I retaliated, and we played like children, in the snow, buffeting each other with snowballs. She and I then made a snowman, standing in front of his snow castle. Then, both hot and beaming, we retired to a stifling

[259]

café and drank hot chocolate until the skiiers returned.

At once, shy Mieko became incredibly bossy, determined to get us into the onsen, that natural pool heated directly from a volcano somewhere beneath the earth, and channelled into a tiled open-air pool. As I had seen before, all reserve was abandoned. The pool was a-babble with chatter and laughter as happy females splashed each other joyously. Middle-aged matrons squatted on their haunches, as dutiful daughters scrubbed their backs; young girls stood, languidly uncoiling their hair, standing like naiads in the steaming water, and Mieko was giggling like a schoolgirl as Fumiko poured bowls of water over her head. As usual, I was the only foreigner, but everyone was having too good a time to notice. The water was hot, but not unbearably so. It had a faint smell of sulphur. After a few minutes I left Mieko, dog-paddling beatifically to and fro, and went back to the locker room to shower and get dressed. Joji drove us home in high spirits after his onsen. He was singing. He decided that we would call on his father, and that his father would lend me his typewriter, to help me write out my exercises.

"But, Joji! You told me your father is now ninety-four years old. Surely we shouldn't disturb him now?"

"No problem. No problem. He will like to meet you. Once he used to teach English. So, you talk to him about Shakespeare, eh? He likes Shakespeare very much," Joji assured me.

Uno-san Senior was propped up in what looked like a bamboo car seat, legs under a kodatsu, watching television with another son and daughter-in-law. He had a delightful smile, but his voice was a mere breath of sound, and I could barely hear him. Bent almost double, he led Joji and I into another icy room to try and locate the typewriter, finally crawling on the floor, scrabbling under shelves.

"Please, don't bother," I begged him. "Honestly, it doesn't matter."

Lying almost full-length on the floor, he stretched out a bony arm under bookshelves, and began tugging. Joji stood watching. I couldn't bear to see him struggling.

"May I not help you?"

Joji's father looked shocked.

"Thank you, Cook-san, but no," he whispered, firmly.

Panting, he at last dragged out a heavy box, and Joji squatted down beside him. The key to the box was missing, but Joji found a screwdriver to remove the lock, and revealed a seventy-year-old black Royal, with round cream keys circled in metal, all oiled and gleaming, in impeccable order. It had its own special little screwdrivers and cleaning brushes still in their original cardboard box, and a heavy wooden board onto which the typewriter had to be screwed before use.

"My mother gave me this typewriter when I was twenty-four years of age," the old man remarked, still prone on the floor. He looked up and gave me a beautiful smile.

"I had just achieved my degree. She had saved the money for it for a long time."

I promised to take very good care of it, telling him that the Royal typewriter was known all over the world. Joji staggered out to the car with it. On its board, the thing weighed a ton.

"Thank you so very much. I am truly most grateful for the loan of it."

"My pleasure," he gasped, "my very great pleasure."

The Royal has made a great difference to my studies. I can now type out exercises, and even make up some of my own, writing questions and answers in Japanese, and translating them into English. Kamada has been photocopying them for other teachers, to help their English grammar.

"These will live on, even after you have gone", she told me.

I wonder, clacking away, what had the young graduate committed to paper on its heavy rollers, long before I was born; did he translate Shakespeare's sonnets? Write about the war? Type paeons of praise to his Emperor, the cherry blossom, or maybe to his love?

―∿―

For at least the last decade, the 25th of December has provided shops with a much-needed winter spending spree, especially since it came so soon before the annual New Year holiday when all workers went away. Post Christmas, however, shop takings slumped, and a new incentive had to be found. Once again, it was a Western custom that came to the traders' rescue; with relief, they adopted 14th February as a 'must buy' solution. Every shop window now boasts plush red velvet hearts edged primly with faux Victorian lace, love slogans on helium balloons, turtle doves a'courting inside frilly hoops, and a myriad of cards, all of them flowery, or depicting cute kittens or bunny rabbits – the humorous variety showing fat ladies or hen-pecked hubbies being deemed impolite.

Florists too, display red roses, but they do not do a particularly brisk trade, because, here in Japan, it is the male who receives tokens of devotion from the female population on St Valentine's Day. Hence, this is the time when sweet shops do their biggest, bumper trade. I went into Daiwa Depato at lunchtime to discover that almost the entire food hall had been given over to a display of confectionery. Behind each square glass-topped counter, assistants were gift-wrapping heart-shaped biscuits, continental chocs, and baskets of sugar fruits and flowers as fast as they could, to supply the demand of queues of schoolgirls and women of all ages.

Various loudspeakers played conflicting melodies, violins keened. Crooners were mooning about June, the moon, and young love, as earnest secretaries counted out their yen with concentration before holding up yet another cellophane parcel of sugar shells, fruit, or birds. Boys, all eating, walked by in pairs, nudging each other and guffawing at this scene of feminine frenzy.

It has become de rigeur in each and every office for female employees to give their male counterparts gift-wrapped sweets. I bought Joji a tray of multicoloured birds that seemed more appropriate to St Francis of Assisi than St Valentine, but thought it appropriate, given his position as authorised Prefectural Nature Explainer. In the library, I noticed the Administrator, Watanabe, had collected a mound of be-ribboned boxes and baskets on his desk. He was punching away at his computer, and beckoned me over.

"I have another enquiry for you. Perhaps you would like to teach a group headed by my young friend, Yoshinobu-san?"

"Yes, please, Watanabe-san. Thank you very much."

"Okay, I fix."

A burst of laughter from the staff room, and two more teachers approached his desk with yet more offerings, a cellophane-wrapped spun sugar iris, resting on a bed of pink sugar rose petals, and yet another raffia basket of life-sized garish sea creatures.

"Dozo, Watanabe-san," they bowed.

He offered me a bright yellow duckling sweet, with an orange beak. I bit into it, and discovered it to be hollow, and having absolutely no particular taste. It was merely very, very sweet.

"Arigato, Watanabe-san. What a popular Administrator you are!"

He beamed, and all the women nodded assent.

Joji arrived home in high good humour, arms overflowing with delicacies, and Mieko and Fumiko had put their own offerings round his plate. I added my birds, and we all scoffed sugary nothings, toasted Joji in beer, and ate and drank for several hours. It was a happy family evening, not even marred by the news that Fumiko had come fourteenth in her Ski Competition. Joji spent some time redesigning her future. Rather than becoming an Olympic skiier, Fumiko is now destined to become either a sports teacher, or enter the police force. The evening ended cheerily, but all that sake, sugar, raw fish, rice and pickle was having a disquietening effect on my tummy. I was just about to get into bed when Mieko gave one of her mouse-like taps on my door.

"Hai?"

She slipped inside, giggling, and gave me a little packet of chocolate animals decorated with a large golden heart.

"Me boy, you girl," she explained. "I love you!"

I stared at her.

And then remembered I had told them that in England, it was the women who received tokens of affection on Valentine's Day. Mieko, now creeping noiselessly down the stairs, had wanted to make me feel at home.

———

The following morning, I was not feeling loveable. My bones ached, and I had a thrumming headache. My throat was sore.

[263]

Sitting in front of Taniguchi, at my lesson, her vivid shawl blurred before my eyes, and her voice seemed to come at me from a long way away, as if from under water. My chair tipped back a little, and the scene went black. It only took seconds, but when I shook my head, the air was punctured with tiny shining dust motes, all out of focus.

"Angela-san? Angela-san... dai jobu desuka?"

Taniguchi put a cool hand on my forehead.

"It's my head. I feel dizzy. My head is going kura-kura," I explained. "Sorry ..."

"I think you should go home now. I think you have the Russian flu. Maybe the Korean flu. You should go to bed."

My journey back to Mattoh was a nightmare. I had another dizzy spell just before crossing the pedestrian crossing to reach my bus, and missed it.

The next bus was a heaving mass of schoolchildren, shrilling and shoving, and, by the time I reached Kanazawa station I knew I must have a fever, because the concrete steps up to the platform kept behaving in a most peculiar way, heaving and tipping sideways, keeping time with the ripples of harp music over the tannoy system.

I knew I had to get back to the Unos, and, at last, sometimes resting on the dead flowering cosmos by the roadside, I achieved their front door, ignoring Koro's welcome.

Back in my room, I lay down, and let the world spin round me. I slept.

The next thing I knew, a bright light was being switched on. The anglepoise on my desk. Mieko was lighting the kerosene stove, and closing my window.

"It is cold in here, Angela-san. Supper is ready."

I was not cold. I was roasting hot.

"No. No supper, Mieko-san. I just need to sleep. I think I have a slight fever. So, just leave me to sleep, okay?"

Her face loomed over me.

"You are ill?"

She looked horrified.

"No, I'm grand. But, please Mieko, just leave me to go to sleep. Really, I mean it."

Of course she didn't.

She brought me up supper on a tray, waking me later with tangerines and coffee; always relighting the stove, and closing the window. I woke again at about midnight to see her shadow through the wall, looming hugely on the panel. She was kneeling, sighing, raising an arm, and then lowering it, stretching it out and repeating the gesture. Perhaps she was praying for me? No, silly, she was doing the ironing! Later I opened my eyes and saw Mieko's worried face hanging over me, a thermometer in her hand.

I felt even worse the following morning. Even the dim light filtering through the screen windows hurt my eyes. All of me ached now. I attempted to lift my head from the pillow, and the room swirled into blackness. This is scary. I have never felt like this. Was I going to die? Away from my children? I counted to ten in my mind, Very slowly. Mieko was still by my bed.

"I stay here with you, Angela-san."

She had cancelled her day's work at the sandwich factory. It was clear to me I needed help. Perhaps, if I could only get Mieko out of the way, I could go down the stairs, and ring Dr Kishitani, and ask what medicine I needed for this flu?

"Mieko-san! Please! I would love to eat a banana."

She nodded. "I get for you."

I heard her slam the front door, get out her bike, and leave. Then, I crawled down the stairs, diary in hand. I reckoned I had ten minutes before she returned. Mrs Kishitani answered the phone.

"Kishitani-san! Sumimasen, er, watashi wa netsu ga arimasu," I told her, swaying on the phone. She sounded understandably confused.

"Who is it has a fever?"

"Oh, sorry … Angela Cook here. Me, I have a fever. Perhaps the Russian flu … please, what, er, please …"

I could not remember the word for medicine, and my dictionary was upstairs. I tried to think of a word that might mean 'pill'.

"Dochira wa no piru ga arimasuka?"

I knew it was hopeless. How could she possibly understand?

"Doesn't matter," I said. "Don't worry ... I'm okay. Really! Sorry to have ..."

"Wait. I get husband," she said.

Dr Kishitani came on the phone. His voice was reassuringly professional.

"Cook-san? Netsu ga arimasuka?"

Yes, I did have a fever.

"How big?" he enquired.

I did not know.

"Where are you?"

I told him I was in Mattoh.

"I come," he said. "Address, please."

"No, no. You mustn't. It's too far. At least one hour. Dr Kishitani, I only want to know what medicine I need ..."

"Address, please, Cook-san," the voice said, decisively.

Mieko returned just as I got into bed, bringing bananas.

"Kishitani-san is coming," I mumbled.

"Hai, hai," she said, tucking the duvet tenderly under my chin, and setting the stove to its highest. She laid a huge bunch of bananas beside me, and settled herself on the floor to watch me, with the air of one expecting a miracle. I ate a mouthful of one and retched.

"Perhaps later, when the Kishitanis ..." I began.

But Mieko, not wanting me to ramble on in delirium, patted my shoulder, and slipped out of the room, murmuring: "You rest yourself, Angela-san."

I slipped in and out of blackness, the room spinning as if I was drunk. This wasn't flu as I knew it, and I was frightened.

The Kishitanis arrived while Mieko was out shopping. I heard Koro barking, and then the sound of the front door being slid open.

"I'm here. Upstairs." I called.

The stern father of Yoshika and Yukika had become a reassuring doctor. His wife, a nurse, took my temperature, plumped up pillows, and laid a cool hand behind my aching neck. They spoke together, nodding. I resigned myself, totally, to their care. Even when the two of them began to circle the room, tapping all the walls, I didn't care. If this was some form of Eastern exorcism, providing it worked, that was OK by me. Maybe I was possessed by affronted Bug Devils? Maybe the gods needed placating? Well, maybe. But I trusted both the Kishitanis. Dr Kishitani was reaching up to the ceiling, his wife crouching behind him, still tapping away, when Mieko returned. She ran up the stairs, laden with a bag of tangerines for her patient, slid open my door, and discovered two total strangers performing some curious rite. She promptly dropped the lot.

"Kochira wa Kishitani-san," I said, faintly, "and, um, dochira wa Kishitani-san. Achira wa Uno Mieko-san desu."

Dr Kishitani began to explain something to Mieko.

"Aaah, so desu!"

She started to tear the polythene bag from the tangerines into strips, and handed them to Mrs Kishitani, who knotted them together.

In my locker was a book, entitled How To Be Ill In Five Languages. I pulled it out. The doctor was now knocking a nail into the window frame, while his wife and Mieko handed him the knotted polythene strips, and he tied them in a makeshift rope onto the nail. I passed over the booklet.

"Mieko? Tell me ... What are you doing?"

Mrs Kishitani smiled at me. "Drip," she said. "We arrange drip, because you need. Alright?"

Mystery solved; together they fixed the drip bottle and suspended it from the strips tied to the nail. A masterpiece of Heath Robinson in that room of ricepaper walls.

Illness in Japan is a family affair. Fumiko and Mieko stood together in the doorway, watching the needle go into my vein with horrified eyes, and mouths agape.

"Aarrgh ... itai! ... itai imasuka, Angela-san?"

In retrospect, perhaps my reply should, grammatically speaking, have been: 'Arimasen, hai' (it isn't sore, yes!) but at the time, I merely croaked, "Ie, dai jobu."

The Kishitanis looked over the booklet and were able to tell me that the first one was a vitamin drip, which would be followed by another glucose one. They asked Mieko for milk for me, and Fumiko was despatched on her bike to get some, with the promise of an ice cream as reward.

Joji Uno returned an hour or so later, halfway through the application of the second drip. He stood in the doorway, staring like a mesmerised rabbit.

"Waaah! What happen?"

The Kishitanis explained that I was badly dehydrated, had a fever, and was anaemic. I needed milk, and yoghurt. All foreigners needed milk, they explained. Fumiko was sent off again to get more, with the promise of another ice cream on delivery. Fumiko was doing rather well out of my peculiar foreign requirements. Reading from my book, the Kishitanis explained to their audience that I needed anti-inflammatory pills and antibiotics, which they would leave. And perhaps just one more drip of glucose, the following day.

"Perhaps Joji Uno could ...?"

His eyes glittered in horror. I had a vision of a punctured arm, and bubbling veins.

"Absolutely not," I told them.

Joji hastily took the doctor downstairs and gave him a beer before he had to leave for hospital duty. Later, he drove Mrs Kishitani home, after the glucose drip had finished.

I did not see Joji for several days.

Two days later, we discovered that my temperature had gone down. Mieko has been instructed to leave a little air into the bedroom, and she never, ever appears without a glass of milk for me. The Kanekos had apparently telephoned each day to find out how I was, and now came to see me, armed with gifts for all the Unos, and me; the twins had made Get Well cards, Yasuko had bought me a green leather purse, a basket of sugar ducks and fishes, and a big bowl of home-made strawberry yoghurt. Joji and Mieko received a big box of prawn crackers, and Fumiko was given sweets. Never before have I experienced such caring from people who had only known me for a comparitively short time; the Kishitanis, who refused to accept any money for their visit, the drips, or the medicines; dear Mieko, selflessly nursing me, and the Kanekos for their concern, and thoughtfulness. I feel privileged to experience something that few Westerners experience – the genuine kindness and friendship Japanese people offer to foreigners once they get to know us. Truly impressive.

———

I phoned the Centre and took a couple more days off to recuperate.

In the evening, having started on a new project Kamada had set me – an attempt to explain the life history of William Shakespeare in Japanese – I went down to the kitchen and offered to help Mieko prepare supper. Unusually, she accepted. Tonight we were to have stew. I took a bag of carrots, and set about peeling four. Mieko was astonished at the quantity:

"Why so many, Angela-san?"

"It is good for my body condition," I told her. "And for Fumiko and Otto-san, too."

I remembered looking for stewing steak in Kanazawa, once before, searching for a butcher's shop, asking passers-by for a 'Neku-ya', without success. Joji and Mieko had been much amused. "No, no, Angela! We have no Cat Shops! 'Niku-ya' is the word for a meat shop."

The stew was delicious, despite the bouillon cube that resembled white chocolate, and a drop-scone object, half pink, half white, added to the onions and fungi. This was fish meal.

We ate the lot, carrots and all.

At least, Joji, Fumiko and I did. Mieko, as ever, sat crouched over her bowl, meditatively stirring morsels of stew with her chopsticks. Occasionally she would grasp a fragment of food, raise it halfway to her lips, and then put it down again, untouched.

"Have some more, Angela-san?" she begged me, pushing the soy sauce and chopped radish closer to my plate.

"No, really, I couldn't, thank you. But you! You are always serving us all, and yet you never eat yourself."

[269]

Joji frowned. He leant over, and helped himself to a piece of meat from her bowl.

"I know. I agree," he said. "And, I do not like this. It is servant-style, no? Not Western style."

His gaze fell upon his own rice bowl, now nearly empty, and an expression of reproach flitted over his face.

"Wife – rice!" he scolded, mildly.

"Hai, hai, otto-san. Gomen nasai."

Mieko jumped to her feet to replenish his bowl, her own still untouched.

The Shakespeare project had taken up four days of study. I had laboured at it mightily, clacking away on the old Royal typewriter, dictionary and grammar book to hand, finally producing two A4 pages for my Monday morning lesson.

"Read it for me, please," commanded Kamada.

I read the lot. Kamada sat, attentively listening, her head on one side. When I had finished, she clapped her hands.

"You read very well," she announced. And, your accent is also very good."

"Oh, I don't know," I said, secretly delighted.

"Of course," she continued, "there were a few mistakes …"

Over the next hour, she decimated page one, sentence by sentence. Barely a word escaped criticism: wrong verbs, incorrect participles, meaning muddled because adjectives were either placed in the wrong place, or badly construed.

The clock struck twelve.

"And now, to page two," said Kamada, her spectacles gleaming.

"I don't see the point," I said, sulkily. "It is perfectly obvious that I can't write Japanese."

She persisted. "But no, it is wonderful!"

I was not in a mood to accept her warped sense of humour.

"Personally, I can see nothing wonderful in producing the very best work I possibly can, all of which is apparently wrong." I said, breathing deeply.

"No, no, Angela-san. You must not think like this. I have classes of advanced students who have never written so much. I am very impressed. You should be proud. Now, to page two …"

Thanks to Watanabe-san I now have a full schedule of classes to teach nearly every evening.

But, that evening, I went to another of my classes, booked for me by Yoshinobu Ikebata, determined, tonight, to show the lot of them that they were the very worst students ever spawned in Kanazawa. And they were. Despite all my best efforts to encourage them to actually speak English, only two of them had dared to try – Yoshinobu himself, and a sweet, earnest young woman who told me that she went to public baths every evening and was trying out her English conversation by talking to her cat. After ten two-hour lessons with me, they had taken a vast number of notes, but refused to take part in role-playing exercises for fear of mispronouncing words, or making a mistake.

Tonight was their final class. As usual, I tried my best to encourage them to speak, throwing an orange to one student, and then one to another, suggesting they introduce themselves, and attempt a basic conversation on a subject – their job, their hobby, their pets, holidays, children, a film they had seen … without success.

"Eee, muzukashi desu, sensei," they moaned.

Not that difficult, surely?

At the end of this last class, they took me out to a nearby restaurant and bought me dinner. A marvellous, filling dinner of scampi, beer, chips, and ice cream. Finally, Yoshinobu made a speech, and I replied in halting Japanese. As I left to catch my train, Yoshinobu asked if I would like to see Wajima, before I left Japan? I knew that Wajima was famous for producing the best lacquerwork in the world, and as his parents lived there, and were actually painters of this lacquer, I said that I would be fascinated to go.

"I try to arrange," he said.

I am reading a book about how Japan was, in the early nineteen hundreds, when it was still a secret place, sequestered from foreign eyes, by order of the Emperor.

Hardly a single European had been permitted to land on its sacred soil for three hundred years. Yet, in 1826, the 'Black Ships' arrived; a huge fleet of vessels from Britain, America, and, subsequently, from Russia. British ships came from a land ruled by King George IV; he who had commissioned the baroque glories of Brighton pavilion. Meanwhile, Byron was writing and scandalising his countrymen with his illicit love affairs, Napoleon was languishing in Elba, and Charles Dickens was a young man. It must have been with mutual wonderment that men from such two different cultures first gazed upon each other. Yet, here they were. Large, hairy, beefy merchants, not only disembarking unchallenged, but openly trading, and even starting up their own factories and businesses. The Japanese sons of the nobility, trained from infancy as Samurai warriors, honour-bound to fight for their Emperor God, and their imperial country, stood alert, ready for the inevitable call to arms.

It never came. The Emperor stayed silent.

Now, extraordinarily, he even decreed that Japanese schools should start to teach written English! This, a canny, statesman-like move, ensured that his people began to understand the methods these foreigners used, to become rich, whilst not defiling their tongues by actually speaking a base language.

His strategy worked.

The invading foreigners had only come to this land to further enrich their coffers. They employed the locals in their factories for miniscule wages, delighted to find such undemanding, productive workers, always so eager to learn …

Unobtrusively, the Japanese gained knowledge of business practice, and, of course, the know-how of manufacture. Gradually, they themselves began to set up competitive businesses of their own, always undercutting their erstwhile employers. Of course, it was understandable that fellow Japanese businesses would prefer to deal with their own people, even if a written guarantee not to do so had been agreed. Many foreign businesses saw the writing on the wall and sold up to their Japanese competitors. One large company, however, did not, resorting to law. To their relief, they won in the Japanese court. Their delight in victory was short-lived, however, as, seemingly unprompted, the public boycotted their wares. They too, were forced to abandon their factory, and leave Japan.

—⁓—

I had been reading for several hours when Joji tapped at my door.

"You study too much. You are too Eager Beaver," he told me, sternly. "You will make yourself ill again. So, tonight, we go dancing."

The dance hall was in the centre of the town. We climbed up concrete steps, and were admitted by a hat-check girl seated under a silk fig tree. Inside were bare walls, a stretch of parquet running the length of the hanger-like room, two rows of old sofas at either end, and a red formica-topped table serving beer and coffee. Joji ordered two coffees, and began to discuss wrestling with the barman. Strains of Victor Sylvester drifted across the room. On one side of it, men approached prospective partners seated, or leaning against the wall on the far side. I was reminded of that old film The Ballroom of Romance, except that here the men sported business suits and serious expressions. Most wore spectacles.

The women were all heavily made-up; the more mature matrons wearing discreet cocktail dresses, younger women displaying miniscule waists tightly belted above circular skirts, their ensemble usually topped by a trim white broderie anglaise blouse. The air was heavy with the scent of face powder and floral perfume. All were competently executing a foxtrot, but at arm's length from their partner. This seemed to be de rigeur.

No one spoke, except Joji and the barman who were now demonstrating football tactics that should have been adopted by their favourite teams. When the tape was changed, amplifiers blared out a rock and roll tune, also executed expressionlessly by the couples on the floor. Once the music stopped, all the couples separated, and made their way back to their sofas, sedately. Joji ordered two more beers, and continued chatting to the barman.

The sugary strains of 'The Vienna Waltz' trickled out, and Joji bounded to his feet.

"Ah! This is for you! We dance!"

I resisted. "Joji-san, er actually, I am not very good at the waltz … I love to dance, but I don't waltz very well … rather badly, actually."

"Then, I show you," Joji said.

As he led me onto the floor, all other dancers held back, watching.

I should have guessed. Japanese-style, the lady reverses, using the opposite leg to our norm. Joji, standing half an arm's length from me, crashed knees on our opening move.

"You spread the leg," he panted, conscious of all eyes upon us.

"Do what?"

It dawned on me that he meant me to reverse with my right leg, but by then he had tried to adapt his usual style to mine with disastrous results.

"Which leg, Joji?"

"One-two-three, one-two-three," he chanted, pushing me backwards like a trolley with a wonky wheel. I noticed that the sofas were still fully occupied, the floor still bare of other dancers.

I put my hand firmly on the small of his back, drawing him closer, and suddenly, we were off, whirling across the dance floor! The music rose and fell, we pirouetted and swirled at break-neck speed, and, within minutes, the rest of the dancers had joined us, revolving more slowly. The scented air rushed past us as, in a daze, we hurtled around the room, only coming to a halt when Strauss stopped. I have never enjoyed a more energetic waltz. We finished our beers, and rested on our laurels, watching other couples perform a passionless rumba before returning home to Mieko who was waiting for us with bowls of green tea. I went to bed, after thanking Joji for a memorable evening.

A glass of milk was waiting for me at the Kishitanis when I arrived to teach their daughters the following Friday. The doctor was on duty, but Mrs Kishitani sat in on the lesson. Yoshika had studied hard, and achieved all the right verbs and adverbs. Yukika had not.

"Come on, now, Yukika," I cajolled. "I left you your own special book. Try to tell me what Sadie is doing?"

As ever, she looked to her sister to supply the answer.

"No," I said, sharply. "If you cannot try to speak, well – zannen ga – because that means you cannot join in the game at the end of the lesson and that means you will have no points, and Yoshika will have them all. And, all the prize sweets ..."

Yukika stared at me, scowling.

"So, I'll ask you again. What is Sadie doing?"

A long pause. Yukika continued to fiddle with her braids, looking down at the table. Then: "She skipping," she muttered.

"Well done, Yukika! She IS skipping. Remember? Tell me the verb To Be, please."

She remembered it. A minor triumph in my teaching career.

We finished the lesson with an extra-long game involving slips of paper with jumbled verbs, adverbs and nouns, and I managed to ensure that both children won the same amount of points – and, of course, sweets. Mrs Kishitani is delighted that her children are so enjoying their English lessons, and absolutely insists on paying me, despite my protests. The following week they are going to take me to dinner as a farewell present.

The last weeks of my time in Japan are rushing by, with promises of sayonara dinners: the Kanekos want me to go to their house for one last night, the water-purifying executives intend to take me out for a meal, Yoshinobu Ikebata has taken time off from his work, and has arranged my trip to Wajima to visit his parents, and ... this is the great weekend when the Unos are bringing me to Kyoto!

Returning on Friday evening, I did not recognise Mieko. She had been to the hairdresser, and looked surprisingly young and pretty, wearing lipstick and a navy skirt and cream jumper. She and Fumiko were pink with excitement at the prospect of the trip to Kyoto.

"Wah, Joji-san!" I said, "Your wife is looking beautiful!"

He looked pleased.

"I have good wife, no?"

For some reason known only to himself, Joji elected we should all leave at 1.45 am. All of us were tired. Mieko had not been to bed at all, worried that lying on her new hairstyle, specially done for the trip, might spoil it. She had also been preparing goodies for the trip, lest any of us might feel a slight twinge of hunger.

Our journey was punctuated by rustles of paper as Mieko, sitting by Fumiko in the back seat, handed over little titbits and chocolate biscuits. Joji refused the chocolate biscuits, saying that his teeth were aching. He lost his way on the outskirts of Kyoto and handed the map reading over to Mieko. I looked over my shoulder and saw her turning it round and round, clucking in dismay. As an appalling map reader myself, I sympathised. However, we made it. A sleepy porter admitted us to the hotel at around 5.30 am – early by even Japanese standards. Nothing daunted, the Uno menage, with me in tow, marched into the lobby, and settled into armchairs. Joji unlaced his shoes, put his feet up on a coffee table, and promptly fell asleep. He began to snore. Mieko rummaged yet again through her assortment of plastic bags, and laid out a selection of mandarins and rice cakes on the table, avoiding her husband's feet. Distributed round us lay our cases, cardigans, and anoraks.

A little later, hoovers began to hum, and women started polishing tables. Mieko, balked of her plan to have a full-style picnic, drank cups of coffee, and smoked, sadly. Fumiko drooped in an armchair.

Joji woke at 8 am. On learning that our rooms would not be available until the afternoon, he and Fumiko devoured Mieko's picnic, and we left to catch a coach and start sightseeing.

As an ex-guide myself, I was intrigued to watch my Japanese counterparts at work. Dressed in natty red cotton suits with matching pill boxes on their heads, they kept up a non-stop monologue in high-pitched, juicy little voices, stopping only when their coach was either parking, or leaving the parking lot. Then, they are obliged to nip behind their coach and blow sharp blasts on their whistles: two short blasts mean 'carry on backing', one long one for 'stop NOW'. I wondered why the drivers didn't use their driving mirrors? Perhaps because, true to form, in days gone by, mirrors didn't exist? We hopped on and off our coach, seeing more and more wooden temples, Mieko always holding the family camera, insisting we face it and smile, whilst Joji and Fumiko made the inevitable V-sign, grinning into the lens.

We saw the main pavilion of Kyoto, named the Golden Pavilion, de rigeur viewing for all tourists: it was certainly bright; bright golden yellow throughout, and highly ornate. The next temple contained about one thousand life-sized figures, in gold leaf, each and every one of them with varying features. All of Buddha. By running, I managed to see approximately 500 of them, standing rank after rank, just getting to the central Buddha, seated and surrounded by golden lotus blossoms, before having to belt back to the coach.

Joji's responses were becoming progressively more monosyllabic. He was now clutching his jaw.

"Joji? Why don't you buy some aspirin?"

No, he would not. He did not approve of painkillers. He was a Japanese man. And, sometimes he had this toothache, but, then it went away. And, he didn't like dentists. We crossed a bridge and walked along the banks of a river, looking at pod-shaped rowing boats, dams, and the thirty-six jagged mountain peaks surrounding Kyoto.

Our final visit was to the Silver Pavilion. This was my personal favourite. It had a fabulous garden created some three hundred years ago by a famous Japanese gardener; ineffably simple, yet so imaginative. The garden was made principally from silver sand, raked early each day into ripples – perfect ripples, of course – representing the sea. At its centre stood a gigantic silver sandcastle. The temple has its name because it, and the garden, was designed to be seen by moonlight.

I was constantly dawdling, lingering to retain things in my mind; envisaging the imagination of those fantastic gardeners who had deliberately selected each boulder, choosing it for its contour within a chosen space, designed to reflect a miniature mountain, or an island glimmering in a lake. Such conceptual brilliance! So many hundreds of years ago, they shaped each lake, chose each bonsai pine or maple, and constructed each silver sand waterfall with an eye to harmony and reflection, exactly as we see it today.

I had been an avid visitor to English stately homes and gardens; but their gardeners primarily planted with living materials, to a landscape approved by their patrons, and, often, when the descendants inherited these gardens, the vogue had changed, and so did the gardens. Not so here. Only the forebears of the white cranes and ornamental ducks have been reborn over the centuries.

Our final coach ride took us to a steep street filled with intriguing little stalls, selling every conceivable sweetmeat: local bean jam, rice candy, jellyfish and fried cuttlefish, as well as charming fans, lacquerware, ornamental chopsticks and gold statues of Buddha. Mieko developed a nervous Lassie syndrome, anxiously collecting me from the stalls and hastening me after the guide.

Here also, in season, is the flourishing insect market. Where some British collect their special 'fancies' – ornamental fowl, canaries, pigeons, or mice, a Japanese collector might amass singing insects, as did Lafcadio Hearne, who wrote of punishing his maidservant because she had forgotten to feed one of his favourite crickets when he was away from home. On discovering that this tiny creature had eaten away two of its legs to assuage its hunger, trapped in its wooden cage, he was sufficiently enraged to beat the servant. His heart, he wrote, had been sorely afflicted, despite the fact that the tiny creature was scarcely larger than a pin. Yet, he had been utterly distraught.

Later, in spring, this, and many other street markets will have bamboo cages hung on their stalls, the occupants all chirruping, humming, or sawing away like a many-stringed orchestra playing something similar to Bartok, or maybe Stravinsky? The Japanese maintain that this delight in something so fragile is indicative of the sensitivity of the nation, and, to their ears, the song of the cicada is as exquisite as any of our caged birds.

Joji's face had now become so swollen that he finally gave in and bought some medicine. We ate a hasty meal in the hotel, and retired at 7.30 pm. It was a fairly large, square room, empty except for a low table in the centre. I paused at the doorway, as Mieko hurried in and began opening cupboards, pulling out futons, rice-stuffed pillows, and quilts, all, of course, impeccably clean.

"This is your room ... where is mine?" I asked.

She looked at me in surprise: "Eeh? This is our room. Oto-san, Fumiko, you, and me!"

She assembled the tatami and laid out Joji's futon in the centre of the room while he washed, placing hers and Fumiko's beside it, inviting me to place mine also in the line. I declined, grabbing my futon and putting it down against a far wall. Joji emerged from the tiny shower room, drew the quilt up to his chin, and, within seconds, was snoring stertoriously. Young Fumiko, vastly over-excited by the experience of being in strange surroundings, and having eaten a strange meal in a hotel restaurant, pranced around to pop music from the built-in TV, giggling, until a particularly noisome warning snore escaped her father, and he heaved over under the covers. She then subsided under an adjacent quilt, shut her eyes, and proceeded to give a tenor accompaniment to Joji.

Mieko, now in a wrapper, made cups of green tea for us, and silently indicated that we go out to the tiny balcony. Stepping over the recumbent bodies of her family, we slid the doors behind us, and sat on wicker chairs, taking in the view of the lights of Kyoto city: Kyoto Tower illuminated, skyscrapers, restaurant lanterns twinkling, and floodlit temples, all backed by a few flickering lights from lone cabins up the surrounding mountains. Very quietly, we lit cigarettes, and sat together, saying nothing, lost in our own thoughts. Before retiring, she produced a can of Kirin beer for me, pouring it carefully into the residue of green tea in my cup. I wasn't about to be fussy. Never has a can of beer tasted so good.

Surprisingly, once I laid my head on the pillow and snuggled under the covers, I fell fast asleep.

Daylight!

I opened one eye and discovered Mieko boiling water for tea, and Joji, now obviously feeling better, playing at being fierce bears with Fumiko. We all inspected the breakfast menu displayed in our room.

The serving of bread was deemed sophisticated and unusual, as was the hard-boiled egg provided in addition to the usual fish gruel and bowls of rice.

In the restaurant, I declined the gruel, but tucked into the generous one-inch-thick slices of bread, topping the hard-boiled egg in its egg cup. The Unos found this very funny. They had also never before seen an egg cup. I demonstrated the old childish game of eating the egg, reversing the shell, and offering it to an adult. Joji, and neighbouring tables were greatly amused by this trick, Joji enquiring if it was a long-standing English tradition, possibly practiced by Shakespeare? Or, Winston Churchill? Or even the Queen?

"Very probably," I replied.

———

Today, the first item on the agenda was a visit to Ni Jo Castle, the ancient home of a Shogun, or Daimyo, the Lord over Kyoto. Other tourists could not detract from the magic of this place; the gates themselves were imposing and beautiful, but, once inside the castle, perfection succeeded perfection. All the inner walls were painted during the sixteenth century – that time of our Elizabeth I, and – of course – Shakespeare. Four-hundred-year-old paintings and murals, all exquisite, under ceilings and walls panelled in a soft gold. The actual paintings were sensational – such deceptively simple animals; cranes, standing on a gnarled willow branch, sparrows chattering on a cluster of bamboos tossed in a breeze, pigeons, plump and docile, and an eagle, its talons gripping a pine branch. Even the pictures of tigers, which the artists had never actually seen, merely painted from hides; those magnificent creatures had been brought to life, springing on their prey, or playing with their cubs. I also remember a sprig of white cherry blossom painted on a wooden panel, so dense and fluffy I could have stretched out a finger to touch its froth.

Each room was reached by walking down long corridors floored by polished wooden boards, each more than a foot wide. These are known as the 'nightingale floors', commissioned by the Shogun, designed to foil any intruder. It is impossible to set foot on these boards without evoking a chorus of squeaks, creaks, and twitters, reminiscent, I thought, of Richmond Park, where I sometimes came upon a tree alive with small birds, possibly starlings or maybe finches, all trilling away, until, at some unknown signal, every bird took flight, leaving an almost startling silence. To ensure that the craftsman who had created these unique singing boards could create no more for others, the Shogun had him executed once he had finished his work.

We passed down these corridors, past the guard posts concealed within walls, past council chambers and audience rooms with models of vassals making obeisance to the Shogun, past truly unbelievable ancient wood carvings; these were placed over the sliding panels now admitting us to view each room; a seemingly delicate painted fretwork depicting peacocks, peonies, storks; or, fans, bamboo, cherry blossom and pine, with kingfishers in full flight.

The astounding thing about these fine, filigree carvings was that, when looked at from the other side, the scene was different, though not apparent when glimpsed from either side. Each carving appeared to be of no greater thickness than a paper doily, but, in actual fact was carved from wood that was a minimum of three inches thick. Unbelievable expertise!

Finally we visited the garden of Ni Jo Castle, walking through many different vistas. I stopped to look at a circular stone, partly submerged in a lake. The stone was facing a small pine-crested island. It represented a baby turtle, returning, against all odds, to its base, but, the creature was so realistic, it was hard to believe it only stone. Conscious of intruding on its repose. I took a photo of a great grey stone under a tree, placed on a bed of raked sand. This perfectly captured the essence of a creature, now lounging at ease, contemplating its viewers with a decidedly supercilious air. Even to my untutored eye, this was a majestic animal.

There were avenues of camellias in full bloom, and another garden set aside purely for a collection of cherry trees, all growing out of a moss garden – pendulous varieties, dwarf trees, ancient spreading shapes – all cherry trees, reached down an avenue of queer convoluted trees called Japanese Pagoda trees.

Ni Jo Castle left me bemused and enthralled in wonderment.

After lunch, we set off to see the final sight of our visit to Kyoto, Kyoto Tower. That tower I had seen, illuminated, from the balcony, the previous night. By day, it resembled a cross between a very white lighthouse and a solid Eiffel Tower. We were ushered into lifts by bowing and smiling lift attendants, all smartly dressed in tartan uniforms, and sailed up to the circular viewing platform on the top floor. As ever, it was evident that Town Planning Departments held no sway over the development of their towns, not even one so internationally famous as Kyoto. But, beyond the higgledy-piggledy mass of ancient houses, shacks, gleaming glass skyscrapers and cream-coloured modern villas were the thirty-six peaks of densely wooded mountains, and, on one, beside a rose-coloured pagoda, I saw the colossal, seated figure of a goddess, carved from what looked to be sandstone. Even seen from a distance, her countenance was amazingly peaceful, gazing serenely over the whole sprawling, ramshackle wonder that is Kyoto city.

Next, we were directed to walk down steps to a lower level. It was here that Fumiko's sightseeing came into its own; both lower floors were amusement arcades of quite staggering vulgarity. The first floor was given over to a series of little scenes depicting well-known Western themes; Cinderella – bearing a strong resemblance to a Cindy doll – danced in glass slippers with her Prince Charming, both in life-sized plastic. Rounding the next corner we came across the pageantry of ye olde England displayed before our very eyes; Buckingham Palace as a backdrop for the Household Cavalry, the entire troup sliding up and down in groove (grooving, maybe?) to the accompaniment of the chimes of Big Ben. Next stop, Vienna, where more plastic dolls revolved to the strains of Strauss waltzes. Paris was represented by ghastly dollies in frilly drawers, jerkily giving their all in a can-can, whilst from Hawaii, well-boobed beauties executed the hula-hula in grass skirts. Finally we came across a scene from Red Riding Hood. This had an additional attraction; from time to time, there was a whizz and a flash, and a wolf's head suddenly popped out from a plastic tree. In the capital city of Italy, I was surprised not to encounter the Pope emerging in a puff of white smoke from the towers of the Vatican.

The last floor had raised models of the principal cities throughout Japan. At the touch of a button, one could make a light come on in any particular town. Kanazawa was duly lit up for a few minutes, and the Unos were well satisfied. Joji began to sing along to the musak – 'Que Sera, Sera' boomed from speakers, Mieko was laughing happily, and Fumiko was licking a giant ice cream cornet. We rounded off our trip by buying omiyage (souvenirs) for neighbours and friends, and set off for home.

The Unos insisted on taking me to dinner at a Chinese restaurant in Mattoh, to round off our trip. I can never repay their kindness to me. Back at their home, the unfortunate Koro greeted us effusively, standing on hind legs, tail going like a windmill, yipping with delight; a neighbour had fed him during the two days we were away, and conceivably might have dragged him across the rice field in front of the house, but, personally, I doubt it. Tomorrow, I will make it up to him, and take him down to the beach.

March is coming in like the proverbial lamb. I see no point in saying this to my teachers, since I have never, ever, spotted a single animal grazing in Japan. No lamb has ever frisked on Honshu island, to my knowledge.

I have been allocated a new teacher. I am told she speaks no English. Reluctantly, I discover her to be a brilliant teacher, always able to know when I understand the lesson, and, perhaps more importantly, when I hadn't.

Kamada has told me, in strictest confidence, that she has been sitting a sort of Master's Degree exam in English, travelling to Tokyo twice, so far. The first exam was a written one, the second an oral, and, at the end of it, she had to meet a panel of examiners – all men – who are the ultimate arbiters of success or failure.

"And, it depends on whether they like you," she explained. "They ask so many questions; would your husband mind moving? Your children? Why do you want to move from where you are? Do you have good relations with all staff in your present employment?"

[283]

It did not seem particularly PC to me.

Once before, having obtained top grades in her written exam, she had failed the oral, because, she explained, one of the old examiners didn't like older women! She has to travel in all, three times to Tokyo, the third time to obtain her results. They have no system of posting them up on boards, and certainly do not send them through the post to the examinees' private home. By contrast, Taniguchi's husband's firm has just relocated him to another town. She will, of course have to sell their house, give up her job at the Centre, and move their children from the school they love, and leave all her relations and friends. Taniguchi is very sad, but resigned.

"But didn't they give him a choice?" I asked. "I mean, couldn't he have refused?"

She shook her head. "Of course not, Angela-san. It's just the way things are."

We went on with the lesson, both of us determined that I would master the passive voice, and the transitive and intransitive tense. And I tried. She tried to explain the grammatical logic underlying Japanese sentence construction. I realised that, try as I might, it simply was not registering in my brain; my stupidity, not her teaching ability. However, this did not prevent me from growing progressively crosser, and when, after an hour and a half she told me that in a newly acquired polite tense the words for 'go', 'to come' and 'to be' were the same, I exploded.

"This has to be the ultimate Japanese secret weapon!" I snarled.

Her hand fluttered to her mouth. She looked at me in horror.

"But no! We do not have such a one! Truly! We never did, and we do not have one now!"

We stared at each other. She distressed, I, uncomprehending.

Then, suddenly I realised what it was I had said. Taniguchi's grandparents, maybe even her parents, had lived through the unbelievable horrors of Nagasaki, of Hiroshima ...

I had just said something unforgiveably crass.

I apologised. It was merely a figure of speech ... it was simply a foolish remark, made by a stupid student who was incapable of responding to her good teaching.

"Could we just stop our lesson now, Taniguchi-san, and perhaps go and have a cup of coffee?"

We retired to the staff room and drank mugs of instant coffee. Senior tutor Kamada came in and joined us, complimenting me on the progress I had made. She and the other staff were amazed at how far I had got, she said, bearing in mind I was Such A Difficult Student!

The Unos were all unusually quiet over dinner that night. Even Fumiko was silent, helping her mother to break raw eggs into soy sauce and whisking them while Micko added grated daikon (white radish) and small parcels of rice wrapped in seaweed. We all slurped appreciatively. When I get home, I mused, I am going to eat solid food, not as good for my body condition as Mieko's, but I am going to ask for a home-made steak and kidney pudding, probably with thick chips, and maybe blackberry and apple crumble and cream to follow. Double cream, whipped. And NO BATH! Then, in the morning, a full Irish breakfast, with all the trimmings – lots of rashers, sausages, fried tomatoes, fried mushrooms, and fried eggs, all fried in lashings of butter … my reverie was interrupted. Joji pushed his chair back, belched, and announced that his father had had a bad fall, and now we would go to visit him in hospital.

All of us.

I protested: "Surely it would be better if I did not go, Joji-san? I mean, your father is not strong. He is an old man, probably suffering from shock. I am sure he wouldn't want to see a stranger at this time?"

But Joji was determined.

"No problem. No problem at all. He will be happy to see you," he declared.

I said no more, realising that it would be rude for a guest, let alone a foreign female guest, to question his decision, although I learnt that the old man had just endured an entire week of agony because the full extent of his injuries had not been recognised until Joji had called round and found his father crawling on all fours, unable to stand, and had taken him to hospital. In the car, Joji explained another reason for our visit. Joji's dentist had told him that he needed to have four teeth extracted – all in one go – but, without his family medical card, he would be unable to obtain the free dental treatment he was entitled to as a local government employee. That medical card had accompanied Uno senior to hospital and he needed to reclaim it.

"Much, much money this dentist wanted this morning," he growled. "And he tell me, no card, no money, no treatment. So, I get the card tonight, and get treatment tomorrow."

The hospital was a modern concrete block building. Old Uno-san was in a ward on the fourth floor, the entire floor containing some one hundred patients, all under the care of one pretty nurse throughout the night. We walked past ward after ward on either side of the corridor, each small square room resembling many of our old cottage hospitals, except that these had no locker space between each bed. When we walked into Uno's ward, eight shrunken old men watched our approach impassively from iron beds, only their eyes moving, like tortoises.

I did not recognise Joji Uno's father. He lay on his side, face and hair as white as the sheet, one emaciated hand grasping the bedrail, his eyes closed in a skeletal face. I thought he had died. Joji's stepmother scrambled up from matting beside her husband's bed, her grey hair dishevelled, her eyes red-rimmed in a blotchy face. She would continue to sleep there each night to attend to her husband's needs, like many other relatives did, because special night care was expensive. Joji made her a perfunctory bow, and motioned for Mieko to hand over gifts of biscuits and fruit. For few moments he stood, gazing down at his father, but the old man never stirred. He was barely breathing. Joji turned away, slowly, and then began a noisy, jolly conversation across the bed, laughing and chatting to the wife, while Mieko, also smiling broadly, handed out packets of crisps to sustain the watcher during the night. He then collected the medical card, bade her goodnight, and we left.

"Very good hospital that," Joji observed, reversing his car with care. "Very new. Modern."

"Good, Joji-san. That's good. Yes, I'm sure it is…"

I was thinking of the last time I had seen his father, only a short time ago, remembering how he had insisted on giving me a bonsai maple tree that he had grown for about fifty years, starting to train it when he had been a schoolmaster in the local school. I recalled him speaking to me in halting, very precise English, describing his admiration for Shakespeare's sonnets and tragedies, and lending me his prized typewriter. Seeing him now, I doubted he would be alive tomorrow.

We drove to report progress to Uno's oldest brother's house where their Father had been living for many years, as is the traditional responsibility of all oldest sons. It is also the reason why most young girls, when being shown photographs of young men by Marriage Arrangers, always want to know their sibling position in the family. Obviously, being an oldest son is a considerable black mark against desirability.

At the brother's house, the TV stayed on. I averted my eyes from a programme shot in the Philippines showing, first, cock fighting, and then a truly revolting bout of horse fighting.

"I am sorry," I said, "but would you mind changing the channel? I cannot bear to watch this." The brother got up and switched it off, looking at me in mild surprise.

"Do you not gamble in England?" he enquired.

"Yes" I told him, "but not with defenceless animals."

Joji said, "But, you hunt the fox, yes?"

"Well, yes … but we don't gamble for or against the fox!"

I stretched my leg under the kodatsu, inadvertently kicking their fourteen-year-old miniature white poodle. The little creature staggered out and lay beside me on a zabuton, panting. It was toothless and half blind; both its ears had been pierced, revealing two pink silk rosebuds to match the bow on its topknot.

While Mieko gave out omijage from Kyoto, the brother, a baker, produced buns filled with bean jam and confectioner's custard, and his wife plied Fumiko with sweets and ice cream, chuckling raucously. Joji demanded the best green tea, and quite a party atmosphere developed. Everyone smoked innumerable cigarettes, and told jokes, roaring with laughter. When the conversation turned to remembering how old Uno had only been able to crawl like a baby after his fall, Fumiko was convulsed with laughter, as were the others.

And yet, I know that Joji loves and admires his father.

CHAPTER SEVEN

Sayonara Times

Only twelve more days in Japan! I can't quite believe it. The concept does not seem real. I have become so absorbed in my life here, and my studies, that I cannot imagine being transported back to another world, on the other side of the globe, although that other world is my own. In the meantime, all my new-found Japanese friends are inviting me to farewell dinners and sightseeing trips; the Kishitani family have invited me to dinner at a famous Kanazawa restaurant; the Kanekos want me to stay with them for a few days, and plan a special 'Sayonara Party' for me, and, tonight, after my final lesson with the water-purifying plant executives, they are to take me out for a meal. Mr Higashino, one of the senior executives in tonight's class, has offered to drive me to view the beauties of Noto peninsula: "My wife is interested in English," he said. "She is a good nurse in our big hospital, and my children would like to see you …"

Yoshinobu Ikebata and Akiko, his wife, have arranged a trip to Wajima, to visit her mother, and to stay overnight with Yoshinobu's parents.

Miyazaki arrived for my lesson with a little violet plant, in full bloom. She and her husband had gone on a mountain trek, and dug it up for me. We explored Lesson 40, the 'If' tense, and I think … I think I am beginning to understand it! Just … maybe.

The end of my last lesson with the executives. They gather round me, all twelve of them, the women linking arms, as we walk to their chosen restaurant.

"The best in Kanazawa for raw jellyfish," Ayashi observed, casually. I know him for a tease, and merely shrugged. I phoned the Uno house, and told Fumiko that I would not be back for dinner, and please to tell her mother.

The restaurant was obviously prestigious. Our reserved table was laid out with a banquet of food – platters of wafer-thin Kobe beef, shellfish, sausages, sushi, pork chops, delicious chips, and a variety of salads.

"You enjoy?" Higashino-san enquired, watching, as I took a second helping from one of the bowls, using my chopsticks with a confidence inspired by copious glasses of beer and sake.

"Delicious! Absolutely delicious," I told him, dousing it in the peanut-butter sauce.

"What is it?"

"Raw jellyfish," he smiled.

Later, came the speeches. And their presentation to me of a lovely miniature gilt screen decorated with a flight of ducks and bamboo. Inspired by gratitude and drink, I responded, wishing them success in America.

"Where Ladies Go First," remarked the Chairman.

"And, if a problem, you ask for …"

"No, no," broke in Higashino, "you SEND for the Manager!" Everyone burst out laughing. Higashino was the mildest of men.

Outside, on the street, I prepared to say goodbye and goodnight. I stood with the other women on the pavement. The men, however, were feeling well-fed and expansive.

"Tell me, Cook-san," said Ayashi, casually, "how you like our nightclubs in Kanazawa?"

The nightclub was suitably dimly lit. Upstairs was a circular bar, and a tiny dance floor backed by a screen, painted with pine trees and bamboo. Ayashi-san took over. A bottle of ten-year-old whisky materialised at our table. Ayashi commandeered maraccas and a tambourine. Miss Kobo danced for us. Higashino sang a passionate Japanese love song, unaccompanied, and Ayashi, rhythmically shaking the maraccas, oscillated to his own version of a Spanish flamenco. I have a dim recollection of teaching Ayashi the Charleston, to great acclaim, as the whisky level diminished. A wonderful night.

My taxi arrived back at 2 am. To my horror, there was Mieko, drowsing under the kitchen kodatsu, awaiting my arrival with the dinner she had cooked and kept for me. Fumiko had neglected to pass on my message.

The following day I woke after Mieko had left for work. I gave my breakfast to Koro and took him for a long walk to clear the cobwebs.

That evening, when Fumiko came in from school, dumping hat and satchel on the floor, turning on the TV, and opening the fridge, I asked her why she had not passed on my message. She lay on the floor, half under the kodatsu, sucking an ice cream, demanding that Mieko cook her sweet potatoes.

"Didn't understand you, Angela-san," she said, casually.

"Now, look here, Fumiko! Don't you realise that your poor mother …"

Mieko flashed me a beseeching look. Joji had just banged his way into the hall. I turned away, and said nothing. Mieko switched on the hot plate and poured me a glass of sake, smiling.

—⁓—

Saturday morning was a brilliantly fine spring day. Fresh wild cosmos is springing up by the roadside, and daffodils are in plump bud by Mattoh station. Regrettably, I shall miss the onset of the renowned cherry blossom, but now the scent of plum blossom, with a fragrance like sweetpea, drifts on the air. I walked to the station early in the morning and caught a local train travelling away from Kanazawa, a direction I had never before taken.

The Higashinos – husband, wife, and their four children – were awaiting my arrival on the platform. Their oldest son, aged thirteen, looked at me with suspicion. No way was he going to speak any foreign tongue. No 'Hallo' would pass his lips. His sister was twelve. She lowered her eyes with a faint smile in my direction. The two younger children, a boy of eight and a chubby little girl two years younger were much excited, out-shouting each other: "HALLO, HOW ARE YOU?" Each took one of my hands and led me to their people carrier, and we set off for Noto.

Their mother settled the children, and motioned for me to join her on the bench seat behind the driver. Beside her were two thick dictionaries, and a heavily bound tome of English-Japanese medical reference. Mrs Higashino, a nurse at a local clinic, had attended her music lesson on the shamisen at 6 am in order to meet me and improve her medical skills in a foreign language. The shamisen lay between us in a case shaped like a fiddle.

"Soon you will see our beautiful countryside in Noto," remarked Higashino, over his shoulder. I doubted it. All the car windows were tightly shut, and fogged with condensation.

His wife nudged me with her elbow:

"How you say this, Angela-san? Boles oppen?"

I peered at the book. "Ah. Bahwls oepen," I told her.

"Aaaa, so desuka."

She wrote elegant squiggles in a notebook. Presumably phonetic squiggles. During the next hour we covered many complaints, from 'tummy atchi' to 'wahoopng koug'.

"Um, 'koff', actually ..."

At last, Higashino drove onto a tarmac area where we were the only car. We all got out and he waved his arms expansively, pointing at a mountain slope that looked to me like a jigsaw puzzle. I forget its name, but it replicated the old practice of dividing land between siblings. Here, because so little of the land was arable or flat, it had been decided in ancient times to divide what there was among all the villagers, each division a demarcation line etched by a ridge. Today, each of these were covered by a thin powdering of snow.

Because of the lie of the land, each ridge was forced to curve, resembling the flow and eddies of the tide over sand. Our ancient ridge and furrow system – the furlong – served the same purpose. Here, the difference lay in acreage available, and population. In this area, some 3000 people all needed their own piece of land, and each member of the community owned his own tiny strip, even if it was in some cases barely allotment-sized, and slotted into its neighbouring plot, curving and curling like a jigsaw puzzle. Below stretched the icy blue sea.

We ate a marvellous picnic prepared by Higashino himself while his wife had been at her music lesson; deep fried bean curd, garlic bread, rice balls in seaweed, various cold meats and an assortment of prettily arranged salads, plus fresh fruit and biscuits. The English equivalent: cheese and ham sandwiches, a hard boiled egg, an apple and a thermos of stewed instant coffee is in a different league altogether!

Just beyond our picnic area sat several old ladies, all trying to sell souvenirs, calling out to us in shrill, reedy voices. One old lady was silent. She simply smiled. In front of her she had spread a cloth. On it were miniscule objects. I went over to have a look, crouching down in front of her. Infinitesimal tortoises, their carapaces made from nut shells, moved their pared-down matchstick legs in the breeze; flying fish fluttered their fins, ladybirds stirred hesitantly. They were exquisite: each one hand painted, and all made from nutshells and matchsticks.

"Did she make these?" I asked Higashino.

"Oh yes. She, and her daughters, and her grand-daughters make them, after the autumn harvest."

"How much is that tortoise?" I asked the grandmother.

She beamed, toothlessly. The tortoise cost all of 35 pence.

"And the fish?"

The fish was more expensive. Price 40 pence.

I made that old lady very happy that day.

We had a walk by the sea, crunching along the sand, chasing the children, before it was time to head back to the station. Mrs

Higashino brought out her shamisen and began to strum it. I promised to send Mrs Higashino How To Be Ill In Five Languages and we drove to the station all singing lustily 'Old McDonald Had a Farm' to the accompaniment of the shamisen.

My train drew away from the station, and I leant out to call a last goodbye to the family, now standing in a group, waving vigorously, the small boy jumping up and down, his sister astride her father's shoulders, bouncing and waving.

Another farewell to new friends on the other side of the world.

Every day is now a 'last' for something; the last couple of nights with the Kanekos, evenings spent eating Yasuko's delicious food, drinking lots of beer, mock arguing with Jin-Ichiri in our usual curious mixture of his poor English and my bad Japanese, and now, the last of my private lessons at the Centre.

The final Friday. Taniguchi had received permission to teach me this one last time, and, to my amazement we spent most of the two hours chatting, actually chatting, in Japanese! All the teachers gathered in the staff room as we had a last cup of coffee, Shinchi-san producing the special ashtray they kept hidden for my use.

"The last time, for your using, Angela-san …"

The inevitable cameras were produced and snapped Kamada and me, Taniguchi and me, Miyazaki and me, me with Saito, and one final one suggested by me; I climbed up an old cherry tree in the grounds, and held out my arms to all the teachers gathered round its trunk, telling them to imagine it was in full bloom, and that I was with them in cherry blossom time.

Last bows in the staff room. Last handshakes. Unexpectedly, last hugs. Taniguchi's eyes were wet, and I had a lump in my throat as I walked out into the pouring Kanazawa rain. Over.

This part of my life, all the resolution, all the hard work is over. I have failed in my intention to master the language, and so will be no nearer getting a well-paid job on my return to England. I love England with every heartbeat of my being, and, I always shall. England is my home country, but, currently, I have no home in it.

And, no job to go back to. Oh, and no money! At this moment, Japan, with all my new-found friends, feels safer than the uncertainties that await me on my return. However, I still have three more days here.

Tomorrow, Saturday, Yoshinobu and his wife, Akiko, are to take me to Wajima, returning to the Unos on Sunday evening. Monday, Mieko is cooking me a special farewell dinner. Tuesday, I leave for home.

Yoshinobu Ikebata arrived promptly at 9 am. I had first met him when he interviewed me to teach at an adult evening class, and had always thought him rather a fussy, precise young man. Boring, actually. Today, however, dressed in slacks and a fisherman's sweater, I saw a handsome young man, with a gentle face, a bit like that of a Tibetan monk. Akiko was a pretty, lively girl, far more volatile than her husband; words poured from her like water rushing over pebbles. Sadly, only Japanese words, but she was appreciative of my efforts to communicate, clapping her hands in delight whenever I got a sentence right. They have only been married a short time, and seemed to have a lovely relationship. She told me that their marriage had not been arranged:

"No indeed," said her husband, "if it had been, perhaps I would have done much better!"

Akiko laughed. Her retort was not translated to me, but there was certainly nothing of the submissive little wife about her, and the teasing came and went, both ways.

We stopped for a few moments in an ancient village for me to take a photo of the houses. These were made from overlapping planks, with roofs thatched either with pine bark, or, in some cases, rice straw, pitched low over the walls, and scooped out over the upper windows like eyebrows, exactly like Tudor roofs, though using local material.

The next stop was at a modern restaurant overlooking the sea, after which the Ikebatas led me to a turnstile set beside a thick, dark curtain. I steeled myself to see an amusement arcade, and was enchanted to enter a museum depicting scenes from the local annual festival. Here were carriages, lacquered rickshaws and floats, and huge ornate dragon's heads with hinged jaws. (In Japan, the dragon is a symbol of good fortune and well-being: St George would not score any brownie points here.) We watched a DVD showing all these museum pieces in action. Some of the most spectacular floats are carried on shafts with some twenty young men shouldering them, bearing first a wooden platform on which pretty girls play a shamisen or flute, all wearing traditional kimonos; stretching upwards from this platform are two upright wooden spars, each the actual height of a two-storey house, topped by a temple-shaped paper screen. In the film we watched as these floats battled, jockeying for position, towering against the skyline, each being manoeuvred to tilt at the other, while the attendants of each float hung onto guy ropes, and took their turn to bear the shafts. They were all dressed in identical white tee-shirts and headbands showing the red sun of Nippon. Practically every man in the locality took his turn.

Although local traditions dictate different battles, there is one that seldom varies. This is the ceremony designed to appease the God who likes to inflict pain. For this, each year, they construct a truly beautiful little wooden building like a miniature shrine, or temple. Local craftsmen carve, and spend many hours painting, gilding, and decorating it. Then, on the day of the festival, it is carried ceremoniously through the town by half a dozen chosen men, and finally tipped into the river. All the bearers jump in after it, bashing and dunking this cherished object, to roars of encouragement from the banks. The final degredation comes when the battered shrine is fished out of the river and carried to a bonfire to be burned to ashes. There is an obvious symbolism here, relating to fire and water, but I would love to know the origins of this practice. Had I only known of this annual festival, I could have gone last September.

We drove away to visit Akiko's mother and grandmother before heading to Wajima.

Both Ikebatas wanted to hear about English festivals – had we similar festivals there?

"Well, not exactly," I said, with truth. I did my best to describe dancing round a maypole, and village competitions where personal honour was at stake in growing the biggest marrow, or baking the lightest Victoria sponge. But, how to explain the church bell-ringing, or the children ringing handbells in the Women's Institute tent while visitors drank a cuppa and ate home-made shortbread? Or my local church displaying the wedding dresses of many of its parishioners over sixty years, dressed with flower arrangements? Various ladies taking turns to play the organ? Judging the best allotment? How to put across the friendly atmosphere and banter in our local pub where the vicar and the local priest each headed up rival darts teams in my local Warwickshire village? Irrespective of the absence of a village pub, the concept of a Shinto and Buddhist priest having a jolly game of darts anywhere seemed both ludicrous and irreverent.

"The same, it is not," I said, lamely.

Akiko's mother and grandmother live in a large house with a deeply sloping roof, facing rice fields sunk lower than the level of tarmac track. Everyone bowed. But, of course, no one embraced. Yoshinobu and I were ushered into the inevitable wide sitting room to sit and await tea. Peals of laughter and shrill chatter came from the direction of the kitchen, where Akiko was receiving, and giving, presents of food.

Yoshinobu, as a much-loved son-in-law, was given permission to show me more of their house. He took me to see their Butsudan, the household shrine, concealed behind ornate tabernacle doors. This shrine was at least 250 years old, and had been in Akiko's family for five generations. Yoshinobu unlocked the doors of the black lacquered cabinet doors, and I saw the small figure of a golden Buddha, surrounded by minute chalices of rice, and water. There were also tangerines, and a small vase of flowers. He selected a stick of incence, lit it, and struck two blows on a tiny brass gong, clapping his hands sharply, and bowing his head. I too bowed my head, marvelling at the purity of tone resonating through the room. I had heard this in several other houses. There must be craftsmen who specialise in forging such exquisite bell notes for Buddha, like our own few remaining craftsmen who still look after our great church bells.

Over tea, the grandmother began telling us about their night of the Great Typhoon – the worst to strike Ishikawa Prefecture in 45 years – the one that I had experienced, cowering on the floor at the Kitamuras, fortunately unaware of its magnitude. Here, at the foot of mountains on Noto peninsula, it must have been terrifying. The grandmother, white hair caught back under a blue cotton kerchief, demonstrated how great trees had been uprooted, how they had watched them, whirling through the air, crashing down on others, bringing those in turn down in their wake, wrecking destruction throughout the valley. Gold teeth flashing, her cheeks exactly like an over-ripe Cox's orange pippin, she described how a neighbour's roof had been torn from his house, landing at the end of the rice paddy.

"So, what did you do?" I asked her.

She hooted with laughter, nudging Akiko's mother. This very thin woman twisted her hands, smiling nervously. She said nothing.

"Do? What should we do? We sat here and waited, of course. And then, next morning, when it was over, we started to clear the mess away. Then, there was plenty for us to do."

Indominitable old women, I thought. The same the world over. Disaster? Illness? Errant husbands or offspring? War? Death, or even Acts of God. There is always plenty to do, and it gets done. I never heard of a Japanese counsellor being called in to assist. We left them, laden, as always, with presents. I was given a big tin of biscuits to give to the Unos, because they were my hosts, and yet again felt mortified that I had come unprepared. At every turn of the road we saw signs of the devastation caused by that typhoon, passing by the neighbour's roof lying, intact, on sandy soil soon to be planted with Japanese tobacco.

We arrived at Yoshinobu's home place in Wajima at five. Yoshinobu had explained to me that although some foreign tourists occasionally found their way to the famous Wajima lacquer showrooms, his parents had only observed them from a distance, and had never actually met a foreigner, so I was deeply aware of the honour they were giving me, on their son's recommendation; accordingly, I was punctilious in the matter of porch sitting, and placing of shoes.

Father Ikebata was a short, stocky man, wearing a navy suit and white shirt without a tie. His wife wore shapeless brown trousers and an equally shapeless woolly jersey of indeterminate colour. Like many middle-aged women, she wore no makeup, and made no concession to fashion. Their small house was full of beautifully painted lacquerwork. I was shown exquisite tables, boxes designed as wedding presents, trays and bowls. Both Ikebatas worked on the process of making lacquer from home; first washing the surface of each item, then cleaning it scrupulously, and drying it in large cabinets fitted with drying racks before beginning the laborious process of painting and decorating. Their table was of black lacquer, gorgeously gilded by husband and wife in a complicated design of birds, pine, peonies, and bamboo, part of a decorative process that takes many weeks, or even months, in a series of painstaking processes and delicate brushwork to achieve. Other prized possessions were also on display around the room: brass souvenirs, china pussycats with pink and blue bows, ashtrays from different countries; all cheek by jowl with hand-painted fans, and their own, special Wajima-nuri bowls, many of which were further embellished with mother-of-pearl.

Ikebata-san ensured that I had a backrest at the table, and kept a constant eye on my welfare, warning his wife whenever my cup was less then half-full, and lighting my cigarettes. He offered me one of his own brand, but, thirty-odd years of addiction had not prepared me for its impact. I coughed and snorted for a few minutes after my first puff, and had to explain that I, as a mere woman, was incapable of enjoying such strong stuff.

We three visitors went shopping to the supermercado, to buy ingredients for shabu-shabu this suppertime. It takes ages to eat shabu-shabu (which means, literally, 'gossip') but very little time to prepare. For it, the hotplate sits in the centre of the table, a cooking vessel is brushed with oil and then stock, sake and soy sauce are all added. Once this has heated up to the correct temperature, everything else is put in: paper-thin slices of meat, shrimps, chopped green onions, fish, tofu, clumps of baby mushroom looking like tiny white Ruritanian castles, the usual radish, and some sort of slimy rice spaghetti. There is a family ritual in selecting your own particular delicacy from the pot, or saving something special, a known goodie, for someone else. The level in the pot seems inexhaustible, and the eaters become more and more expansive as everyone starts topping it up and adding more sake, both to the pot, and individual glasses. I found myself able to chatter volubly to Yoshinobu and his father, using Japanese words I did not know I knew!

I was given the privilege of the first bath, followed in turn by Ikebata-san, Yoshinobu, his mother, and Akiko, and we all returned to the kodatsu, wearing cotton yukatta robes, to munch on nuts and drink more tea. Tomorrow, I was told, we must leave here at 5.30 am.

My room smelt delicious. Standing in an elegant lacquer vase flowers drooped gracefully, leaning at an angle from the door to the bed quilt, its welcoming message unmistakeable.

Mrs Ikebata smiled: "My husband is Ikebana teacher," she murmured. It was only 9.30 pm. I lay down, listening to the sound of waves against a sea wall, and was asleep within seconds.

The tap on the door woke me: "Angela-san! It is 5.30! We wait for you …"

I fumbled for my clothes in the chilly darkness and went downstairs to where the others stood, muffled against the cold. All of us walked down by the sea front, our footsteps echoing on the pavement. The only other sound was the lonely cry of the kites as they swooped overhead, or perched on rooftops calling to each other. Later, when it grew light, I counted at least thirty of these great birds, whose wingspan stretches five foot or more. Now, as we neared a quay, cyclists began careering along the pavement, none with lights; when alerted by the twang of a bicycle bell, both parties swerve automatically – hopefully in opposite directions. The sound of a harp, coming from a loudspeaker, disturbed yet more kites and seabirds, and I saw a flotilla of cuttlefish boats – roughly the size of our fishing smacks – each hung about with globular lights to attract the cuttlefish; great goldfish-bowl lights dangling from boats festooned with coloured bunting, or little fairy lights. The effect was festive.

The pre-dawn hazy light now revealed people under a roofed jetty. Men in oilskins, wearing baseball caps, and motherly souls, wearing plastic aprons and short wellies, all yelling and shrilling their wares. Wajima fish market was in full swing. Gnarled old ladies trundled through the crowds, pushing barrows on which they had threaded small fish on a daisy-chain principle. I imagine they are sold a necklace at a time. There were wooden boxes full of what looked like red mullet, all neatly facing the same way, straw log baskets full of writhing crabs, mostly vivid blue, and everywhere lay fish of every conceivable description being bargained for by official fish merchants, who were also collecting bids, and buying for hotel chains and restaurants. Ikebata-san knew them all, occasionally stopping to exchange a word, and introducing me as his English guest. We stopped to watch the auction of a huge sea bream, called a Tai. This is the expensive, popular dish eaten at banquets, or wedding breakfasts. The bidding was brisk, but there was disappointment when it was knocked down with a blow from the autioneer's wooden mallet for the equivalent of £15. In Tokyo, apparently, its price would have trebled.

The Ikebatas were growing anxious, glancing at their watches, and urging me outside.

"We walk to here, and, now, we stop." In the chill pale grey light we stood, shivering as, one by one, the round cuttlefish lights were extinguished.

"Aaaa, yes! See, Angela-san?"

Ikebata pointed to a mountain range that stretched beyond the bay. As we looked, a sliver of sun appeared, growing plumper and more dazzling with each second. The mountain tops lost their angularity, turning a soft pink under the canopy of early morning darkness. The morning light had sped down the mountains, turning even the lower slopes shades of violet, as the risen sun shone on the sea below, waves sparkling, cormorants diving. This is the memory of old Japan, a changeless scene that my hosts had planned for me to see in the Land of the Rising Sun. We stood there in silence, as, one by one, the goldfish-bowl lights on each fishing smack were extinguished. Mooring chains clattered. Kites screeched overhead. An unforgettable experience.

Back at their home, Mrs Ikebata had laid on a truly enormous breakfast spread. Many of her neighbours had also been invited to stare at the unusual spectacle of me, all the way from England, kneeling in their home, eating with chopsticks. They were all nice people, full of questions, amazed that a lone female foreigner had turned up in their midst. It began to seem likely that there would not be time to explore the renowned Wajima Market. Akiko caught her husband's eye.

"Husband? Perhaps we should leave now, to give Angela-san one last memory of Wajima?"

I wished I had the skills to thank Yoshinobu's parents for their hospitality, and for the unforgettable memories they had given me. I tried to express my feelings, and hoped they understood. Ikebata senior leaned through the car window. He spoke in English.

"Goodbye. And, welcome!" he said, handing me a pretty lacquer bowl as a farewell present.

Wajima market was great fun. Like Yasuko, Akiko dragged me away from stalls, telling me to buy with my eyes, not with my purse. I bought a pretty hand-painted fan, and an intricate rice straw boot to house chopsticks, for the Unos (I was learning). On our way back, Yoshinobu stopped the car to let me take a photo of an outcrop of two rocks in the sea, joined by a hemp rope; the final stage in a pilgrimage that must have tested any prilgrim to his utmost.

Before we left Noto, I was taken to the island of Noto-jima, to visit the Museum of Glass, seeing extraordinary exhibits, some by Picasso and Chagall, all displayed in an spectacular modern building overlooking the sea. Here, in Japan, each exhibit was given plenty of space, and sensitively lit. Driving back to Kanazawa I said that the whole weekend had been a magical experience. I told them how much I had enjoyed everything.

"I suppose," I said, dreamily, "that if I had the choice of beautiful objects in that glass museum, I'd probably choose that violin sculpture … or, maybe the Chagal teapot. How about you?"

Yoshinobu and Akiko looked at each other, and then back at me, worriedly.

"But, I am afraid that will not be possible," he said.

I laughed. "Well, of course not! It's just a game. Like, pretend you could buy any car you liked, what would it be?"

"Maybe, one day, we visit Europe," he said.

Yearning after the unlikely, wishing for the impossible, or even imagining it, is a foreign concept. They have their aspirations, but only those that are credibly achievable. Perhaps this philosophy breeds contentment? Nonetheless, we played the wishing game all the way back to Kanazawa.

Yoshinobu brought my case to the Unos' front door, and held out his hand. He cleared his throat. "I wish," he said, with a small rueful smile, "that you were not going away so soon. There is so much more we would like to show you of our country."

I took his hand. "And I wish I could take you and Akiko back with me, and show you something of my country."

Dawn over Wajima in the Land of the Rising Sun is a memory that will stay with me for ever.

—⁂—

Monday morning. I walked down to the local post office with a parcel of shoes, clothes, and some of the gifts given me by my host families, and students. Not a particularly big parcel. I walked back to the Unos with the same parcel. Even sent by the slowest post, overland, via Russia, the cost was prohibitive – about £40!

Back in my bedroom, I stood and contemplated my belongings. No way would they fit into my one suitcase, one grip, and briefcase. All my clothes now lay heaped on the bed, my shoes (virtually unworn over the months) circled the plastic hat stand: folders, exercise books, Japanese language cassettes presented by my teachers and textbooks were piled high on the desk. Shampoos, conditioners, cream, nail varnish and make-up had miraculously multiplied, currently wrapped in one of my two large bath towels. Next door, seen dimly through the rice panel into Mieko's drying and ironing room, hung my macintosh, fur jacket, and Naoko's gift, the kimono. On the floor I had assembled my omijage: a wall clock from the Unos. Screens, prints and Japanese calendars. The wooden kokeshi dolls I had bought as presents for my children, plus the fragile items: a jewel box, given to me by students, Mrs Kishitani's hand-painted shells, the delicate jet bead brooch knitted by Yasuko's mother-in-law, a small glass horse bought for my son by Yoshinobu, to celebrate the fact that he had been born in the Year of the Horse, and the delightful cardboard mobiles that I could never resist – geishas paddling a canoe, a fisherman reeling in a fish, two young girls on a swing – plus expensive sheets of hand-made Kanazawa ricepaper. Humphrey hot-water bottle, propped against the mirror in his tartan case, overlooked the confusion. If ever a bear could be said to have his tongue in his cheek, he had.

Two hours later, I had folded, scrunched, rolled, discarded, unpacked, and re-packed several times. I abandoned a bath towel. The Unos could make four of it. And, I would return to England as God had made me; make-up-less. I heard Fumiko come in from school and asked her to sit on my suitcase, Both of us struggled, but it would not close, and the grip was virtually unliftable.

Joji took me down to the station to buy my train ticket. He had coached me over supper, giving me the correct construction and conjugations, and we practiced the sentences in the car. It was essential to be specific: I understood that I required: 'One adult. Unreserved seat. Single ticket to Osaka. Tuesday morning. On slow train. Leaving Mattoh, 9.10 am.' This must be said in reverse order, to be understood.

Joji stood back, smiling encouragingly, as I approached the ticket window, where two bored, uniformed officials waited. I launched into my prepared speech. Both men stared, and then turned from the window. From their expression, I might have been ordering a rickshaw in Mars.

Loudly, I tried to gain their attention: "Sumimasen!! Ticket of …

Osaka to … seat on … unreserved is … Tuesday date, er, yes! Morning is …"

It was kinder not to look. Obviously, I was a deranged foreigner. They turned their backs.

Joji bounded up to the window, tapped on it, and bought my ticket, explaining that I was his house guest, and had only been in Japan, attempting to learn Japanese, for six months. The two men nodded at me, chuckling kindly, as I hunted for the correct change in my purse, Joji all the while making jokes like a benevolent ringmaster displaying his inadequately trained circus act. Clumsily, I dropped the purse. Notes and coins fell on the ground. Joji and I grovelled about and picked them all up. He collected the correct amount, paid, and gave me my ticket.

"I'm sorry, Joji-san," I said, in a small voice.

"No problem, no problem," Joji said, bestowing smiles all round. Amid bows, we left the station.

That night, in bed, I had a brainwave. I would wear nearly all my clothes, except, obviously, shoes. Any garment that did not fit into my case or grip would be either worn, or carried over my arm. I spent most of the following day sewing, breaking several needles in the process. But I was making progress. My macintosh was now lined with a heavy tweed cape. My thickest cardigan I sewed into the lining of my fur jacket, and the fairisle jersey joined a tracksuit top. Pleased with my ingenuity, I sewed two skirts together at the waistband, and decided to wear leggings and jeans underneath – the jeans, to my surprise, actually zipping up! I would leave behind my short wellies, and wear long black leather boots.

I took Koro for our last walk. It was a glorious spring afternoon, actually warm – not the kind of day I required for tomorrow. Clipping his lead back onto the kennel, my heart bled for Koro. I gave him a last cuddle. If I could have, I would have … Trustingly, he settled down, giving my hand a lick. Huffing and puffing, I got the case to shut.

My last job before joining the Unos for the special tempura Mieko was making for me was getting rid of all unnecessary paperwork – masses of it: museum tickets, unintelligible bank statements, old exercises, brochures, etc. Pleased with myself for finding a solution, and achieving order out of chaos, I managed to squeeze my suitcase shut, and ran downstairs for supper.

I entered the kitchen cheerily, and then stopped short. The three people in the room appeared frozen, as if in a video on pause. Fumiko, white-faced, stood against a wall by the table, staring at her father, Mieko beside her, gazing at Joji like a mesmerised rabbit. Joji was seated at the table, glaring at them. I recognised the symptoms; Joji had passed the stage of lament, and was now entering an ominous crooning, crooning with rage. He looked up as I came in. The video momentarily shivered into life:

"Angela-san. Please to sit down," he said, formally.

I took my usual place. Fumiko sidled into hers, and Mieko bustled to the hob. Her hands shaking, she began to serve us all. I smiled at her. "Why, thank you, Mieko-san, this looks delic ..."

Without warning, Joji's rage exploded. He leant across the table and slapped Fumiko across her face, roaring with anger. Fumiko, beside me, screamed, knocking over her glass of water, spilling it across the table, as Joji, now beside himself with fury, picked up his rice bowl and hurled it at her. She ducked in time, and it grazed my cheek, breaking into shards on the floor. I jumped up, just in time to avoid the second rice bowl.

"What the Hell do you think you are doing?" I shouted, " Stop it! How dare you ..."

Fumiko was now screeching non-stop. She made a dash for the door, but ended up half under the kodatsu, her father behind her. Once more, between the two, stood Mieko.

I walked over to the door, opened it, and closed it behind me. I walked upstairs.

Tomorrow, thank God, I was going home. I opened my copy of The Hobbit, that I intended to re-read on my journey, and tried to close my ears to the din below.

Much later, Mieko tapped at my door. "Please, Angela-san – you will come down now?"

"No thank you, Mieko-san."

Her face appeared round the door, looking distraught. "I so sorry this – problem – disturbs your 'Sayonara supper' … I make special tempura for you. You will like it. Please, please, will you come?"

Stonily, I looked at her, bobbing in the doorway.

This was Mieko-san. Gentle Mieko who had looked after me, nursed me, and provided for me. She and I had played snowballs, and swum in the onsen. We had sat together on the balcony in Kyoto, smoked, and gazed out at the unseen night city.

I followed her downstairs.

The kitchen gleamed. The floor shone. A fresh white tablecloth was laid, and a huge bowl of tempura bubbled on the hotplate. Fumiko sat at her place, sporting an unnecessarily large white bandage, affixed by Joji. She was still heaving great shuddering sobs, and he kept solicitously damping the bandage with cold water, telling her to keep it on, and to be careful of the cut.

"Aaa, Angela-san! We must have beer tonight, on your last night," he declared. The three of us drank beer, and ate the tempura, toasting my visit, and my return. I did not feel disposed to chat. I gathered that Fumiko had shown disrespect to her father by either losing, or destroying, an article written in a local newspaper that featured Joji talking to the host families of Kanazawa. I helped Mieko wash up, and bade them goodnight. For the last time.

"Oyasumi nasai Joji-san, Oyasumi nasai Mieko-san, Oyasumi nasai Fumiko-chan," I said, formally. "I would like to go to bed now, but thank you for everything – and, the tempura was delicious, Mieko-san."

I retired, taking my dignity, and my stiff British upper lip with me.

Half an hour later, I discovered I had lost my train ticket.

I did not have enough money to buy another. I would not be able to get to Osaka to catch my plane. Frog Prince, Tadpole, and all their minions would come and arrest me for over-staying my permit … fingerprinting … prison … British Embassy …

I called down to the Uno family: "Joji! Mieko! I have lost my ticket!"

The four of us looked everywhere. We searched the room. I unpacked suitcase and grip, scattering the contents. Mieko stripped my bed, and Fumiko crawled under it with a torch. Joji upended all the empty drawers onto the floor. Desperate, I unpacked my satchel, handbag, bag of presents, and two polythene bags.

No ticket.

"I will go down to the station, and try to explain," Joji said, glumly. For once, he did not preface the statement with a 'no problem'. I sat back on my heels and knocked over the wastepaper basket, the contents joining the utter chaos on the floor.

Joji pounced. "I look here." He picked out cigarette butts, empty shampoo bottles, torn fragments of bank statements, and, suddenly, let out a shout of triumph: "HA! Ha … Hora!" In his hand he grasped a fragment of torn paper.

"Hora!" he bellowed again, "Kore wa densha no kippu desu, Angela-san!"

Piece by small piece, they found more bits of the ticket, and Mieko was despatched to find the family sellotape. Like that Biblical widow, finding her talents, we all celebrated. Joji insisted on driving us to his favourite restaurant that featured a pair of the swans sailing past on a river. Here, he bought Fumiko (now minus bandage) an enormous, multi-coloured knickerbocker glory, and Mieko and me o'sake. The three of us toasted each other, laughed, recalled events, and made little speeches, until suddenly noticing Fumiko, empty ice-cream glass on its side, curled up on a banquette, quietly snoring. Time to go back.

———

I awoke early, and got up to look out over the rice paddies; over to those dark distant mountains, now still shrouded in mist. Shortly, the usual sounds of men leaving for work, purring engines – then chatter, doors slamming, kids' voices complaining as they were chivvied into cars, and the noise of older engines stuttering into life. So what was so different?

This day dawned with clear blue skies, promising a rare, hot spring day. I turned from the window and dressed for the thirty-hour journey from Japan, as planned: two woolly jerseys sewn together, etc. etc., tracksuit bottoms over two pairs of jeans, and the conjoined skirts. I brought my luggage downstairs, panting.

"No, thank you, Mieko-san. Really! No breakfast … I couldn't … Well, thank you, but, just one bun … yes, I do mean it, okay?"

The morning sun beamed pleasantly over all. Getting into Joji's car, I wore my fur jacket lined with two cardigans, and slung my satchel, heavy with books, over one shoulder. Across the other was a canvas bag filled with presents – the fragile ones. My handbag hung from my neck like a nosebag, and over one elbow, I clutched my mac, now lined with my tweed cape.

I staggered out into the warm air, and into Joji's car, its engine already running. Mieko and Fumiko carried the rest of my luggage, suitcase, grip, and wheels, into the boot.

Koro, straining at his leash, howled.

———~~~———

Not only do trains arrive on time in Japan, but they also leave on time. To the minute. The precise amount of stoppage time allocated for this train to allow passengers to get on or off in a small station like Mattoh is approximately 30 seconds, and is strictly adhered to, no matter what. I wrenched open a carriage door, and lumbered weightily down the train corridor. Joji pushed past me, determined to stow my luggage. A whistle blew, the train jerked suddenly, and took off. Turning, I saw the leaping figure of Joji hurdling over baggage, thrusting his way through the throng still clustered by the door.

"Joji! Be careful! Don't…"

As the train gathered speed, he hit the platform, running. Mieko had her hand over her eyes, her mouth a round O of horror. My last sight of the Uno family. All three standing in a row, waving. The train rounded a bend, and they were gone. Passengers were settling into their seats. But, which was mine? That 'unreserved seat, Osaka to …' The Hell with it. I found an empty seat and collapsed into it. All carriage windows were hermetically sealed, and sweat fell like the gentle rain from Heaven, dripping into my eyes.

Only twenty-nine and a half hours to Heathrow.

Half an hour later I could stand it no longer, and began to rid myself of my garments, bit by bit, watched curiously by the rest of the long carriage. Women with food trolleys began to make their way along the train just as I had removed the two skirts to reveal the tracksuit bottoms. Crimson in the face, I was patently the cynosure of all eyes; an inelegant, well-past-her-sell-by-date stripper. The pile of garments on the seat beside me was growing in bulk, but I still had to rid myself of just one last jersey. The train was slowing down. Tugging my navy fisherman's jumper over my head I saw that we had stopped at a station. Through my window my discomfiture was observed by a giant gilded goddess gazing austerely in at this ridiculous alien figure. I dropped my eyes.

The wheels of the train click-clacked rhythmically on, passing dragon-crested mountains and curly-roofed houses, past endless rice paddies and gullies. The rest of the passengers ate, drank, smoked, and slept placidly as the train rocketed through towns and villages, its wheels sounding : 'No-more-Japan, no-more-Japan, no-more-Japan ...'

Had the experience changed me? I wondered. Was I now a different person, returning home? I doubted it. I believe that our intrinsic personality is formed fairly early in life, but that layers of experience can guide one's instinctive reactions sometimes providing a patchwork of coping stratagems and knowledge. So, what had I learned over the past six months? Not fluent Japanese, that was all too evident. But I now knew myself to be more resilient, although recognising that I sometimes needed help from others. Perhaps I had learned a bit more patience, and a smidgeon of humility? Probably others would be better judges than I.

'No-more-Japan, no-more-Japan, no-no-no-more Japan ...'

And, no more smell of kerosene stoves. No more radish stalks for breakfast. No more incessant rain. No more frogs croaking from bushes. More importantly, no more utter bewilderment, or frustrating lack of comprehension. No more misunderstandings.

But flip the coin: no more Kitamuras, no more Kanekos, no more

Unos, or Kishitanis, and no more Ikebatas; no more wonderful teachers who had tried their best to impart their knowledge into my slow and resistant brain; Kamada, Taniguchi, Shinchi, Saito, Miyazaki. All those wonderful, kind people who have shown me uncommon warmth, and loving friendship in their magical country. All my life, I shall carry them in my heart.

JAPAN! Always surprising; a country where, to me, nothing is quite as it seems, I am captivated by this land. And tomorrow seems a long time away.